ASHES

to ink

A Memoir

LISA LUCCA

ju ju house publishing

Published 2021
ISBN: 978-1-7377502-0-8 (Paperback)
ISBN: 978-1-7377502-1-5 (eBook)
Library of Congress Control Number: 2021916504

JuJu House Publishing
Las Cruces, New Mexico
www.jujuhousepublishing.com

Cover design: Lisa Lucca
Interior design: JohnEdgar.Design

A Note from the Author

This is a work of memoir, which means my story comes from the vault of my memories, a collection of experiences, thoughts, conversations, and moments that have passed through the filter of my emotional perspective and the veils of time. The names of most people have been changed to protect the privacy of those who have not chosen to share their lives publicly, and who may remember these events differently. It is my truth that is revealed on these pages, with no malice intended toward anyone living or dead who resides within them.

The language used in my story is representative of the time in history when hate speech toward LGBTQ+ people wasn't only tolerated, it was used on network television where I learned those offensive words as a young girl. I have included words in the book that remain true to the language used at that time and by no means condone the use of anti-LGBTQ+ slurs of any kind.

For My Parents.
There is no me without both of you.

Prologue

"I'll take his brains and heart," I whispered to my sister when the funeral director presented us with the ashes of our father. Half are enshrined in a plain blue box, the other half in a tube with a photo of a golf club adorning the outside. My father never golfed a day in his life. His interests were more suited to belting out show tunes or shopping for drapes. Since both Deena and I will be scattering Dad's remains, we chose between the two free temporary containers Saxx Funeral Home had lying around.

I picked the one Dad would hate the least.

Now, that box sits on the coffee table where I put it yesterday after returning home. It draws my attention as I turn on the TV to chase away the quiet. When the screen flickers on, an elderly Frankie Valli appears, singing "Can't Take My Eyes off of You," a song that flowed from the stereo in the dining room of my childhood.

"He looks pretty good, Dad," I say to the box, remembering when my father performed that song in a talent show at Nippersink Resort in Wisconsin when I was twelve. Handsome and confident, he sang with gusto while his biggest fans—Mom, Gram, my sister, and I—applauded from the audience.

That was the summer of 1973, before I found out my father was gay.

While Frankie sings, I go into the kitchen and open a bottle of Cabernet, pour myself a generous glass, then sit down on the couch. Frankie's voice is the opposite of soothing, so I turn off the TV. When the mellow effect of the wine doesn't take hold, I pull a throw blanket around me even though it's not cold and accept that nothing feels comforting tonight. Then, I let the tears come.

I will never hear my father's voice again.

Memories flood in, his death breaching a dam we'd constructed in recent years to keep a fragile peace. So much time spent alternating between longing for and rejecting each other. So much stubborn selfishness.

He can't really be gone.

Yet here he is inside this boring blue box. Half of him anyway, less the small amount his partner, Benny, will keep ensconced in a gold rose he picked out from the funeral home catalog. Even though there were many signs Dad's health was failing, the reality of his body reduced to ash startles me each time I glance at the container. It occurs to me that this plain box won't do until I scatter his ashes. A decorating diva, my flamboyant father could barely stand to see a wall with more than twelve inches of blank space.

Until then he needs something with a bit more flair.

Pouring myself a second glass of wine, I slide the Fleetwood Mac *Rumours* CD into the player and collect scissors and a glue stick from my desk drawer, then pull a handful of magazines from a basket beside the couch and sink back down. Flipping through while Stevie sings of crystal visions, I rip out clichéd words of bereavement and inspiration; pictures of hearts and clocks are torn out along with a tampon ad filled with butterflies. Some things for my father— *Threshold, Serenity*—and some he has left behind for me—*Wisdom*. A love that can endure. They all land in a pile on my lap.

A large, colorful *Feeling Good* gets fastened across the top of the box. To be pain-free is the thing Dad wanted most and what eluded him for the last decade of his life; so many years were focused on numbing his pain, real and imagined. As I glue each slip of paper, tears fall. Sadness and relief fill my broken heart in that peculiar way they do when someone you love dies and their freedom from pain is a blessing—no matter how hard the hurt is for you. Like a ransom note, I piece together the words *Remember your family all love you*—a message to be deciphered in the afterlife since I'm not sure he knew this while he was living, at least not all of us loving him at the same time. Now the tears and wine are really flowing.

Christine McVie sings about Daddy making her cry. *Oh, Daddy, you made me cry, too,* I think, then drain the last of the bottle into my glass, letting my feelings for him soften with each stroke of the glue stick. A deep feeling of compassion settles me as if now that he can't upset me anymore, everything between us is okay. My sticky fingers smooth the edges of the paper and I sob, shaking loose thousands of memories of my father. An entire lifetime of joy and sorrow, inquiries and lessons, scathing tirades and tender hugs. All the secrets that broke my heart. All the resentment that broke his. I see the futility and the necessity of all of it.

Flipping through the last magazine, I find the letters RIP on one page in an elegant, curvy script; an exciting find. *Rest in Peace.* I cut them out and carefully glue them beside a purple heart for the wounds he suffered—especially those inflicted by me.

One

When I wake with a start, I'm still on the couch. The clock on the cable box reads 3:03 a.m. Across the room, the dark television screen reflects an image of a middle-aged woman with a colorfully decorated box in her lap. This is a new version of me, one altered by my father's death. It's barely visible, but I know she's changed.

I peel off my clothes and crawl into bed knowing my head will hurt in the morning from wine and crying. A car passes below my window and a streak of light falls across the room as the sound fades. Tossing and turning, I think about my grandmother, wishing I could talk to her. The anniversary of her death just passed—thirteen years—on the day before my father died. *This week will be even sadder now,* I realize. The death anniversary week.

"Gram, do you think my dad will take us out tomorrow?" I said as we watched *The Song of Bernadette,* an old black and white movie she loved. I was on pins and needles waiting for my father to call about going out on Sunday.

"Oh, I don't know. Maybe so." She swept a thin, wrinkled hand across my bangs, her red fingernails grazing my cheek as she tucked my hair behind my ear. Gram was a comfort on Saturday nights after my parents divorced, staying with Deena and me while Mom went out. Her steady love was a life raft to save me from drowning in the tumultuous sea of my adolescent emotions. "You'll see him soon," she said, before sending me off to bed. "Try not to get too worked up over it."

But I couldn't help it. Waiting for Dad to call had become my weekend obsession, as if sitting by the phone would make it ring. Without any set visitation, Dad was able to see his daughters whenever he wanted to, which wasn't every weekend.

"We'll see, honey," he said each time I asked when we'd see him again, hoping to pin him to a date. "I'll call you. Maybe a movie next weekend." What I heard was: "I will see you next weekend, and maybe we can go to a movie."

By Sunday morning I was in a panic, listening to the phone ring off the hook as I dialed his number over and over while my insides knotted like tangled yarn.

"Lisa, call one of your friends and go do something," Mom suggested, but I was sure he was just at the store, or in the shower. *But he said...* So I kept dialing. When he finally answered sometime Sunday evening, the sound of his voice untied the knot in my chest, allowing me to breathe again, as if my very existence depended on hearing him say hello.

"But you *said* we could go to a movie on Sunday. I tried calling you all day!" I wailed.

"Lisa, that's enough. I never promised to see you girls today. I said we'll see. Now if you don't stop crying, I won't see you next week, either. Just stop it," he warned.

"But I thought you said—" I caught myself. *Don't argue with him.* It was clear that letting him know how upset I was would make him withdraw his attention even further, instilling in me the notion that compliance with a man's desire would keep his affection. So, rather than risk losing my daddy's love, I kept my mouth shut while my anxiety grew sturdy stalks of insecurity, its deep roots taking hold.

. . .

"Girls, this is Terry," Dad said, holding the seat forward for me and my little sister while we climbed into the back of his Cutlass Supreme. A young man was sitting in the front.

He's cute, I thought, and nudged Deena with a slight shove. "Move, Deen." She shot me a look and scooted over. "Thank you." I shot her one back as I flipped down the armrest to separate us.

"C'mon, you two. Be nice," Dad said, though without his usual authoritarian tone. He was in an exceptionally good mood.

"Good to finally meet you, girls. Are you ready for bowling?" Terry flashed a bright smile at me, and I could feel my cheeks burn. *Man, he's a fox.*

The warm rush I felt when a good-looking guy glanced my way was unnerving but felt good. This new friend of my father's looked to be about ten or twelve years older than I was, halfway between my dad's age and mine. *Kinda young to be friends with Dad,* I thought.

At the bowling alley, we got shoes and balls, then found an end lane. As usual, I jockeyed to sit next to my father, soaking up as much of his attention as I could during the few afternoons we spent with him each month. Not that it mattered where I sat this time. Dad was preoccupied with Terry, a constant source of playful joking around, making comments only they would understand.

"Just wait till you live with me, honey," he quipped, smiling at Dad before sashaying down the alley to throw the ball. *Live with him? Is this guy gonna be his roommate?* I shrugged off the thought for the rest of the game and, by the time we got to Eva's Diner later, had forgotten all about it.

But that night in bed, the excitement of the day still buzzing in my mind, I remembered Terry's comment, and began wondering why my father didn't have a girlfriend. Not that I wanted to share him with another female—my sister was bad enough—but while

Mom had started dating Harry, a nice Jewish man who took her dancing, Dad never mentioned dating anyone. As someone so smart and handsome, it seemed to me any woman would be thrilled to date him. Drifting off to sleep, I realized it was fine with me if he never remarried. I always wanted to be his favorite girl.

· · ·

"Hey, Dad?" I asked when he picked me up from school a few weeks later. It was rare to see him during the week, alone. "You know, Mom has been going out on dates. Do you date anybody?" We had opened my first bank account with money from my recent fourteenth birthday, a rite of passage he had suggested. I was a little nervous asking him such a personal question, and I studied his face for signs of disapproval. "I mean, do you have a girlfriend? I'm sure you could find one if you wanted to." He glanced over from behind the wheel and smiled as he pulled into the gravel parking lot of the townhouse I shared with Mom and my sister.

"Well, honey, that's a complicated question, but no, I don't have a girlfriend."

"Why not?" I pushed, feeling like there was something he wasn't telling me. Terry joined most of our outings, but Dad never brought a date.

"Having a girlfriend doesn't fit in with my lifestyle. Let's just leave it at that."

Lifestyle? "Okay, Dad. I just thought—" He gave me a look that said, *enough*, then leaned over to kiss my cheek.

"I'll talk to you soon. I'm happy we got your account set up today," he said. "You sure are growing up. Say hello to your mother and Deena," he added before I pushed open the door.

"I will." As I walked up the porch steps, a thought stopped me in my tracks: *Terry.* Turning back to look for Dad's car, I caught only a glimpse of his taillight as he merged into traffic.

He spends all his time with Terry. I realized I hadn't been to my dad's place in a couple of months. *Did he move in? Oh my God, what if that's why Dad doesn't have a girlfriend?*

Suddenly, snippets of television references to men being queer ran rampant through my head; my stomach churned at the thought of what this might mean. I dropped my book bag inside the front door and went straight to the kitchen to call my mom. After dialing her number on the wall phone, my stomachache worsened while it rang. *What do I even want to know?*

"Demar Plating, this is Peg," she said from her desk in the small office where she was a secretary.

"Hi, Mom. So, Dad dropped me off after school, and before he left I asked him why he doesn't have a girlfriend. He said—"

"Lisa, do we need to get into this now? I'm at work."

"I know, but yes, we do need to talk about it now. Dad didn't really give me a straight answer when I asked him. Something about his lifestyle, he said. I mean, what lifestyle? He hangs out with that guy Terry all the time and I think he's moved in. There isn't even a spare room. I mean, that's pretty weird." I coiled the long yellow phone cord around my finger as I rattled on, forming a picture in my head I didn't really want to see.

"Lisa, please. We'll talk when I get home."

"*Mom.*" I plowed ahead, unable to contain the question I wasn't sure how to ask. "Uh, does Dad like guys? I mean, like *that?*" A growing panic seized me. "Is he *queer?*" The word felt like profanity when I said it to my mother.

She released a heavy sigh. "*Please.* I'm at work. We can talk more about this when—"

"Ma, I need to know now! He's my *father.*" Tears stung my eyes as I waited for her answer, though I already knew the truth.

"All right," her voice was not more than a whisper. "Yes."

Yes? Oh my God, my dad is a fag.

A deep, guttural laugh escaped me, turning to heaving sobs as I slid down the wall and sat on the floor unable to catch my breath as any remnants of my childhood evaporated like drops of water on a hot stove.

"But Mom, I don't understand. I mean, how could he do this to us? Don't you hate him?"

"Lis, c'mon. We'll talk tonight. Why don't you go to Mrs. McCall's and wait there until I pick you up after work? I don't want you home alone right now." Her insistence that I go to her best friend's house was a gentle order, not a suggestion. "And please don't tell your sister, do you hear me? Please. I'll have someone pick her up from practice." Her voice changed in a way that told me someone was standing at her desk. "We'll talk about it more when I get home. Okay? Now go to Mrs. McCall's."

"But—"

"I have to go. It'll be okay. We'll talk later."

I reluctantly hung up, then ran toward Maureen McCall's house, the heaviness of my new discovery crushing my chest. *My dad is queer.* I didn't even fully know what that meant. All I knew was what I had heard Archie Bunker say about queers and fags. *They're fairies.* As I ran, each tiny piece of information I had ever heard about homosexuality began to fit together all at once, revealing the whole picture like a jigsaw puzzle.

Dad seemed utterly comfortable in a room full of women; at a party he hung out with the wives instead of drinking beer with the men. He didn't watch ball games and was meticulous about cleaning. "Don't make me do a white glove test," he warned while overseeing Saturday morning chores. He might have been joking, but I never doubted a white glove could be produced at any time to challenge my diligence. He liked things to be perfect and taught me to comb the fringe of the Oriental rug with an actual wide-tooth comb.

He's always been different from other dads, I thought as my feet pounded the pavement. He's never golfed or wrenched on cars. Instead, Dad sang and danced his way through *Anything Goes* as a stowaway belting out "You're the Top," dashing in white trousers and a navy jacket. I was so proud to be my father's daughter on that opening night, thrilled by the chaos and glory of being backstage at the theater. Now that I knew his lewd secret, I felt ashamed.

Our whole life has been an act! How could he betray us like this?

The late sun cast long shadows of the bare trees as I traveled block after block, tears clinging to my cold face. A memory from the year my parents divorced played like a movie in my head, of the night before Easter when I woke up to hear my mother crying softly in the living room. Sneaking down the stairs, I found her hiding Easter eggs, alone. It was after midnight and Dad was still out. She was startled, caught in front of the mantel, a blue plastic egg in her hand, poised to disappear behind a picture frame. She stifled a sob when I hugged her waist. "Are you okay?" I asked. She nodded, and we stood there for a long time. Then she sent me back to bed, her eyes red. I cried myself to sleep that night when it dawned on me how often my father went out without her.

Where did he go on those nights out?

I stopped running to catch my breath, bent over, and held my knees, my lungs burning. I wished I had my Primatene Mist. *Did he go to gay bars?* The thought repulsed me as I pushed away the image of a bar full of men drinking and dancing together, making out in a dark corner of the room. *Is that how he met Terry?*

With a couple of blocks left to go, I slowed to a walk, letting the pieces connect and make sense of things I hadn't understood before. A snapshot flashed in my mind of sitting on the hand-me-down sofa in Dad's studio apartment a few years before, while my parents were separated. I was ten years old and desperately wanted to know why he left us. He'd told me there were things that I was too young to understand. *He left because he liked men. Did Mom know then?*

A year later, they got back together. All my anxiety over losing my daddy vanished when he moved us into the beautiful house in Oak Park. We were happy there for three years, until Dad started going out without Mom. What a shock it was when he sat us down on the white brocade couch and told us they were getting divorced.

"We still love each other, and of course, we love you girls," he said. My mother nodded quietly. Bereft, I begged to know why he and Mom would break our world apart. They didn't have a good reason.

Now I know why.

Trees swayed as I walked, resentment at my dad growing as the wind kicked up. I pulled my jacket tighter around me. *Poor Mom.* My anger at her for moving us back to River Grove subsided as I thought about how hard this must be for her.

I'd begged to stay in Oak Park the day they announced their divorce, arguing that she couldn't drag me away from my friends in the middle of junior high. But my mother wore Oak Park like a too-large coat, one that looked ill-fitting and heavy on her. She never seemed as happy there as in the working-class suburbs to which her Italian family had migrated in the 1950s from Chicago. She found her joy in the backyards and basements of her sister and cousins, sharing meals and stories with those she loved while the newest family member was passed from lap to lap. Her decision to move us back to River Grove at the end of that school year produced a fierce rage in me that could not be quelled.

"Lisa, that's enough! Your mother can't afford to keep this house even if she wanted to. Besides, she wants to live near your grandmother and Auntie."

Dad's words had been final, each one delivering a heavy blow to my young life until it was shattered into little pieces. No more sleepovers in the grand parlors of my friends' homes, no more walks to Marshall Fields for chocolate after school. It had seemed so unfair to move from a canopied street lined with stately homes in a Frank Lloyd Wright neighborhood to a dumpy complex lined with bent screen doors, a dozen hard-luck stories living behind each one.

Nothing is fair, I thought as I slowly made my way down the final block in a daze, my nose and ears frozen. By the time I got there, Mrs. McCall had been briefed by my mother, and I poured myself into the sanctuary of her warm, ample chest and wept.

"Shh, shh, it'll be all right," she said, holding me.

I looked into her face for validation that it really would be. She smiled, raising the mole above her lip ever so slightly. My breathing returned to normal as she pulled me in tighter.

The phone rang.

"Hello?" she said, answering on the third ring. "Yes, she's here. Uh-huh. Do you want to talk to her?"

"It's your dad," she said, handing me the phone. Panic shot through me. "It's okay. Talk to him."

I took a deep breath and put the receiver to my ear. "Hi, honey," he said. Even though I had seen him only an hour before, he felt like a stranger now.

"Hi, Dad." I felt sheepish, as if somehow I had done something wrong.

"I'm sure you're a little surprised by what your mother told you, but you seem to have figured it out all by yourself. So, I suppose you're old enough to understand what this all means."

I'm not really sure I am, or even want to. He kept talking.

"It's important that you know there is absolutely nothing wrong with me, and at some point, I want you to go to the library and read about homosexuality so you can understand that this is normal."

How is this normal? Fresh tears stung my swollen eyes as I listened to him go on and on, barely comprehending his words about genetics and tendencies as they roared through my head. *Understand you're a homosexual?* The word felt dirty, like the bad swear words my older cousin taught me. The ones my parents never said in front of us.

"Do you have any questions? You can ask me whatever you want, Lisa."

Of course, I had questions. Sex was never talked about in our house, especially by my Catholic mother. Everything I knew, beyond what we learned in sixth-grade health class about getting our period, came from my friends. And Erica Jong. It had been thrilling to discover *Fear of Flying*—her ode to the "zipless fuck"—in my mother's nightstand after my parents divorced. Having sex crept into the minds of young teenage girls, like me, even though we were told to wait for marriage. We stumbled around in conversations about what it might be like to "go all the way." I couldn't even imagine my parents being sexual, let alone doing the things Erica described. And I was intrigued by the passion she wrote about.

But nothing had prepared me for the thought of my father having sex with a man.

I felt nauseous imagining my father sharing that passion with Terry. *What did they do? Did he feel like this before he met Mom?* Embarrassment rose like bile at the thought of asking my father these questions.

"No, Dad, not now," I said. *Just let me off the phone.*

"Fine, honey, everything will be fine. I'll talk to you soon. Maybe we'll see you and Deena on Sunday."

"Okay. Bye." I hung up the phone.

Things did not feel like they would ever be fine.

Two

Being far from where I grew up, finally at home in my own world, feels like kicking off too tight shoes. Relief wraps around me as I lie in bed grieving my father's death alone. The morning light peeks out from under the blinds, and my head throbs. Flooding in comes the day when all the pieces of the puzzle came together, scattering the shards of my ordinary eighth-grade life to the cold wind. It has become one of those moments that gets branded onto your psyche, seared by a scalding hot truth into a vivid memory. The kind of moment that shapes us by taking something away, like our innocence, or safety, or hope.

Pushing back the covers, I begin my day wondering how it has been only a week since the call from my sister that propelled me to the airport, to Dad's deathbed, and to the rest of my life without him in it.

In the days following my discovery about Dad, the awful secret took up residence inside me, too shameful to tell my friends, too embarrassing to discuss with my parents. Sworn to secrecy, to shield my little sister from the truth, I had no one to talk to about this new information. I carried it inside like a small, scared animal. At times it lay still and quiet, something I hardly knew was there. At other times it thrashed and gnawed at my insides, demanding it be fed and released, threatening to chew a hole through my soul. Sometimes it just ran around in circles until it fell in a heap, exhausted.

It was vital to me that the world think my parents were normal. As far as I knew, I was the only girl—aside from my oblivious little sister—who had a gay father.

Dad's suggestion that I research homosexuality at the library horrified me. The mere idea of standing in front of a librarian to check out books on the subject was unimaginable. Like most secrets, the shame of its potential discovery was the hardest thing to bear. If Dad being gay was a secret, then it must be bad. And if it was bad, then Dad must be bad.

Carefully weighing my shame against the heaviness of the secret I carried, I finally allowed it to break free in my friend Phyllis's kitchen. Over steaming bowls of SpaghettiOs, I spilled my family guts.

"Phyl, uh, I want to tell you something really weird about my dad. I mean, I haven't told anybody." In the dim, cozy kitchen, it felt safe to utter words I didn't even know how to say. "It's really bad."

"Like what? It can't be that bad, your dad seems nice." She tilted her bowl against her lips, slurping the last drops of orange sauce.

"I guess he is, but this is pretty bad." I stuck the last spoonful into my mouth and went to the stove to get more. Food had become a salve that numbed my pain.

Before I turned around, I said, "He likes guys. I mean, he's a fag." Silence filled the room as I sat back at the table, my eyes cast down into my bowl. *Is she still gonna be my friend?* I looked up to gauge her response.

Her huge blue eyes were wide with surprise. "Is that why they got divorced?"

"Yeah, and the thing is, Mom still talks to him like everything is fine. I mean, how can she do that? I don't ever want to talk to him again. I know that's mean, but I just can't even look at him without thinking...you know. And he has this young boyfriend that I actually thought was cute."

We sat quietly for a moment, letting my news sink in. Not knowing what she thought made me nervous. "Wow. I can't imagine my mom ever having sex with anyone," she said. Phyl, the youngest of three sisters, was more experienced in sexual matters, and was quite promiscuous in junior high compared to the likes of me. "It's been so long since my dad died, I don't think she even remembers what it was like."

I rinsed the dishes in the sink, relief flowing over me like the water that spilled over my hands. *Thank God she doesn't think I'm weird.* "My mom dates Harry," I said, turning back to face her. "But I can't imagine them doing it. She and Dad probably did it only twice to have me and Deena. In some ways, you're lucky your dad died and isn't around to be ashamed of. Sometimes, I wish mine had just died instead. I know it's wrong, but—" I burst into tears as I made my confession, choking on the words, then ran to the bathroom.

The shame and relief of saying out loud that it would have been easier if Dad had died made me feel like I might throw up. I splashed water on my face and went back into the kitchen where Phyl was putting the dishes away. Her sister had come in and I was relieved that the subject was dropped.

· · ·

Of course, once I knew the truth about Dad and Terry, the shame and humiliation were enough to make me want to stay away. "Why don't you go to the show with your dad and Deena this weekend?" Mom suggested when he made plans with my sister. She encouraged me to see him, but my desire to punish him won out.

"No way. He won't go anywhere without Terry, so no."

The truth had opened a portal to things I didn't want to see. Now that Terry had moved in with him, and the cat was out of the bag, I found it uncomfortable to be around them. Dad seemed unwilling to spend time with only his girls; Terry had to be with us whenever we saw him. What was once the thing I wanted most—time with my daddy—I now refused out of awkwardness and spite. Each time I saw my sister climb into the back seat and drive off with them, envy of her innocence and carefree oblivion filled my heart, sinking me further into an angry gloom.

Glimmers of my silent belief that it might have been better if he had died, rose to the surface when I realized my father would never again be the man I'd adored as a little girl. *It's like he's dead already.* Immediately my vile thought was replaced with deep shame that I still wanted to punish him for lying to us and sneaking behind Mom's back.

Talking to my mother about Dad was uncomfortable, like talking about sex. Her own silent shame created a barrier to openly expressing my confusion and disgust. So enmeshed was his lifestyle with his sexuality that any mention of him and Terry felt illicit. Mom clearly didn't want to talk about it with me, treating him like he was just her friend now.

Each day, I sat on my red bedspread under posters of The Jackson 5 and Cat Stevens, listening to my cherished records for hours. *Tea for the Tillerman* comforted me. Over and over, Cat's words to "Sad Lisa" were cranked up high in my headphones while I wrote "Dear Diary" in my large loopy script. My diary became a private repository for my deepest thoughts, a safe place to record tearful meltdowns about my dad or my current best friend, and the detailed recaps of nights drinking beer in someone's basement while hoping that some guy likes me. Each page was gilded with a gold edge, a tiny lock securing the tab that bound them.

I wrote volumes about attracting the attention of a cute boy in class or the loathing I felt toward my father who dared to be so different from everyone else's. So different I couldn't even talk about it with my mother. I wrote as if I were the character in Cat's song "Father & Son," who kept all the things he knew inside, then vowed to go away. I couldn't wait to grow up and leave. I didn't yet realize that you cannot run from the truth.

While my parents were coping with the changes in their own lives, it never occurred to them that I was struggling to understand what happened to our family and might need to talk with someone about how it felt to hold a secret so big and restless. Like most teenage girls, I was a hormonal stew bubbling over with all the flavors of adolescence; my need for understanding and attention was insatiable. I missed my dad, even though I said I never wanted to see him again and refused to speak to him. He didn't try too hard to change my mind, content with just seeing my sister. Deep down, I wanted him to fight for me.

"You just don't understand how hard this is for me!" I screamed at my mom. The fact that she still talked to him made her an accomplice in my despair. "I can't help it that this doesn't make any sense to me. That I can't forget how happy you guys were when you were married. How weird it is that Dad is with Terry."

"It's not easy for me either, Lisa. Can you imagine how I feel? Let's just drop it." As usual, Mom was quick to point to her own suffering, then want to change the subject. Her discomfort with my anger and confusion made her unwilling to let me run off the rails with my feelings, in an attempt to avoid the train wreck that roared inside me. Also, she still liked my dad and didn't want me talking against him.

Finding out my father was gay had answered some questions about their divorce but challenged everything I knew about who my parents really were, and about marriage itself.

When they were a young couple, Dad left our two-bedroom Georgian home each morning for his job as a rising star in the new world of computers. He put on a pressed shirt, carefully ironed by Mom after she sprinkled the crisp cotton with water from a Coke bottle, then he expertly knotted a striped tie in front of the bathroom mirror before coming downstairs for coffee and toast. Mom was a consistent figure at the kitchen sink, washing the most recent meal's dishes or standing at the counter preparing whatever would be served on them next. The rest of the time she cleaned and did laundry, shopped for groceries, and coffee-klatched with the neighbors while we kids ran around. Their marriage modeled the cooperative managing of a household and the raising of children. Their displays of physical affection were limited to a quick kiss when Dad came in the door. They laughed a lot and seemed to have an endless list of things to talk about. They bickered a little but didn't fight. And each night they seemed content to watch television after supper in matching recliners while my sister and I lay on the floor, our fists tucked under our chins.

I love that Rhoda has her own show! I wrote in my diary when Mary Richards' sidekick got her own spin-off. *And she's getting married! Joe is such a fox.* Rhoda getting herself a husband seemed to validate her after all that painful dating, and while it wasn't likely that she would become June Cleaver in a headscarf, she settled into a new version of herself, someone I wanted to be when I grew up.

My idols from *Mary Tyler Moore* and *That Girl* were the flint that sparked the romantic fantasies of my girlhood. Even though I dreamed of a chic apartment of my own in some exciting city— the perfect backdrop for my life as a sophisticated and smart career girl looking for love—I identified more with Mary's best friend Rhoda: loud and curvy, a creative window-dresser with a tiny bohemian apartment, often in the throes of unrequited romantic attraction. I thought my father would be like Ann Marie's, attentive and protective of his little girl, imparting his wisdom and support when she needed him. I swooned over the starry-eyed kind of love portrayed by my first crush, Davy Jones on *The Monkees*, whenever he looked at his dream girl-of-the-week.

No, the romance I watched on television was not what I saw growing up in my house. Until I noticed my father look at Terry with those stars in his eyes. This made me squirm. I had never seen him looking at Mom like that.

Three

While my coffee brews, I watch the neighborhood come to life. It's a cloudy Thursday. *May gray, June gloom,* the weather phenomenon that blankets the sky with dense coastal fog on early spring and summer mornings. People are walking their dogs, driving to work. It all looks so normal, and yet I feel like I'm swimming in slow motion through thick air.

An eerie calm comes over me while I take a mug from the cabinet—then I think, *Dad is dead* and burst into tears. Sobs shake me hard; a little earthquake that lasts a dozen seconds or so then subsides. An aftershock shudders through me.

After fixing my coffee, I wander into the living room and confront the box on the coffee table, now deceptively cheerful for something containing the charred remains of a living, breathing human being. "You could have taken better care of yourself, Dad," I say, then I realize he'd been living on borrowed time for half his life.

"It looks nice, but it's pretty low-cut. Let's see it with the jacket," Mom said while we shopped for the perfect dress for my eighth-grade graduation. I had picked out a yellow polyester sheath that hung from spaghetti straps over my blossoming curves down to the floor.

"I love it!" I tied the matching ruffled jacket across my chest, covering my ample cleavage enough to satisfy my modest mother. She nodded her agreement and smiled.

Meanwhile, my father and Terry were miles away, driving seven hours to Minnesota to borrow a kiln to fire Terry's pottery. As my mom was handing her Master Charge card to the store clerk at Madigan's Boutique, Dad was in the back seat bleeding internally, with a Kotex stuffed in his skivvies.

The shrill ring of Dad's call awakened us before dawn the next morning, a time when phone calls only bring bad news. "What? What happened?" I heard my mom say as I padded my way to her doorway.

"Oh, my God, Don."

I sat on the bed next to her, trying to hear what I could of my father's responses. She let me stay. "I knew I was sick when we left town," he said, weaker than I'd ever heard him, "but I thought I'd get better. We just needed to fire Terry's pots, then go back home. But I collapsed when we got here, and he took me into emergency. The doctors want to do surgery, but I just want to come home."

He admitted that for a few weeks he had been bleeding internally and had lost a lot of weight, ignoring the signs of a serious problem. He said something about severe ulcerative colitis, and a perforated colon.

"What am I supposed to do, Don?" Mom looked like she wanted to cry.

"Go over and tell my parents. They'll help get me home." She wrote down the phone number for the hospital. "Thanks, Peg. What would I do without you?" The question hung between them before she agreed to call him back and hung up.

"Mom, this sounds really bad." Panic rose in my chest. "Is he gonna be okay?"

"He'll be fine. I'll go make coffee, then go to Grandma's. You stay here with your sister."

By daylight, Mom was at my grandparents' kitchen table explaining what had happened. She shared the option of flying their son by air ambulance back to Illinois, and they agreed to pay whatever it took to get him home.

When he arrived in the emergency room, I was waiting there with my mother. As the ER doors swung open, my father was wheeled in on a gurney. After months of not seeing him, I was shocked by how thin and pale he was. When he saw us, he cried—something I had never seen him do. This made my unyielding rejection of him even more shameful, bringing my own tears as I realized that he might actually die.

"His insides are leaking into his system," the doctor explained. "We need to remove the damaged colon and fight the infection before it gets any worse. He needs a colostomy. I'm sorry, but without this surgery he is not likely to make it."

Still, my father resisted. The doctor's explanation of what was happening inside of him sounded scary, and of course I had no concept of the repercussions of such a surgery on a recently outed gay man. Any hopes for a less drastic procedure were dashed when the doctor explained that if he wanted to live, he had to let them operate.

"We're optimistic," the doctor said, "but there is still less than a 50 percent chance of survival with this surgery." It was scheduled for the following morning.

I lost the argument with my mother to go to the hospital with her during his operation and was left at home with my sister and Gram. Mom knew better than to add my emotions to the already stressful scene. For hours, she and my father's parents propped one another up while waiting in his room, sustained by weak coffee and hope. Grandma sat in a plastic chair, each exhale a sigh as she chain-smoked her Pall Malls.

Terry and the friends he shared with Dad had taken over the waiting room, a group of strangers anticipating the same results as his lover's parents and ex-wife. Eventually, Terry dissolved into a dramatic mess, trying to get into the surgical area and generally wreaking havoc for the staff and my family. Mom tried to ignore him.

"Just shut the hell up!" Grandpa yelled at this queer boy who had replaced his beloved daughter-in-law in his son's life. Grandpa hadn't said much about the divorce since Grandma's preferred coping mechanism was denial. But he was fond of my mother and had a hard time understanding his son's new life. "If you say another word to her, I'll throw you out the goddamn window," he said to Terry.

Dad's two lives slowly collided during those twenty-four hours, revealing the juxtaposition of his gay life with his family life. Both were meaningful to him, but he had purposely kept them separate, knowing neither group was comfortable with the other. To an onlooker, it would have been inconceivable that these two groups, huddled apart against the threat of death, could possibly be waiting on the results of a single surgery patient.

I will be a good daughter and try to understand him, I prayed to God that night as guilt pulsated through me. *I didn't really mean it when I wished he was dead. I swear I didn't, I am so sorry. Please save my dad.*

• • •

Seeing Dad after his surgery took my breath away. My strong thirty-five-year-old father had been reduced to skin and bones in a matter of weeks, as pale as the white sheet that covered him. But he was alive.

The promises I'd made to God about being good, about trying to be a better daughter if He spared my daddy, were now mine to keep. Each day, I pushed down my lingering confusion over how my father would suddenly want to love a young man instead of Mom—the one person Dad still seemed to need most in the world, the one who had run to his side when he got sick. I swallowed my antipathy toward Terry, who sat beside Dad's hospital bed in the chair that should have been my mother's, holding his hand in front of us.

As grateful as I was that his life had been spared, fury sucked the air from my lungs as I sobbed with shame in bed at night. *How can I be a good daughter if I still hate to see Dad with Terry? If I still hate how Mom acts like it's all okay? I am so sorry.* Eventually, I worked myself into a full-blown asthma attack.

"Please do something, Mom," I pleaded, exhausted and tearful. Sitting on my bed, I rocked back and forth, clutching my pillow to my chest.

"C'mon. Crying only makes it worse," she said, rubbing my back. "I think I better take you in to the ER, Lis. They'll give you a shot and a treatment. You'll feel a lot better."

An hour later, as I sat behind a curtain in the West Suburban Emergency Room—the same hospital where we had greeted my father's air ambulance just a week before—a shot of epinephrine coursed through my body, making me feel all jittery inside but opening my airways enough for me to catch my breath.

"Rest for a few minutes while I go up to your dad's room and tell him we're here. Okay?"

I nodded, and tentatively leaned back against the raised head of the gurney, hearing my heartbeat in my ears. My thoughts went straight upstairs to Terry sitting at Dad's bedside, and the tightness in my chest returned. By the time she got back I was wheezing again, and they decided to admit me. An IV was poked into the vein of my right hand, and I was settled into a room on the second floor, where I was given continuous oxygen, and a heavy dose of prednisone. Every four hours a respiratory therapist appeared to administer a treatment. Mom floated between my room and Dad's.

Although I was finally breathing more easily, the treatments and medication did nothing to quell the panic I felt while occupying the same hospital as my father and his boyfriend, who curled up in the chair beside Dad's bed each night, refusing to go home.

"Did you hear about the fags on the fourth floor?" I overheard a nurse say to another one in the hall outside my door. My ears perked up. *That's my dad*, I thought, both terrified of anyone knowing the truth and desperate to share it with someone who would listen. Someone who would help me understand how I could feel fear, anger, hurt, and shame—all at the same time—while still wanting to love my dad.

"The guy's *friend*," she said, exaggerating the word, "barely leaves to go home. A prissy thing, too. Very demanding."

My faced burned with embarrassment at the thought of mentioning that we were related.

"How are you? You look better," Terry said late one night when he came to my room. He pulled up the visitor's chair close to the bed and sat down. Not waiting for my answer, he continued, "It's crazy that you would end up in the hospital at the same time as Don." He looked at me squarely. "He was really sick, you know. We almost lost him. I don't know what I would have done if he didn't make it. I couldn't live without him."

Why is he telling me this? It still unnerved me to be near him, especially alone together. The initial crush I had when we first went bowling was tangled with thoughts of him and my father that I couldn't bear to think about. I pulled the covers up close to my chin. "But he's gonna be okay, right? We don't have to worry because he's getting better," I said, parroting what my mom had been saying since Dad's surgery.

"Yeah, he's getting better." He eyed me closely for a moment, started to say something, then stopped. A dazzling smile bloomed across his face before he spoke. "You know, sweetie, your father loves me. I mean he *really* loves me." He paused just long enough for his words to pierce my heart, then tear a gash across it. "He loves you girls, too, of course, but we're in love. You just need to know that, sweetheart."

"Okay," I said, my throat closing as the heaviness in my chest returned; a wheeze rattled each exhale. *Please just leave.*

"When he gets out of the hospital, we will need some help. Don's going to need someone to look after him while I open the shop." *Oh, yeah. The shop.* Dad was leaving his successful computer programming job to open a gift shop in Oak Park with his artist lover. Lost in the shuffle of his surgery, the opening day loomed and would coincide with my father's release from the hospital.

"This is all happening so fast, and I just can't be in two places at the same time. You'll be out of school when he's released so we thought maybe you can come and help."

Come and stay there with both of you? No way. My immediate instinct was to reject any suggestion that had me sleeping over in their small apartment. *But Dad will be so mad if I say no.* I pictured Terry telling my father I wasn't willing to help him. I remembered my promise to God.

"I'll ask my mom," was all I could muster. I tried to hold my breath to mask the embarrassing sound of my wheezing, making it even harder to breathe. *Please go.*

"Good. I'm glad we could talk." He got up, smoothing the creases that had gathered down the thighs of his tight jeans. "Now, feel better, okay?" He patted my leg through the thin blanket that covered me. "You have a big day coming up! You wouldn't want to miss your graduation. I better get back to your dad. Nighty, night."

Once alone, I settled against my pillow, slowly drawing in oxygen from the tube beneath my nose. Fat tears rolled from my eyes into my ears as I cried myself to sleep.

Four

A fabric bag emblazoned with Saxx Funeral Home's logo leans against the wall beside my front door. Inside are pictures I took from my father's buffet the day after he died. I dump them out on the coffee table beside the decorated box of ashes and sift through them.

One of the first photos to surface shows Dad gaunt and sickly in a hospital bed, but he's smiling with his daughter in the pretty yellow graduation dress standing beside him, the daughter he had barely seen for months. Behind her smile are the conflicted feelings she has for this man she truly loves but struggles to understand.

In another shot Terry stands beside the bed, his arm draped above Dad's head, both of them happy—the relief that he is still alive fills the frame. A Polaroid of my father sitting on an unfamiliar couch, presumably in a hospital lounge, shows his legs sticking out of his robe like bent toothpicks. I'm struck by how emaciated he is, how sick he must have been.

I'm struck by how much time I wasted being mad at him.

So much of my young life was spent trying to win my father's attention or getting back at him for withholding it because of judgments I carried over things I didn't understand. I dragged them through my adolescence like a sack of heavy stones while I tried too hard to be heard, to be seen. Along with this load, I carried the erroneous expectation that parents automatically put their children before themselves, as if a switch is flipped the moment they are born. I assumed that families should be like every TV sitcom that filled our living room, with a belief that once they got married and had kids, Mom and Dad became a fused unit, erasing who they might have been before parenthood.

I open a sleeve of photos and there is one of Dad and my sister at his sixty-fifth birthday party. My stomach churns when I think about Dad's will, then roils with shame for even caring. *It wasn't all his fault. But it wasn't all mine. What was he thinking?*

After a few days of treatment for the asthma attack, I was released from the hospital to my final days of eighth grade. On the night of graduation, Mom took me to see Dad. Mostly, I wanted him to see me in my yellow dress. *How do I look, Daddy? See how grown-up I am?* After Terry's visit to my hospital room, when I became keenly aware that it was he who held the highest place in my father's heart, I had secretly begun to crave Dad's attention even more than before, regardless of my lingering anger.

"Let's get a picture with your dad, Lis," Mom said, aiming her small Kodak Instamatic at me standing next to his bedside. The flashcube popped as I gave her my widest grin.

"You look very pretty, honey." His voice quivered with weakness and pride. "My gosh, you look like you could be graduating high school." I beamed under his praise.

By the first of June, Dad was healing and almost ready to go home. Terry prepared to open the shop. A cheerful green and yellow awning greeted us as Mom and I approached the storefront to talk to him. I took a deep breath and opened the door. *Here goes*, I thought as a bell jangled to announce our arrival. Terry turned from his perch on a ladder in the middle of the large space. Boxes in various stages of unpacking filled the room, along with a few young men who were painting.

"Well, hello ladies," Terry said, still standing on the ladder.

"Hi." I shuffled my feet and looked around the shop, stalling. "Uh, there are just a few things I want to tell you before I agree to come help Dad." Mom stood quietly beside me while the guys around the room stopped what they were doing.

"Well, okay." Terry glanced at one of his friends with a smirk.

My heart pounded. "I'll agree to come under one condition: I don't want to be subjected to anything that will repulse me." *Whew. I got it out.* I looked over at my mother, then back at Terry across the silent room.

He leveled his eyes to mine and laughed. "Well, honey, that won't be a problem. He's just getting out of the hospital, after all." His friends snickered.

My mom gently took my arm. "C'mon, Lis, let's go." She hastily guided us out the door to the car. If she shot Terry a disapproving look, I didn't see it.

Terry's laughter was still ringing in my ears.

· · ·

My parents slept in the same bed until the day they divorced, and then my mother slept alone. Her dating life was chaste, a social opportunity that provided dinners out and nights on the dance floor with a nice man she had no intention of marrying. Her beau Harry's friendly hello when he picked up her up was the extent of my relationship with him. I never imagined her being full of butterflies and expectations, like I was when I thought about boys. Sex was the furthest thing from my mind when I pictured my mother—which was exactly what she wanted.

Yet, Dad seemed to flaunt his chemistry with Terry. It was like a vapor you could almost get a whiff of if you got too close. Any value judgment my mom carried about her daughter staying at her gay ex-husband's apartment while he slept with his young lover, she didn't share with me. Like in their marriage, Mom rarely challenged my father.

Off I went to stay with them.

My dad's departure from our family, and finding out he was gay, had made him into a different person in my eyes. Like a snake who had shed its skin, he was made new, and I grieved for the lifeless, discarded layer that was my Daddy. This reborn creature wound around another life now, curling beside Terry instead of us. Entering their den made me wary.

Tension replaced any compassion I may have felt toward my frail father who sat on the couch on a donut pillow, his skinny legs crossed beneath a navy bathrobe. At barely 130 pounds, he looked kind of scary.

"How about you make beef stew for dinner tonight, the way your mother does," Dad said. "There is a pound of meat in the freezer you can defrost."

I had been preparing simple meals since my parents' divorce, my repertoire consisting mostly of Shake 'n Bake and Hamburger Helper. I called Mom to walk me through the beef stew recipe over the phone. "Add a can of tomato paste, then a few cans of water, a little salt." Her measurements were in the Italian tradition of *a little of this* and *a pinch of that.*

"It's much too salty," Dad declared, wrinkling his nose when he tried it, killing my fragile confidence. "It was a good try, though, honey." I felt judged and incompetent, unable to feel comfortable around this man with whom I had lived most of my life, especially beside this young guy I barely knew. Terry's jealousy of me floated like bubbles between us, his visit to my hospital room still fresh. My jealousy of him made me anxious.

"I may need you to sit at the store for an hour while I run errands tomorrow. While your dad takes a nap," Terry said during supper.

"Okay." I was immediately concerned that there would be customers and I wouldn't know what to do. Dad just smiled, apparently fine with the request. "Will you teach me what to do if someone buys something?"

"Sure, but I doubt we will have much traffic." Then Terry said something to Dad about one of their friends, launching into a conversation that didn't include me. I cleared the table and went in and washed the dishes, feeling like a maid.

In the quiet, dark hours after they went to bed, I leaned out the window smoking cigarettes I had swiped from Dad's pack. Even a solid wall between the couch where I slept and the bed they shared wasn't enough to shield me from the reality of them as a couple. The thought of them kissing, and God knows what else, made me feel sick inside, vanquishing the promises I made to be a good daughter while Dad stood at death's door.

The warm night air soothed me, and I thought about what it would have been like to have a new stepmother. There would have been jealousy, most likely, but perhaps she could have become another adult who loved me. Would I have been as squeamish about their bedroom life? It certainly wouldn't have been the taboo reality of my father in the next room with a young man, a truth especially disturbing since it seemed that I was the only girl in the world whose dad did this. The idea that Terry could be an ally seemed impossible, given his competition with me for Dad's love.

After the second night, I said I wanted to sleep over at Phyllis's, and would help them out during the day. My father wasn't happy about it.

"I see no reason for that, but all right," he said, bristling over my discomfort with staying with them, but he allowed Phyl's sister to pick me up each night.

. . .

My time with Dad and Terry that week took more of the mystery out of his new life than I could bear. How much we shield our children from aspects of adult life varies wildly between households, and across generations. My mother hung a thick velvet drape between her sex life and her children, while a sheer gossamer veil was all that separated us from my father's romance with his boyfriend. Such confusing messages brought up mixed feelings about love and sexuality. This made it impossible to talk with either one of them while my curiosity about sex was developing, like a pupa in a silk cocoon. Mom would be mortified, and Dad would want to chat about it like girlfriends.

Kissing Scott Shepard under his porch in seventh grade and playing spin the bottle at parties were my own secrets, along with the stirrings I felt when a boy I liked looked at me or sat near me. My desire for boys' attention became an ache, like the one I felt when Dad ignored my pleas to see him. It felt as if getting a boy to love me would make my upset feelings about Dad go away.

Along with basement make-out sessions, I had begun seriously flirting with rebellion, experimenting with cigarettes and beer, but not fully committing until the day I hopped on a bus to Wisconsin with Linda later that summer, to run away to Nippersink Resort where we had met when both of our families were still intact.

"We're gonna get killed when they find us, so we better have as much fun as possible," I said as we shared a smoke at the Greyhound bus station. "If anyone asks, we should say we're sixteen." Linda was fifteen—a year older than me—and already in high school. A city girl, she was much more savvy. I followed her lead.

"I don't even know who my dad is anymore," I said, watching out the window as the bus rolled down Highway 12 past cow pastures and small towns. "It was hard when my parents first got divorced, but I knew who they were, you know? They were still *them*." Linda pulled a bag of Fritos out of her backpack, nodding. "But now, I don't know my dad at all. He doesn't even look the same as when he was with Mom. It's like he's become a completely different person. Mom hasn't changed at all except she works full time and dates that guy, Harry." It occurred to me that, unlike Dad, I hadn't thought much about my mother and her life apart from us. She was always just Mom.

I plunged my hand into the bag when she offered it. "My Mom and Dad seem like the same people," she said, "but our lives are different. I mean, we're still in the house and everything. Mom is just really angry all the time. I see my dad every other weekend." She leaned close to look out the window, her breath smelling of corn chips. "We're almost there!"

The International House of Wine and Cheese greeted us, indicating we had crossed state lines and were within minutes of arriving at the resort. Soon after, we were sitting on bleachers watching the college-age staff play baseball in the hot August sun. The thrill of independence washed away our teenage angst, and we felt very grown up—until the sound of my mother's voice crashed our reverie.

"Lisa! Get over here right now!" Mom yelled when she and my aunt found us, swooping in like a SWAT team. "You, too, Linda. Your mother is worried sick."

Holy shit. How did they find us? We didn't dare say a word. In ten seconds, Mom was right beside us, her eyes red from crying. "Thank God Linda's brother told us where you two went."

My aunt reached the bleachers and grabbed me by the arm. "You are in big trouble, young lady! Get moving. Now!" Auntie's stern demand turned the heads of everyone, stopping the game. My face burned with a humiliation worse than the punishment I knew would be coming. On the way home our purses were confiscated, the cigarettes found.

"You're grounded for as long as your mother says so," my father declared when I was required to call him that night. "Right now, it's a month. And no trip to Hawaii with Grandma Haute on Christmas break. That's for smoking, too. For God's sake, you have asthma."

"So does Mom, and she smokes. You smoke." *So what if you're pissed off. I'm pissed, too.*

"Well, we're adults and she hasn't been in the hospital for it like you have. What were you thinking? What were you going to do at night without a room?"

"I don't know." *It's all your fault, Dad. Everything is your fault.*

• • •

Once freshman year of high school got underway, I hung out with the fringe kids, a breakfast club of burnouts who drank Mad Dog 20/20 wine during school, sneaking out after first period to someone's car. My best friend, Vicki, was smoking pot and experimenting with other drugs while I was still getting good grades and had a reasonable fear of consequences.

Vicki glided through life confidently on her long legs, constantly tossing her thick hair off her freckled face to reveal a tiny pug nose. I both adored her and envied her, with my thin, straight hair, too-large nose, and thick thighs. She swung effortlessly between the cool kids and the cheerleaders, holding court while I mostly hung back, sucking in my pudgy stomach so I fit in. But I didn't really fit in, instead I was grateful to just be her sidekick.

We talked endlessly about boys. Mostly about my current crush, Will McDongal. We had a movie date that ended with us making out in front of my house. The next day, as we drove around during sixth period in his Riviera, he dropped the bomb.

"Sorry, Lis, but I like you too much as a friend to go out with you."

"It's okay. We can still hang out." It was not okay, but I didn't want to upset him and lose his friendship.

The next day I saw him in the hall with Vicki, who was laughing too loudly and standing too close. *All the guys want her and not me.* I held back tears for the rest of the day and noticed that Will didn't find me to drive me home after school. He gave her a ride instead.

While I sobbed in my room alone, I picked up the small ceramic figurine Vicki gave me for my birthday. *Best Friends Forever.*

"Yeah, right!" I screamed out loud and hurled it across the room, shattering it into pieces. I picked up a broken shard, then ran my finger over the sharp edge. As I began poking my wrist with it, the pain absorbed the one in my heart. *I'll show them.* I cut along the surface and watched a thin red line snake across my wrist like a strand of crimson thread. I was hypnotized, the magnitude of the gesture so big, so *final*. I didn't really want to kill myself. I wanted them to see my hurt feelings.

After that fleeting moment, the sight of blood completely freaked me out and I went to the bathroom to run my wrist under cold water to stop the bleeding. I wrapped it up in gauze and taped it, letting the throbbing remind me that although my heart was broken, it kept on beating.

• • •

That Father's Day, Deena was spending the weekend at Dad's place without me. As I stood in the card aisle at Walgreens, thumbing through colorful drawings of fishermen, mechanics, and golfers, all I felt was dread. *They don't make cards For My Gay Dad.* I skipped right over the Best Dad in the World cards and chose a generic one with a tie on it to send with Deena to give to him, along with two packs of

Camel cigarettes I got my mom to buy.

Sadly, my rejection of my father meant that any love he offered me I refused. It wasn't as if he didn't invite me when he took my sister out. But seeing him meant seeing him with Terry; he had made that clear. To receive Dad's love, I had to accept Terry completely. My refusal was how I punished him, though it hurt me, too. Probably more.

I settled for the groping hands of teenage boys and called that love instead. I became a magnet for indifference, my heart a holy grail to be retrieved only from the object of my romantic affection.

How agonizing for this young girl that the adults who surrounded her didn't notice the extent of her pain. Dad was a betrayer and a fraud in my young eyes, a fallen knight. My distrust of his conditional love made any contact with him intolerable. Meanwhile, doing her best with a full-time job and two daughters to raise, my mother was taking care of us with everything she had. She was a "good girl" who had followed the rules: she got married, had babies, and stayed close to her family. Nothing had prepared her for her husband's announcement that he was gay, let alone her grief-stricken daughter's reaction. She was as ill-equipped to deal with a teenager who rejected her homosexual father as any Midwestern mom in the 1970s would have been. It was easier for her to dismiss my anger than to wade into those uncharted waters with me.

So, we didn't talk about my emotions; I simply expressed them. Fights about my curfew, drinking, and having friends over when she wasn't home were balanced with crying jags that went on for hours when I was missing my dad. Mom didn't know what to do with me. Clearly uncomfortable talking about Dad's boyfriend, she encouraged me to accept the situation.

It was never discussed that perhaps I needed to talk to someone else. Someone who wasn't one of my parents.

...

"I can't believe how Mom can be nice to Dad after everything. I mean, she should hate him even more than I do. He was her husband!"

At fifteen, I found Nancy with Northwest Youth Outreach, a social work intern who racked up hours by volunteering to talk to the fucked-up kids after school. We met on Tuesdays after class in a drafty church basement, where she let me smoke cigarettes while I poured my heart out about all the things I didn't understand, and the things I wanted to change but couldn't. She was my salvation, simply because she listened.

"Why do you hate him, Lisa?" Nancy asked questions no one else did.

"Because he's not normal!" I took another drag of my Salem, then loudly exhaled. "Why can't he be like regular dads who are married and go on family vacations and have nice houses? Some of my friends have stepparents, not some rude fag like Terry. We lived in such a nice house in Oak Park. I loved it there. Then all of a sudden, Dad has to go off and fall in love with some *guy*! I mean, that's just gross. No one else has a dad like that. Seriously. No one."

"Is that why you won't see him?"

"Yeah, kinda, but I want to punish him, too. He loves Terry more than us!" *There, I said it.* The memory of Terry's smug announcement of their love was still vivid. "I want him to feel bad, like maybe he misses *me* for a change." I lit another cigarette, dropping the match in the empty Coke can on the floor beside me.

"Do you think he misses you?" Her eyes were kind and stayed steadily locked with mine.

"Maybe." The truth was, I didn't really think he did.

I told her about how I got drunk with Vicki, sneaking booze from her parents' stash, always taking the vodka since her mom couldn't tell when water had been added to the bottle.

"And it's not just Dad. Mom and I fight about everything. She screams at me over anything I do."

"You have to remember they are people, too, Lisa. Individuals with desires and dreams of their own. I know you want to be their top priority, but sometimes parents need to focus on adult things. This new information about your father's life is a shock, I know. But that doesn't mean he's a bad person. Try to give your mom and dad a chance." Thinking about my parents as individuals was a notion I hadn't fully considered.

"Until the divorce, they were just my *parents*, you know. I didn't exactly think of them separate from that." They had been a unit I could count on to take care of me, whose lives revolved around Dad's work, and the house, and us. "Now my father has turned into someone I don't know, and my mother is trying to act like everything is fine."

Nancy looked up from her notebook where she had jotted something down. "Well, even though they have gotten divorced, it's likely that you and your sister still matter most to them."

"I know we still matter most to my mom, but not Dad. He has a life that we aren't even a part of." *Maybe that's the real reason I'm so angry with him all the time.*

By the end of that year, Dad and Terry broke up. This softened me. I began to speak with my father again. Still, seeing him was always on his terms. He didn't commit to weekend plans, but that was fine since now my attention was focused on my new boyfriend—and the milestone I reached the week before my sixteenth birthday.

"I went all the way with Johnny," I told Nancy as the light outside the dirty church windows faded on a cold day in December. "He said he loves me, and he gave me his ring." I twirled the band of gold around my finger. It was heavy, with "Class of 1977" flanking a yellow topaz in the center. I had wrapped a wad of pale blue angora yarn around the back to keep it on my finger. "It hurt the first time, but then it felt good when we did it again." The memory of his hands on me, and the aroused feeling of being naked together, made me blush. The sex itself didn't feel all that great, but the sensation of merging together was incredible.

"Have you told your mom?" she asked, even though she probably knew the answer.

"Uh, no. But I got birth control foam from the drugstore, so I'm careful." Vicki was just one of my friends who'd had an abortion while I was still a virgin. It seemed like a good thing to avoid.

"That's a very good idea." We talked about the implications of being sexual; she gave me pamphlets on birth control. When I broke up with Johnny a month later, for lying to me about doing drugs, she met me at the church and held me while I sobbed.

· · ·

"You look like you just broke up with your boyfriend," the guy at the counter said after ordering an Italian beef sandwich and fries. He was wearing a Beatles T-shirt and had become a recent regular at the hot dog joint where I worked after school. He was with his friend, who barely said a word. I nodded and burst into tears.

"Yeah, yesterday." My swollen eyes burned. *Oh, my God. I must look awful.*

"I'm Gregg. This here is Tony, our guitar player. Come down and listen to us play. You'll feel better. We practice behind the barber shop down the street. What's your name?"

Tony nodded. *He's cute.*

"Lisa." I bagged their order, giving them extra fries. "Maybe I will."

After work, I made my way to their make-shift studio, a room filled with band equipment and egg cartons fastened to the walls.

They introduced me to the drummer and the bass player. Not finding a chair, I sat on the floor to listen to them play, mostly cover songs by The Beatles and the Stones. By the end of their rehearsal I was crushing on Tony, the quiet one whose long dark hair fell over his face as he completely immersed himself in playing his red electric guitar.

From then on, I spent every free moment at the studio. Unwilling to be just a groupie, I started making calls to book the band at bars. Each booking made me feel like a triumphant part of the band. I became their manager and pretended to be of age while accompanying them to their gigs, fighting off bar owners who tried to cop a feel as I settled up with them for payment at the end of the night. I was so naïve, unaware of how vulnerable I was to predatory club owners, lucky not to have suffered anything more than humiliation. Each weekend I lied to my mother that I was at a friend's house.

Tony was aware that I was underage and shied away from getting too sexual with me. As a result, I clung to our friendship and occasional make-out sessions with hope it would lead to more, aching to be his girlfriend.

On my seventeenth birthday, I stood in the wings at the Uptown Theater in Chicago with a backstage pass dangling from my neck while they sang "I Saw Her Standing There." Just like in the days of my father's musicals, I loved being behind the scenes. Only this time I was part of it all.

A few days later, Deena and I went to Dad's for Christmas Eve at the condo he shared with his new boyfriend, Ralph. After Terry left, it didn't take long for Dad to meet a new man, and they moved in together after a couple of months.

"Don, did you hear me? Get me a drink," Ralph barked, rattling the ice cubes in his empty glass. Dad scurried to the kitchen to pour him three fingers of scotch. It was startling to see how mean this man was to my father, belittling him in a way no one had ever dared to in the life we shared with him. Neither the beauty of the glittering tree in the corner, nor the elegantly set table, could hide Dad's discomfort. As his lover drank several cocktails and openly criticized the meal, my father cowered.

When I saw my father being treated this way, I imagined he felt like I had as a child under his scrutiny. It was painful to watch him trying so hard to please someone. Instead of being glad that he was getting a taste of his own medicine, I wanted to be nicer to him.

. . .

"I'm going to keep ditching school anyway, so why pretend I'm getting anything out of it? I'll just quit." I announced this to my mother after another fight about getting detentions for cutting class. "It's a waste of my time. I'd rather be at the studio."

"Those guys are in their *twenties*," Mom cried. "They're much too old for you to be hanging out with. Call your father. See what he has to say about this."

Reluctantly, I dialed his number. "This is not a smart idea, Lisa. You used to get straight As, and you have so much potential." Dad paused to light a cigarette. "It's a shame for you to lose your education, but I don't suppose we can force you to go. You already have enough pink slips to paper a room."

"Doing this work with the band is what I want to do, Dad. You know how much music means to me." Talking to him felt like a relief after screaming with my mother. He seemed an unlikely ally, though I knew there would be conditions.

"Well, you need to get a better job until this band starts paying you. And you can always get your GED, I suppose. You're smart enough to make some kind of success of yourself if this band thing doesn't go anywhere." It shocked me that he didn't sound mad.

"I already have an interview for a new job as a purchasing assistant, and I'll pay room and board to Mom. But I won't need to get a GED. I plan to tour the world with rock stars someday." My belief in the band was more certain than anything in my life.

"All right, then. You'll have to go to the dean with your decision."

By Monday I was free of school, and the happiest I had ever been as I dedicated myself to producing a show at the local community center. We made over $500 in profit, enough for a new amp for Tony, rent for several months on the studio, and a half-dozen joints.

My bliss was fleeting, though. Within a few months, Tony found a new, older girlfriend and the band fired me, ripping the scab off all it had healed. I was raw with the heartbreak of fresh rejection.

Still licking my wounds, I spent an afternoon with Linda at our beloved Nippersink over Memorial Day weekend. I came back with a summer job as a cocktail waitress.

"So, you think you can move to Wisconsin, just like that?" my mom said when I told her my plan. "You're only seventeen! They're not going to let you serve drinks. C'mon."

"Mom, we can change my birth certificate, can't we? I said I'm eighteen on the application. That's the legal age in Wisconsin. I'll be living in a dorm, like college. Linda got a job as a maid, so she'll be there, too. You'll be coming up in August with Gram and Deena. Please! I need to get out of here and I know you'll be thrilled not to have me around to fight with." My words gushed at her like an open hydrant.

"All right, all right. But you have to get your father's permission. And you better think about what you're going to do when the summer ends, kid. You need a real job or to finish school." With Mom on board, I knew I could get my father's blessing.

"I know. This will be good. For both of us!" I hugged her neck and ran to find my birth certificate. By the following day we had made a copy and changed my birth date with some Wite-Out and

Mom's Selectric typewriter.

Just like that, I was eighteen and leaving home.

Five

I've been home several days, and my father's photos are still scattered across the coffee table, providing a sort of comfort. I find one from the first year we went to Nippersink when I was twelve—the only year Dad was with us. Mom captured me perched on his shoulders in the pool, poised to leap off in a dive over his head. We are both laughing.

Permission to do anything risky always came more easily from my father. Of course, he would require us to do our homework, with an extensive gathering of information to defend our desires; rules would be followed to mitigate risk. Mom was a fraidy cat, the kind of person who equated risk with danger. But if Dad said it was okay, she would go along with it.

The memory of that day in the pool at Nippersink, when we were a happy family, has faded like flowers tied with a ribbon and hung upside down to dry. You can faintly make out what was once so pungent, so vibrant. The yellowed photo of my dad and me, with the familiar lodge in the background, still carries a whiff of summer. It's enough to bring Nippersink and my eighteenth year to life—and the three months I spent like a character in *Dirty Dancing*.

The weekend after Mom helped me change my birth certificate, I felt the familiar excitement of crossing the border from Illinois into

Wisconsin on Highway 12—only this time, I felt an extra rush of adrenaline, knowing I would not be leaving after a week's vacation. I would be part of the staff. By Saturday afternoon I was loaded into my dorm and settled in.

My roommates were the other three cocktail waitresses, all of them several years older than me. We shared the largest room in the dorm, with four twin beds and a couple of dressers. The sweltering heat of early summer filled the room, and I immediately gained their favor by bringing a fan.

"Highball, screwdriver, Tom Collins. And a vodka martini, up." The girls rattled off each cocktail after they chose the right glass, iced it, and adeptly shot the assorted mixers into it from one of the two guns at our garnish station. Bill, the bartender, poured in the booze and made blended cocktails. I had barely ever stepped foot in a bar. Silently terrified I would look stupid; I watched their every move until I had it down pat. As a reward for our busy nightclub shift, Bill poured drinks for us around 10:00 p.m., allowing anything but top-shelf liquor. Suzanne and Connie opted for stiff belts of whisky and tequila, while I drank White Russians because they tasted like chocolate milk. The booze went straight to my head, the cream went straight to my thighs.

Some of the social staff were guys I had crushed on throughout my teen years as a guest. I'd dreamed of going to the wild after-hour parties I overheard when walking back to our cottage. Now I lived among the dozens of college kids who didn't want to go home for the summer, and took jobs as busboys and waitresses, caddies and housekeepers. We rubbed up against each other in the hot, humid night, loosened by moonshine punch and weed. Even though I was happy to participate, beneath the surface of my excitement bubbled the awkwardness of landing there straight from junior year of high school.

Stumbling back to my room one night as one of the social staff was leaving his, I threw myself in his path and asked if he wanted to smoke a joint. "Sure," he said, and led me back to his room. It was dank and warm, much smaller than mine, with a single bed. We sat on it and I pulled out my stash, expertly rolling the leaves in a Zig-Zag paper, then handing him the joint to light. The sweet smoke filled the room.

"Where do you go to school?" he said, exhaling a long stream of smoke and taking another hit.

"I haven't decided yet," I lied. "How about you?" *He thinks I'm in college!*

"I'll be a junior at University of Illinois this year."

My mind immediately went to the driving distance between where I lived and the downstate campus. It was only a couple of hours. *I could go see him, stay the weekend.*

His kiss interrupted my fantasy, wet and hard, arousing in me all the possibilities. *He really likes me. Oh, my God. He wants to have sex with me.*

After Tony, who'd only slept with me once (since I was jailbait), every guy who gave me the time of day expected sex, and if he didn't, I felt ugly. It felt good to be touched, so I went along with it, believing it was the doorway to love.

Maybe we can really be together after the summer. He lifted my shirt over my head. *Oh, my God, this is really happening.* He pulled my shorts down my thighs. *Oh, my God.* I let myself get carried away with the idea of falling in love with a college boy as he climbed on top of me. "Oh, yeah, you're tight." It was fast and furious and over in a few minutes. He laid back against the wall and lit the joint again. "Thanks," he said. Like I had done him a favor.

I got dressed and walked back to my room alone, the humidity clinging to my skin, mixing with the faint scent of sex and sweat. Something inside me felt emptied out, hollow. *Who am I kidding? He won't be my boyfriend. This probably won't happen again.*

By August, when my family came up for a visit, I was ready to go home. Over the summer, I had been homesick enough to call Dad a couple of times to say hi. He quizzed me about my plans for the fall, requesting answers I didn't have. When I came home from Nippersink, I asked him for money to go to beauty school, since I had started cutting hair in the dorms, mostly in exchange for reefer. He agreed with his usual conditions about keeping up good grades.

Before long, I added Beauty School Dropout to my résumé.

A couple of months later I took the GED on a bet with another smarty-pants dropout who I was crazy about. His feelings for me were never discussed, even though we spent all of our time together, often sneaking into an empty room at the Ramada to have sex during his shift as a janitor. Sex which I thought meant something but was actually closer to the lyrics of "Night Moves," a song that made me cringe a little each time I heard it on the radio.

My 96 percent score beat his by six points, swelling my heart with pride. It was better than graduating.

. . .

I was still eighteen when Vicki and I moved into our own apartment. By day I did data entry in the purchasing department of Melton Steel and by night I donned my hot pants and heels as a cocktail waitress at the After the Hunt lounge in the Holiday Inn. I started dating a manager at Melton, a tall blond in his thirties who had the right lines and the perfect Southern drawl to deliver them—all poured snugly into a pair of Levi's. He drank bourbon from his home state of Kentucky and smoked Lucky Strikes. I wrote the bad poetry of a smitten teenager when a whole new part of me awakened, sensuous and curious. *We write our story on sheets of linen, like sheets of paper...*

After my hit-and-run experiences with guys my age, and the

college boys at Nippersink, sex with this older man became as much about pleasure as it was a way to get him to like me. Passion came at me like wild surf, sucking me under, then depositing me on the shore, gasping like I had a survived a shipwreck. While I was still insecure about my pudgy thighs and pendulous breasts, I was able to freely let go and explore my sexuality for the first time. Plenty of booze and pot helped dissolve my inhibitions.

"Let's keep this cool, baby. No need to tell anyone at work that we're gettin' it on," he said, so I agreed to keep it quiet while secretly weaving fantasies of a future together.

Equating sex with love was all I knew, fully believing that if I was desirable then I was lovable. The young women of my generation were hypnotized by the prospect of romance in songs and movies, while a parallel message of free love played in the background like elevator music. We were told to love the one you're with until you walk down the aisle in a white floppy hat to "We've Only Just Begun."

It wasn't long before Vicki ran off with my lover, only this time her betrayal left me homeless when she moved into his house. Even two jobs didn't pay me enough money to keep our place. I broke the lease and found a little basement in-law apartment. Later, I found out the two of them had run off to Vegas, gotten married, and eventually lived in their car after spending all their money on coke. Somehow, that made me feel better.

The men who paraded through my life, and my bed, filled my heart with hope and my head with bullshit. The dangerous allure of bad boys who promised to call after a weekend of sex and drinking permeated those first couple of years on my own. It was the 1980s, when men called back when they felt like it, resulting in a few unintended one-night stands, and a couple of two- or three- month relationships in which I chased them, and they used me.

They're a blur of disappointment in my memory, a matched

collection of losers who were the opposite of my father. Some part of me rebelled against my gay dad's white-collar intelligence and elegance. I was drawn instead to vulgar, masculine men, or moody musicians, who were indifferent to me. As far from Dad as they were on the outside, they still left me with that familiar feeling of rejection and anxiety as I waited for them by the phone.

As always, my best friend—Kathy at the time—was my refuge. Kathy had an audacious sense of humor, and a mystical quality I wanted to emulate. We went to clubs where we pursued cute guys and good music until she moved to California. By then I was breaking up with Phillip, an adorable alcoholic who played bass in a band. He was the first guy to really stick around, moving into my tiny apartment one sock at a time. His brand of indifference was more palatable than the rest, lulling me into a false sense of security until he turned on me in a rage when he drank. After a year of alternating between being madly in love with him and having screaming fights over his drinking, I reluctantly ended it.

Seeking solace in my fury, I called Kathy. And that phone call changed everything.

"Lis, you have to come for a visit! This place is so amazing." I pictured my friend on a sunny beach, a margarita in her hand.

"I wish." My nearly bone-dry bank account meant the numbers didn't add up to make the trip. Yet, I could feel there was something waiting on the West Coast that had my name on it. Something I couldn't put my finger on.

All week I thought about movies I'd watched as a little girl, like those beach movies with Annette Funicello romping in the sand, and how I had believed that someday that would be me. Now that I was older, my spirit felt pulled westward to an extraordinary life I knew I would never have in the dreary, flat suburbs where I was raised. I wanted the kind of exciting adventure that touring with the band was supposed to have been.

I called her back.

"I'm thinking of just packing up and moving to California, Kath. This breakup beat me up pretty good, and I hate my job. What do you think? Can I stay with you for a while?" A small kernel of an idea started taking form as the words tumbled out of my mouth, breathing life into my dreams of escaping the Midwest. Each word sprouted a new leaf. "I have just enough money for a one-way ticket, with a few hundred dollars left to get settled. I'm sure I can find a job."

"Let me talk to Joan," she said, referring to the roommate she had moved there with. "Oh, my God! It would be so cool if you moved here!"

Joan agreed to only one month of couch privileges, so once I got there I would have to hustle. Clearing my apartment of everything I couldn't take on the plane proved to be slightly less daunting than telling my mother I was leaving.

"Oh, why do you have to go so far way?" she said, surprised by the announcement. Even though I talked to her often, sometimes stopping by on a Saturday for coffee with her and Gram, I was careful about sharing the intimate details of my life. "You're only twenty-one." Her reaction was predictable, coming from a woman content to stay close to home and family.

"Because there is something there that I can't have here, Ma. The ocean, warm weather, cool people, I don't know." *I'm just not happy.* "There's something calling me to California, and I'm not even sure what it is. But I gotta find out." Making her understand something I didn't understand myself was futile. *I just don't feel like I belong here in an ordinary life, like yours.*

"What if something happens?" Her cautious mind was already conjuring up all the dangers that could befall me.

"I'll only be a plane ride away, Ma."

"But I hate to fly."

In my final days in Chicago, I donated parkas and snow boots, heavy sweaters, and corduroy jeans. My mom gave me her old luggage into which I crammed everything I possibly could. Two boxes contained my record collection, the most essential thing I owned. Wrapping my few precious knickknacks in a towel, I stuffed them under the wooden lid of a vintage picnic basket I'd found at a garage sale. It would be perfect for seaside lunches.

I was almost ready to go.

My bedroom set was the only nice furniture I had, a hand-me-down from my Uncle Ted. I wanted to keep it along with boxes of kitchenware, and a few end tables—a kind of insurance in case things didn't work out in California. Grandma Haute agreed to let me store these items in her basement.

"As long as I don't have to feed it, I don't care," she said. I promised to take up only a corner of the unfinished space beneath her house, where she barely went except to do laundry and play poker once a month with her girlfriends.

A couple of nights before the move, a friend helped me transport my stuff with his pickup truck. As we pulled into the narrow driveway, I saw my father's car parked in the back.

"Well, hi, honey," he said through the kitchen screen door at the top of the back steps. "What brings you here? Coming to say goodbye to your grandparents?" He was seated at the Formica kitchen table with his mother and didn't get up as I climbed the stairs to greet them.

"Hi, Dad. Yeah, and Grandma said I could store a few things here when I move. Mostly the bedroom set." I leaned down to plant a kiss on his cheek.

"Oh, how nice." He lifted his china cup as my grandmother got up to pour him more coffee.

Dad supported my move across the country more than Mom

did. "As long as you can afford it." Those were his exact words when I shared the news that I was moving to San Francisco. Not that I really cared what he thought. We were speaking, but I still carried scars of disappointment and lingering feelings of the abandonment which had weighed so heavily after the divorce. California would be a new start away from my family and the need for anyone's approval or permission.

"I cleared a corner for you, dear. You'll see it down there," Grandma said, "You can use all the space you need."

"Thanks, it's not that much." I kissed my grandma's velvety cheek, her Coty powder tickling my nose with the scent of old perfume, then went down to the musty basement.

For the next hour, my friend Jeff and I hauled my furniture, mattress, and boxes down the seven crumbling steps to the basement of my father's childhood home. It must not have occurred to him to offer to help, to insist that his daughter enjoy a cup of coffee with her grandmother while he took on the heavy lifting. But it was just the kind of thing I longed for him to do.

Six

After nearly a month of mourning my father, I watch the California sun sink low in the sky out my window. I carry a glass of wine down to the dock to sit in the golden light with my journal. Most of my life has returned to normal; still, everything reminds me of Dad.

My thoughts turn to how pleased I am to have found something meaningful in which to keep a pinch of my father's ashes before I scatter the rest. After picking up every small box, bottle, or jar I encountered in the tiny gift shops along Fourth Street in Berkeley, nothing felt right until I spotted an antique ink bottle inside a glass case displaying fine pens.

"Can I see this, please?" I pointed inside the case.

The shopkeeper shook his head when he saw what I was pointing to. "I'm sorry, that's not for sale. It's just a display."

No. This is the one. "Sir, please. I'm a writer and my father just died. I'd like to store his ashes in this. Please." *What's wrong with me? It's not for sale.* I was near tears, already seeing it as a home for a bit of my dad.

"Okay, twenty bucks and it's yours."

"Sold." Something quieted inside of me as he pulled the scuffed empty jar from the case and handed it to me. Wrapped around the peeling red and yellow label were the words, "Sanford's Indelible." There won't be a headstone in a cemetery to mark his final resting place—instead, a little bit of him will hang out on my desk or bookshelf, urging me to write our story.

I'll scatter the rest of his ashes here in the lagoon, I decide, as I write about finding the inkwell, *where he can float beside the Victorian painted ladies that line the edge of the water like a string of vibrant jewels, reminiscent of the houses he loved in San Francisco.* Diamonds of light dance across the water as another thought occurs to me. *I will scatter them on his next birthday.*

The morning I left Chicago for California, after partying until dawn, Linda and I watched the sun poke its brilliant head up over Lake Michigan. As it inched up, too brilliant to look at, I imagined seeing the same sun sink into the Pacific Ocean in the days to come. *Everything in my life is about to change*, I thought as we headed to the airport. *Forever.*

I wore a fedora hat. And a suit and heels because it felt right to get dressed up to fly. Excited, terrified, and slightly hungover, I spotted Mom, Dad, and Deena waiting to see me off as we approached the gate. Teetering over to greet my family, I felt sophisticated and slightly intoxicated by the moment. Dad being there made me happy, even though I was reluctant to let him see how much it meant to me.

My father and I had come to a neutral place following my decision to move to California, a detente, of sorts. He didn't object to my move as fervently as my mother did, and his support of my independence eased Mom's fear. "She's been on her own for a few years, Peg. She can take care of herself," he told her, a reminder that worked in my favor.

When I reached them, I hugged my mom first. She was already crying.

"Don't cry, Ma," I said, her warm tears wetting my cheek as she held me close.

"Well, this is it." She pulled back from the hug reluctantly, smoothing my hair from my face. "Take care of yourself and call me when you get there, do you hear me? I love ya, Lis."

"I love you, too. I'll be fine. And I'll be back for visits, I promise." All the love she ever had for me rose up in her eyes. "And I'll call you every week," I vowed.

"You better. And be careful."

Linda took a few pictures, but the shot of me and my mother captures the moment—her eyes are red and she's hanging on to me for dear life, smiling half-heartedly. I look somewhat sheepish, as if I'm getting away with something, yet my posture is confident, like an adult's.

"That thing adds ten pounds of class to your head. You always look good in hats," she said. Her smile was genuine, her pride silent.

"Thanks, Ma." I turned to my father and hugged him. "Bye, Dad."

"Good luck, honey," he said. "You'll be fine." I kissed his cheek and nodded, my own tears coming as I looked at these people who were so familiar, yet I knew didn't quite understand me. Did they think I was crazy? Did they know how scared I was to start a new life, how excited?

I turned to my sister. "Be good, kiddo. Good luck in school. You'll do great."

"I will. Have fun in California!"

"Come visit." The gate agent announced our boarding. I gathered up my things and gave my mom another hug. As I entered the jetway I turned back and waved. "Love you guys!" I said one last time, as they moved to the window to watch me take off.

With $400 in my purse, a suitcase of clothes, two boxes of albums, and a picnic basket filled with treasures, I boarded a plane for San Francisco, sight unseen, like Dorothy on her way to Oz, answering a call that came from both far away and deep inside of me.

. . .

All my senses were intensified by an assault of the color and texture of California. Palm trees and hills replaced the flat concrete and green lawns of the Midwest. On my first day, we climbed to the top of Mt. Diablo, its dry, tawny grass a far cry from the lush backyards at home. You could see for miles up there. It was like being at the top of the John Hancock building in Chicago, only I was atop an actual mountain, filled with joy for having made such a bold move.

A couple of days later, Kathy took me to the coast. The swell of the waves mirrored an emotional current cascading over my soul. The continuous flow of the surf, out and back, felt like the relentless push-pull inside me, gathering the momentum to propel me toward something bigger in my life. I sat on the sand mesmerized, big emotion welling up in my eyes.

This was not the beach I imagined from movies, though. Instead of white sand meeting turquoise water, a rougher shore confronted me, rocky and wild, a coast that connected to my turbulent interior. The cold, briny wind pelted my face, slapping me out of any complacency I had thinking that the move here was the finish line. I felt small beside the vast sea, but awake and fully alive. Getting here was just the beginning.

As Kathy drove us over the bridge back to the East Bay, I realized how much I had missed my friend. She suggested we see one of her new favorite bands. "Merlin is playing tonight. Kinda rock and jazz fusion, like Squonk at the Nickel Bag. The ones who played all the Genesis. You're gonna love these guys."

We settled at a table for two and ordered drinks. The music was already underway, the band's sound full and rich, mystical. Normally my attention was drawn to the guitar players, their instrument slung low across their torso, out in front all nimble-fingered and loose. The drummer usually faded into the background. But not this one.

He had thick, shoulder-length dark hair and a trim beard. His limbs moved like those of a dancer, elegant and fluid; he stood out even though he was hidden behind a circle of drums and the rest of the band. His face was beautiful, mostly because of the blissed-out look he had on it while he played.

"Go up there and talk to him," Kathy insisted during their break. "Buy a record."

Nervously, I stood in line to greet him as he sat on the edge of the stage, peeling an orange while selling albums. He smiled when he caught my eye.

"Hi, I'm Mark," he said when I reached him. He popped an orange crescent into his mouth, holding my gaze. My cheeks burned as I lifted my hand to wave.

"Hi!" I said a little too enthusiastically. "I'm Lisa. From Chicago. I just moved to California a few days ago. You guys sound great!"

In an overwhelming onslaught of joy, I shared with him the details of my recent arrival. "And I just saw the Pacific Ocean for the first time today! It was incredible. I mean, I was in Florida as a kid, but this was just—" I ran out of words.

"Well, that's very exciting. I've lived in California all my life so I can't imagine seeing the ocean for the first time. So, what brings you here tonight?" He leaned in close, the faint scent of citrus on his breath.

"My friend Kathy loves you guys and knew I would, too." He smiled as I told him about our love of live music, yammering on while I fished a ten-dollar bill from my purse to buy one of his records. I removed it from the plastic wrapper and asked him to sign it. He thought for a second, wrote a few lines, then slid it back into the sleeve.

"I gotta get back up there and play," he said. "But how about you come down for tea sometime and we can finish our conversation."

As I watched him write his phone number down on a cocktail napkin, my mouth went dry. I nodded, speechless.

"It's so nice to meet you, Lisa from Chicago," he said, taking my hand in both of his. His hands were large, and warm; on his right wrist he wore a copper bracelet.

"You, too, Mark, thanks." He smiled, then jumped up on the stage and slid behind the drums.

"What did he say? You guys talked for a long time!" Kathy was anxious for details as I sat down at the table and exhaled deeply, finally able to breathe.

"He's lived here all his life. That's about all I know, I talked so damn much. But he gave me his number and asked me down for tea." I set the napkin and the album on the table. "Who has *tea*? He's not like anyone I've ever met."

A crystal ball filled the center of the square black background of the album. *MERLIN* was scrawled in curvy, red block letters across the middle; beneath, it said *Alive at Last.* I turned it over to find a black and white photo of the band. The two hottest guys were in the center of the photo; Mark was one of them, wearing a black knit sweater and light drawstring pants covering legs firmly planted. His eyes were gazing straight into the camera with a disarming, graceful confidence; his arm was wound across his chest, with the same copper bracelet on his wrist that had grazed my arm moments before.

I was captivated as I pulled the disc from the cover to see what he'd written on the sleeve:

To Lisa: Welcome to California ... you are loved. - Mark

• • •

His sentiment lingered with me all week. *You are loved.* The words felt intimate, laced with romantic innuendo. A bit unsettling, coming from a virtual stranger, yet they excited me as I read them over and over. That a guy so attractive, so interesting—a musician with an *album*—would write those words to me moments after we met? Maybe that meant I was a contender with the beautiful girls after all. *He must have liked me. Why else would he write something so personal?* I was a little afraid to find out, the mystery being so delicious.

At night, I lay awake on Kathy's couch, dreaming about finding my own little place in the city and fantasizing about calling Mark. I tried to picture our conversation over tea, deep and provocative, an education in California culture and West Coast men. *I wonder what kind of place he has. Does he have roommates?* The thought of his undivided attention sent a rush of hope through me. The thought of him not remembering me, a rush of anxiety.

All week his open invitation gnawed at me, egging me on to contact him. I decided I would wait and call the following weekend. Until then, my days were spent pounding the pavement until I finally found a job in San Francisco at an employment agency.

On my first day, I took the BART train across the bay. Pushing through the glass doors of our building on Montgomery Street, I made my way to the elevator that would take me up to the fourteenth floor. Sharon, the receptionist, showed me the coffee room and got me set up.

I asked her to lunch on the second day. Over sandwiches I told her about my recent move and how my only friend in California was preoccupied with her boyfriend.

"Well, then you can hang out with me. I have lots of friends!" On Friday after work we went out drinking at the Tiki bar in West Portal, where six of us sucked down thick brown rum and fruit juice through long straws in a coconut bowl. Later that night we made our way to Sharon's, where she deposited me in the basement room that was once occupied by her brother.

"Make yourself at home," she said, so I did.

For much longer than I expected.

It took all weekend to screw up my courage to call Mark. On Sunday afternoon, I unfolded the napkin I had kept in my purse and punched his number into the handset, nervously twirling my finger in the coiled cord as it rang. Once, twice...

"Hello?" I recognized his voice. He sounded quiet, relaxed.

"Hi, Mark? This is Lisa, remember from the show in Walnut Creek a couple weeks ago? You said to—" *What if he doesn't remember me?*

"Hey! Lisa from Chicago. Of course I remember. You were just discovering the Pacific Ocean. How are you?"

"Fine. I'm fine, thanks," I stammered. "I got a job this week and I think I might have a place to live in a co-worker's basement. It's a funky little room behind the garage, but it's in the city and it's near the beach. I think I can fix it up real cute and—I'm sorry, I'm babbling. How are you?"

He chuckled. "I'm good. Really good. And happy to hear your great news." The knot in my chest loosened. "You seem to have landed on your feet, Lis."

Hearing him say my name—especially the shorter version reserved for those closest to me—made me shiver. "Yeah, I think so, too. It's all starting to come together. I really can't wait to move to the city. The job's just okay but I'll find another one eventually. I'm gaining great job-finding skills there, at least!"

He chuckled again. "I'm sure you are."

"So." I paused before launching into my real reason for calling. "You said something about coming over for tea sometime. Where I come from, we drink coffee or pop. Maybe a beer. But tea sounds nice."

"Tea! Yes. It's a California thing. Come down for tea. How about next Saturday afternoon?" His immediate invitation was thrilling. And unnerving.

"Sure. Saturday's great." We made plans for him to pick me up from the train at 1:30, then said goodbye.

It felt like an eternity until the weekend. The outfit one wears to tea with a California drummer became my obsession; Kathy and I decided jeans and a casual top were a good choice. It was still warm enough to wear sandals, even in late October—another phenomenon in my new life—and I carefully painted my toes Cotton Candy Pink.

Mark was leaning against his Pinto wagon when I emerged from the BART station on Saturday afternoon. He looked just like Kenny Loggins, his wild hair flying around his head in the breeze, smiling as I approached. We hugged briefly before getting into his car to take the short drive to his place, during which I had to remind myself to breathe. Sitting so close to this mysterious stranger in the light of day felt exotic, yet somehow natural.

Still, I was self-conscious. In the confines of the car I felt heavy and plain. Even though I had lost ten pounds during my move, my thighs seemed to fill the width of the narrow bucket seat. Sitting up straighter, I pulled my legs in close together, hoping they didn't look huge. *Man, he's gorgeous.* I barely heard a word of what he said about the landmarks outside the window, sharing bits of his history in the town where he'd lived since high school.

Mostly, I stared at his profile and thought about kissing him.

"...and here we are," he said, pulling into a parking space in front of his building. Butterflies fluttered in my belly as we climbed the steps and approached his door. I followed him into the small studio apartment.

"Hey, sweetie, we're back," he announced. A tall, pretty woman with frosted blonde hair turned from the stove and smiled. She was dressed in a peasant blouse, and an Indian wrap skirt that grazed her lean, tan legs as she walked toward us. She was barefoot. *That's how you dress for tea in California,* I thought, and watched as Mark's eyes never left her. She greeted him with a kiss, then turned to me as he said, "Lisa, meet my girlfriend, Eileen."

The crushing blow of meeting Mark's girlfriend was tempered by the reality check that he probably would never want to go out with me anyway. *Of course, he has a thin, blonde girlfriend. Who was I kidding?* I thought as we sat at his small table for tea all afternoon. We talked easily about music and California, swapping stories of where we each came from and where we hoped to go. I relaxed as the monumental question of his romantic interest in me was taken off the table. Instead, the bud of a friendship with both of them began to blossom. We promised to get together again.

The next day, I moved my belongings to Sharon's basement. My room looked out on the yard through a large picture window and had thin indoor/outdoor carpeting covering the cement floor. It was sparsely furnished with an old beige Naugahyde sofa bed and a 13" color TV. There was a half-bath in the adjacent laundry room. I had showering privileges upstairs.

Since there wasn't a closet, I hung a clothesline across one wall and fastened a colorful orange and purple curtain in front of it. An Indian shawl covered an old table I found, which I paired with a couple of chairs from the garage. An old fridge came from the want ads for twenty-five dollars, delivered by the owner for an extra five bucks. Thrift stores and a garage sale yielded pillows, posters, a hot plate, and kitchenware.

Unpacking the knickknacks from my picnic basket, I placed my handmade wizard from the Renaissance fair on built-in shelves, alongside the chipped red stone heart Dad let me take from the "damaged" bin in the back room of his gift shop in Oak Park. I tucked plants into every nook and cranny. Within a week, my place was transformed into a little bohemian studio apartment, just like Rhoda's attic above Mary Richards.

I finally had a home in San Francisco.

Mark and Eileen came over for wine one night to celebrate. The three of us made easy conversation, and Mark started telling me more about metaphysics and the power of manifestation. It was a new and magical discussion I was both intrigued by and leery of, one I had begun with Kathy when we played around with her sister's tarot cards back home.

My Catholic upbringing had been abandoned but was not forgotten, so my secret delight in anything witchy carried a hint of sin. I gobbled up every morsel of his information, hanging on every word about crystals and astrology charts. He also suggested I travel the area as much as possible.

"Lake Tahoe, Yosemite, Monterey are all just a few hours from here. There are so many places you need to see, Lis. Mountains and desert. Ocean. We have it all." As an adventurous native Californian, he knew nearly every inch of the state. I imagined him exploring it with Eileen, my envy shimmering around images of their sunset beach walks like a dry heat.

· · ·

Months passed, and my dreams of seeing more of the Golden State became obscured by thick gray rain clouds. By February, my initial excitement over moving to the West Coast became completely waterlogged, as the relentless rain poured down over every plan I made to experience the wild beauty of California. My days were spent either in my one-room apartment curled up with a book, on the L-Taraval streetcar jostled amid the other malcontents battling the downpours, or at a desk helping others find employment.

Sometimes I snuck and looked for my own.

I worked, I read, I slept. I wrote. I went out for drinks on the weekends with Sharon and her friends. I watched TV. Without a car, I had to walk and take the bus everywhere. In the rain, that meant dragging groceries on the streetcar in soggy paper bags. I hated the commute from the Outer Sunset district to downtown, a mass of rats all chasing the same cheese.

Much of my life felt the same as when I lived back home, only harder. At least there I'd had a car and my own bathtub. But more than anything, I just wished it would stop raining.

What if my great escape has failed and I made a mistake leaving Illinois? I missed my one-bedroom apartment, and my friends. I even missed my family.

Pep talks to myself came in the form of poetry. After spewing rants in my journal about the deep loneliness of being in a dark and dreary basement room, cursing the rain and myself for choosing this place and not sunny, warm Los Angeles or San Diego, I reminded myself that San Francisco still felt like where I was supposed to be. No matter how uncomfortable it was, I knew there was a freedom there I hadn't quite tapped into yet, a state of mind that mirrored my own, lying beneath the soggy winter. A place where I fit in.

"We're getting married!" Kathy said on the heels of her beau being stationed in San Diego. "I know it seems fast, but we've been together over a year."

"That's great, Kath. I'm really happy for you." My excitement for her was tinged with disappointment. The only link I had to home was abandoning me for matrimony and sunnier shores. Her departure reminded me that to craft the kind of life I wanted in California, I needed to take some chances, and meet new people.

In the fall, I signed up for a few writing classes at City College. My schedule allowed me to take them during the day with underclassmen who were a few years younger than me. I felt ancient and stupid, paralyzed when called upon, and unable to tell if my papers were any good.

A part of me was terrified of making a mistake or looking foolish. As a kid, I had always gotten good grades; I was used to being smart. But in these classes, the challenge to stretch my ability required a confidence I found had left me.

"There are no sacred cows in journalism," the professor said, collecting our papers. I wasn't even sure what he meant, which sent panic through me that I had botched the assignment. It made me cringe to think of him reading my words and I skipped his next class. Within six weeks I quit altogether. In yet another attempt at school I couldn't stick with, I had quit before I could fail. By wanting to avoid looking stupid, it's far too easy to forfeit what you could become. My commitment to an overarching desire for excitement and freedom fostered a discipline that was next to nothing, the perfect temperament for my rock-and-roll pipe dreams. An aversion to criticism made it hard for me to try anything new. And too often, I thought I knew everything. Just like my dad.

Without a career to bring me the excitement I craved, I sought it from men. Like in Chicago, the men I dated were either too old for me or unavailable; they promised to call but didn't, and I waited by the phone because I had nothing else to do. Wanting someone to love who loved me back didn't feel like too much to ask. When that didn't come easily my loneliness took charge, making room for the kind of imprudent decisions you know aren't sound, but at least put you in skin-to-skin contact with a hot guy or afford you a nice dinner out. The kind that allowed my old boyfriend Philip to come and stay with me for an awkward couple of weeks.

Fixating on a guy to make me happy was always running in the background, like an operating system. It was as if nothing else could function without the whirring hum of a man to obsess over. When

I met someone I found attractive—and they were *all* attractive—I chased after him shamelessly. Most of the time we'd meet in a bar, have a fun conversation, and share a few laughs, exchange numbers. Sometimes I'd go home with him and have the mediocre sex of strangers, high on a little attention. But when I didn't hear from him the next day, I would start calling endlessly with some excuse or another to talk to him. It didn't occur to me that the awful feeling in the pit of my stomach was humiliation.

I jumped into bed with most men who gave me a second look, believing each and every time that he could be The One. It didn't matter if he drank too much, had no job, or did drugs that scared me. I gave him all my love, forgetting to keep some for myself.

Seven

When I finally collect all my dad's photos, to put back into the Saxx bag, I find the pearly blue globe paperweight at the bottom of it that I had stuffed in my purse the day he died. Spinning it around slowly to look at the abalone Europe and mother-of-pearl Canada, I try to remember for which of my father's birthdays, decades earlier, I had purchased it. Sometime in his forties, I think. He had kept it on his desk ever since, presenting the perfect thing I could swipe to take home with me that wouldn't be noticed, knowing no one else in my family would want it anyway.

Most presents from Dad had notes stuck to them explaining the meaning behind his gift. When I asked to see his will the day after he died, it was because I was certain there would be letters to each of us attached to it, his final words of wisdom and advice. After meeting at the funeral home to make the arrangements, we went to Dad's house. My sister pulled the will from his safe and handed me the thick sheaf of papers. Emblazoned in bold across the top it read: Last Will & Testament of Donald M. Haute. Below, it named the Trustee: Deena K. Haute. I didn't see that coming. Mom and Deena didn't look surprised. *Again, my family kept a secret from me.* There were no letters from Dad.

Pushing thoughts of the will aside, I take the paperweight to my office and make room for it on my desk next to the chipped red stone heart.

For all the ranting and raving I did over the years about Dad being gay, it became clear in my twenties that it wasn't him being gay that was so upsetting, it was that he knew who he was, and he got married and had a family anyway. How could he marry a woman and have kids only to have to undo it all and cause so much pain? The shame of having a father so willing to hurt us doused the spark of love for him that had been struggling to stay alive since my teenage years. His cavalier approach to disrupting our lives, and expecting us to hold no malice, seemed selfish, almost cruel. Years after the divorce, I seemed to be the only one still suffering over this.

Mom had calmed down quite quickly after the sting of the divorce wore off, settling into a close friendship with this man she still loved dearly. Deena didn't take the news badly at all when she was finally told at fourteen or fifteen that Dad was gay. She could talk to me about it, which was unlike my solitary experience of finding out when it was a shameful secret. The world had become more tolerant, too, with more television shows depicting gay characters. But my sister's easygoing reaction wasn't because Steven Carrington came out on *Dynasty*. There was an affinity between her and my dad that was more than all that; Deena's calm acceptance matched their relationship. They shared an even-keeled camaraderie, a give-and-take that didn't ruffle any feathers.

On the other hand, my father and I alternated between arguing and reconciling. I had enough expectations for the both of us of the kind of father I wanted him to be—loving, protective, devoted—and carried all the disappointment when he let us down. There was a kinship between Deena and Dad I couldn't put my finger on, which only made me jealous. I noticed it when I went home for my sister's college graduation, a feeling of being left out of the little triad they shared comfortably with Mom. My physical distance from the family created an emotional gap even greater than the one I'd felt when I left home. Casual conversation at the table that night about things that didn't include me left behind a faint residue of desire for closeness with them. It lingered long after I returned to California.

• • •

"The corporate world is so stuffy, besides being really intimidating," I said between bites of pungent crab drenched in Thousand Island dressing, a treat for me since Dad was paying. He had come to visit me in San Francisco, the first in my family to do so after I'd lived there for two years. I was so anxious to show off my West Coast life to him, to prove I was making it on my own. A secret part of me was also excited to have my father all to myself for a few days in a world far away from my mother and sister. I remained ever hopeful that a magic moment of connection would happen between us in the way I had always imagined it could, one that had me loving my dad like when I'd been a child. "Not going to college always makes me feel like I'll be found out as a fraud," I said, without mentioning my failed attempt at taking college classes.

"As I said when you quit high school, you're a smart girl. I'm sure this job isn't the last one you'll ever have," he said, lighting a cigarette after we finished our lunch on Fisherman's Wharf. "It sure helps to do something you enjoy. That's my biggest advice to you. Figure that out and you'll be fine."

"Yeah, back then I wanted to manage the band. Hopefully, I'll find a job around music someday." I took in the view of the San Francisco Bay, comfortable to be sharing my dreams with my father. "It seems like I have a better chance out here of finding that."

"Well, don't give up hope, honey." He motioned to the server to bring the check, then took care of the bill.

Once outside, we walked along the wharf in the warm October

air, perusing the artists' wares lining the water. Small booths held baskets layered with watercolors of the Golden Gate Bridge and flocks of seagulls; others had tables of colorful beaded jewelry.

Dad pointed to a pen-and-ink of the Transamerica building. "That reminds me of the pair of paintings your mother and I got in New Orleans on our honeymoon. They were of the Court of the Two Sisters."

I nodded, remembering the paintings that still hung on my mother's wall. Interior design had always been a hallmark of life with my parents. *I should take him to see my place.*

"You want to see where I live?" I said, ignoring my embarrassment over living in the back of a garage.

"Sure. I can cab back to the hotel from there." His arrival the previous day had landed him in a hotel in the Castro district, the predominantly gay neighborhood in the center of the city.

We walked a few blocks to the Beach Street turnaround and boarded a cable car. Climbing up Hyde Street, we were rewarded with a panoramic view of the Bay and Alcatraz. My pride in being a resident of this beautiful city swelled in my chest. At Market Street, we caught the L-Taraval out to my tiny apartment.

"You sure know your way around town," he said. "There's such good public transportation here. And the views!"

"Well, I wish I had a car. When I work the late shift, I take an umbrella with me and stand in a phone booth while waiting for the next bus. In case I need to use it as a weapon."

"That's so clever!" He was oblivious to my hint that maybe I could use help getting a car, that it would be safer than taking buses late at night on the weekends. *Should I ask him to help me get one?* I was proud that I hadn't asked for money since being on my own. *Better not risk ruining our good day.* I changed the subject until we arrived at my place and went through the garage to my room.

"It's small but you fixed it up so nice, honey." He looked at the shelves, studying my photos. None of them were of him. If he noticed the red stone heart, he didn't say so.

"Thanks, I got the decorating genes from you and Mom." He nodded and smiled. My movements felt measured and capable as I got the coffee going in my little makeshift kitchen. I hadn't really entertained my father before, not even for coffee. The desire for his approval bubbled up in me like the percolator I filled with water and a Mocha roast.

As we sat at my small gate-leg table—a new purchase from the House of Teak—I studied his face. He still looked like Dad, but I saw another side now: the gay guy. There was nothing intrinsically different about him, but I could *feel* it in a way I never had before. He looked like men I saw around town, men I could tell were homosexual by the way they walked or carried themselves, or a tone in their voice. Before moving to San Francisco, I tried to avoid the reality of Dad being gay, distancing myself from him with his partners, trying to push it from my mind since it started out as a secret, meant to be hidden, forcing me to see him in a sexual way. A way I didn't want to see either of my parents. But here, men were openly gay in public, holding hands. It seemed normal, albeit a bit startling. It was as if I needed to be around gay men in my everyday life to see my own father.

We talked for half an hour about his plans for the visit, which would include Halloween in the Castro. As he walked out my door and got into the cab, I was struck by how handsome he still was in his mid-forties, with a lean build and a nice face. His dark hair was graying at the temples, but he touched it up. He had warm brown eyes the color of mine and an open smile beneath a perfectly groomed mustache. All of this was enhanced by the confidence of someone used to being the smartest person in the room.

He won't have any trouble finding a date. The same thought I had when I was fourteen.

A few days later, he was in a plaid shirt and jeans when we met for breakfast before his flight home to Chicago.

"So, how was Halloween?" I asked, pouring cream and sugar into my coffee.

"You can't even imagine the costumes. They were fantastic!" His eyes gleamed with a joy I wasn't sure I had ever seen. Not when I came home with a good report card, or on Christmas mornings, the reference points of a child's memory.

"That's nice." I buried my face in the menu. "Did you dress up?" I wasn't sure if I truly wanted to know.

"Oh no. No, not really. I had my black leather vest and cowboy boots with me, and a bandanna to tie around my neck. Nothing like the costumes I saw." He gazed into the distance, then back at me. I was trying to imagine him in cowboy boots. Usually, he wore loafers. "You know, your mother and I loved to dress up for Halloween. We had parties at the house on Elder Lane when you girls were small. Remember that?"

"Yeah, of course." I saw Dad in cutoff shorts and a Hawaiian shirt tied up above his navel, and Mom in a muumuu with a huge paper lotus flower pinned in her hair. They wore plastic leis around their necks. I remembered the Tiki torches that lit the backyard and their friends drinking fruity punch spiked with champagne, which my five-year-old sister and I were forbidden to taste. They all did the limbo under a broom handle.

I remembered all of that. But I did not remember this man sitting across from me talking about someone named Robert, and how they met. "I actually met him the other night at the Twin Peaks. There was such an attraction. And last night was wonderful." He was on a high, his voice rising ever so slightly while he recounted every moment of the evening he dared to share, a couple of times wanting to tell me more, caution sweeping over his face as he stopped mid-sentence. *Should a daughter know all this about her father?* It was like a car accident on the freeway; I couldn't look away before taking in a few of the gory details. It occurred to me that we had not exchanged much about our personal lives during my teens once I started keeping my distance. Both repelled and fascinated, I listened silently, repeatedly folding and unfolding my napkin.

"I sure wish I wasn't leaving today," he said, finally ending his school-girl rambling.

"You can always come back to visit soon." He nodded, smiling.

I couldn't even believe this was my dad.

. . .

Two weeks later Dad announced he was moving to San Francisco. His impulsive decision seemed so reckless that I wondered what was wrong with him. This man, who was the epitome of informed decision-making my entire life. The guy who made you do your homework, who was calm in a crisis, reliable, and steady. My father's decision to move across the country and in with a man he'd met for a few hours was beyond any of my own ill-advised impulsiveness. Yet, he was uprooting his whole life to move into his lover's studio apartment after only a couple of nights together.

The irresponsibility of that choice was staggering—not to mention the fact that my escape from the land of my youth to a place where no one knew where and who I came from was about to be permanently interrupted by my gay dad.

Mom didn't want to talk about it.

"You know your father, he's hard-headed. I can't understand what he's doing, but what am I gonna say? God knows I can't change him, Lisa." As usual, Mom didn't like talking with me about Dad. She changed the subject. "Let's talk about what we're gonna do when your sister and I come to visit. It's just a few weeks away!"

It wasn't enough that Dad was moving to California at the end of November, but he would arrive the day my mother and sister went home from their visit to celebrate Thanksgiving and Deena's twenty-first birthday.

. . .

"How can you even drive here? My God, it's terrifying!" Mom said as I drove us down the rocky coast to Carmel on Thanksgiving Day, the Pacific Ocean to our right off a sheer drop. My elderly neighbor had lent me her car during my family's visit. "I don't know where you girls get it from, maybe Grandma Haute, but neither your father nor I like to travel much. Except for Nippersink." Beyond our beloved resort and a few conferences with Parents Without Partners, Mom rarely traveled outside her ten-mile comfort zone.

Out of the corner of my eye, I watched her trying to see this new world through her oldest daughter's eyes. The idea of living so far from where she came from was completely foreign to her, let alone the willingness to leave your family. Like so many women of her generation, Mom's devotion to her mother had been handed down to her from Gram, and to Gram from Nonna. The expectation that her daughters would follow that lead was rooted in my mother, tangled up with my choices, and Deena's. It was easy to let her down by simply wanting a life different from hers.

If she was proud of me, she didn't say so. Mom wasn't one to offer praise, especially the older we got, so as much as I wanted her approval, I knew it would not be forthcoming. She could ooh and ah over the scenery, but not over my ability to live in this place on my own. Winding down Highway 1, the breathtaking coastline unfolding in front of us, it was pride in myself that propelled me.

"So, Dad gets here the day you guys leave," I said, looking in the rearview mirror at my sister. She rolled her eyes. We hadn't talked much about Dad's move since they arrived.

"I just can't believe he's doing this," Mom said, her sigh carrying the weight of her bewilderment, her eyes sad. There wasn't much more for any of us to say about it.

. . .

The first thing I noticed in my father's new home was the lack of his own things. Most of Robert's entire studio apartment was visible from the front door. It consisted of a large room with hardwood floors covered in Oriental rugs, a table for two nestled in the bay window, a leather couch and two chairs in the center of the room facing an ornate fireplace, and a trifold screen shielding what must have been the bed. It was all trimmed in mahogany wood against white plaster walls, with a few pieces of art on them. The room smelled like vanilla, the sweet scent wafting from a lit candle on the mantel. It was nice, but it wasn't my father's usual organized clutter.

"Hi, Dad," I said, shaking off the December chill. The room felt dark, cozy.

"Hi, honey! Let me take your coat." I heard Robert before I saw him, then he emerged through the kitchen doorway to the left, wiping his hands on a dish towel.

"Robert, this is my daughter, Lisa," Dad said, an expectant look moving back and forth between us.

"Hello." He held out his hand for me to shake. Tall and thin, he looked a lot like Dad's most recent ex, who he now referred to as Asshole.

"Hi. Nice to meet you." I shook his hand. *Not really. It's weird.* I was still uncomfortable meeting my father's lovers.

Robert took a tweed coat off a hook near the door. "I'll be back in a few hours, Don. You two have a nice time. Glad to meet you, Lisa." He smiled at me as he went out the door, taking a good part of the discomfort with him.

Once my father and I settled in for the evening at their table overlooking Polk Street, a bottle of white zinfandel underway in front of me, I started talking about how I felt about my parents' divorce. I couldn't stop.

Halfway through the first glass of wine, I casually asked the question that had clenched my heart for a decade. "So, why did you even get married?"

Dad looked startled by my bold question. "I wanted to be married, have a family. That's what everybody wanted in the fifties." He lit a cigarette, exhaled slowly, then placed it in the ashtray beside the one I was already smoking.

"I loved your mother. We were friends. I knew we could have a happy life. We had you girls, and my career took off. Life was good, until something changed. There are things you don't know." I poured more wine as the first glass kicked in. His explanation sounded self-serving and unfair to my unsuspecting mother, whose eyes shimmered with pain when mentioning Dad during her visit. It made me wonder what lay beneath her composed veneer.

"How dare you lead Mom to believe you were in love with her." He looked at me. "And what things don't I know?" Out the window, the flickering red light of a neon sign in the market across the street distracted me from his answer. Downing my glass and pouring more, I realized I was getting drunk, and thought I heard something about Daniel and Betty, my parents' best friends since high school, who had been like an aunt and uncle to me when we were little.

"... so, we met on Monday nights while the girls had ladies' night at our house with you girls. Then Betty wanted a baby, and they were trying to get pregnant. Daniel said he couldn't do it anymore, wanted to focus on his family."

Dad and Daniel? All those years ago when we were little kids?

For a moment, I thought about how long my father had endured hiding who he was, what it must have been like to live a lie like that. I remembered him once telling me of his attraction to Tarzan when his friends drooled over Jane. He said he had kept it to himself, except for Daniel, apparently. Still, I couldn't focus on anything but my mother's pain and humiliation. Any inkling my mother may have had that something was amiss was likely a whisper that didn't interrupt too much of their daily life. Perhaps remaining blind to the secrets in her marriage was far less painful than learning the truth. But when Dad's secret was shouted into the daylight, it changed everything. Since then, watching her husband live an openly gay life was mostly a quiet matter for her.

But not me. I bit my tongue while he continued his story.

"So, I looked elsewhere. Rex at work and I started flirting and it was my transition to a whole new world. That's when your mother and I separated the first time."

The memory of opening the medicine cabinet to find his things gone when I was ten years old flashed through my mind, dropping another puzzle piece into place. Through the haze of my buzz, and my shock, I could hear him still talking.

"As exciting as it was to finally be honest about my life, I decided to come home a year later and try to make it work with your mother. It was too hard to be out back then. Financially, and hiding it at work, of course. It was easier to be married, and I loved living with your mother. And you girls."

Tears filled my eyes as those hours of yearning for him came flooding back. Just like that, I was a child again waiting for his calls, praying for him to come home.

"We got the house in Oak Park and I poured my passion into decorating it. Eventually, I went back to the bars. For a while, I had the best of both worlds. But when I told your mother, and suggested we stay married, she said she wouldn't agree to a double life. You know the rest."

The words I wanted to express during his story had backed up like raw sewage. I wanted to spew every vile word at him through the fire hose of my fury. I couldn't breathe until I said them all, until the stench of my pain was all over him.

"How could you believe that Mom could be happily married to a man who secretly wants to fuck other men?" I screamed.

"Lisa!" He glowered at me.

"How could you do that? How could you do that to Mom?" Pity for my mother fueled my rage. "No woman wants her man to leave her and her kids, and especially not for a *guy*! Holy shit, Dad! Or worse, let him stay and make her live a lie!"

"You don't understand what it was like for *me*." He spoke in the monotone he reserved for his deepest anger, the one he used before doling out punishment.

"No, I don't." I drained the rest of the bottle into my glass. "But I can imagine how Mom felt. You totally compromised her sexuality, Dad, I mean, she was a *virgin*. She was only nineteen when you got married, for God's sake! Fuck. I shouldn't have even been born."

"Lisa, that's enough! How dare you? I told you I loved her. I always will. Now stop it!"

I couldn't. "How could you get back together with Mom and move us to Oak Park? How many lies did you have to tell her to convince her you'd changed?"

He didn't answer. He lit another cigarette, his hands shaking. Smoke hung in a bitter fog around us, mingling with the too-sweet candle. It made me nauseous.

"Now you move in with a guy you met for a weekend? What the fuck? Do you think for a second if me or Deena did this you would be cool with it? Hell no. You insisted we make informed decisions. *You* taught us that. Is this informed? How much do you even know about this guy?" He stared at me, then attempted to jump in to defend himself, but I put up my hand to stop him.

"I'm not done. Every impulsive thing I ever did was scrutinized by you. All my life you punished us for lying. What you say doesn't mean shit to me now that I know you lied your whole life." I spoke like a grown-up about grown-up things, wanting to shock him, to make him hear me after a decade of holding in so many conflicting feelings. I wanted to hurt him as badly as I hurt.

"You're crazy to be doing this, Dad. And you know what? Who fucking cares? Go ahead, do your thing. Hope you're happy." I slumped back in the chair, exhausted. The neon outside the window blurred to an angry red smear as my head spun with words and wine.

"I am happy, dammit. Robert makes me happy." He stared across the dimly lit room. "I love him."

I didn't really want to hear how much he loved Robert, this one-night stand he thought could last. *Would he have done this with a woman if he were straight?* That a woman would invite him to move in after a weekend seemed incomprehensible. *This isn't normal.* I wanted my parents to be normal, regardless of how exotic I wanted my own life to be. It may not have been fair, but I ached for a dad who would help me navigate the treacherous waters of young adulthood, one whose love I could trust, instead of this man who dished about boys, like a girlfriend. I wanted my Daddy back.

He poured me in a cab and sent me home.

Eight

That night on Polk Street is the furthest thing from my mind when I flip through the pages of my father's will, still astonished to find my sister's name at the top of every list of the recipients of his most treasured possessions. It seems unfathomable that Deena will receive all the paintings and antiques he cherished, her pick of the belongings that came out of storage when Dad moved into his own condo after he and Robert broke up, just a few months after we sat at that table speaking the truth. It tortures me to read through his will again, to see my mother's name is second on these lists; his partner Benny's, third. My name is at the bottom, along with his only grandchild. To see none of his favorite things were left specifically to me is suffocating.

Through a veil of tears, I study the pages of my father's meticulous notes about the management of his apartment building, as well as the disposal of his computer, with detailed instructions about deleting the porn from the G:drive. Still desperately hoping for a personal note to any of us, it's as if by reading it over and over, some sort of acknowledgement of how far we had come will appear in the pages, like magic, written in invisible ink. But no matter how many times I read it, there are no words of endearment for me.

Only a reminder of how deeply he could hurt me with his silence.

Dad didn't call me for weeks after the dinner at his apartment. Even in my anger at him I felt a hole in my heart, which I filled with food and wine while yearning for a love of my own. When I couldn't stand it anymore, I called him.

"You hurt my feelings, Lisa," he snapped. "You need to apologize."

"I know what I said hurt you. I'm sorry, Dad." I knew he would want more contrition than that, but it was hard to muster. My own pain wasn't mentioned.

"Well, that's just not good enough. I'd like you to apologize for saying that I hurt your mother by marrying her. That I, uh, *compromised* her. Choices were made at the time that I thought I had to make, and they didn't work out. I gave her a good life while we were married, and I paid every penny of child support. We are still friends."

"I know, you did. I'm sorry. I'm sorry I said that." I could see my parents sitting at every kitchen table they'd ever had, drinking coffee and talking. I knew she still loved him, and in his own way he loved her, too. "You're always there for her."

"Well, that's right. Okay, then." He let it go at that, then told me about the new job he'd landed in San Francisco. "I'll be IT Director in the banking industry, a new field for me. It sounds interesting." Now that he had been proven right by getting the apology he felt he deserved, he sounded fine. We made plans to meet for brunch on Sunday.

After the call, any lingering bitter feelings I had about him got stuffed down with more chocolate and wine.

Taking the L-Taraval streetcar up to the Castro to meet my father for brunch became a monthly ritual. On Sundays, the outdoor patio of Cafe Flore filled up by 10:30 a.m. with chirpy men and their dates from Saturday night. The steady stream of mostly male patrons didn't let up till three o'clock. Dad's date from the night before might join us, something I hated but tolerated. I was glad to have some of my father's attention, and the fact that there were men holding hands at the next table was just part of the deal.

"Hi, what's your pleasure?" the waiter asked my father, his delivery dripping with innuendo. "What would you like to eat?"

"I'll have the Reuben," Dad said, keeping it PG, but underneath I could see he was eating up the attention. My embarrassment was palpable. This neighborhood offered the kind of people-watching one would expect, and it still made me uneasy to include my father among this crowd. While Dad didn't have the effeminate flamboyance of some of the men in the Castro, he did have a penchant for preening. He and the guys he dated carried the mustached clean-cut image of a look-alike tribe that emulated one another in button-down shirts and tight jeans. Trim hair with a side-part rounded out the look. It was as if he loved falling in love with himself.

"I'll have the Cobb salad. And a mimosa." The liquid courage was for the news I came to share with my father. Once the waiter was gone, I spilled the beans.

"So, they let me go from my job. I mean, I'm not really sure why, I was late a few times, and got a little snippy with my boss once, but I know I'll find another one soon." I picked up the drink the waiter put in front of me and took a long swig.

"Well, that's too bad. I know you'll find something; you've never had trouble finding a job. You didn't seem to like it there very much. Just get out there and pound the pavement. That's what I did when I got here."

I nodded and ate my salad, listening to him talk about his condo and the renovations he was doing, as discontentment churned inside me. *Doesn't he care that I lost my job?*

In moments like this, childhood memories still cast him as a hero in my mind, devoted to his daughters, even if that wasn't a true depiction of him. If he cared, wouldn't he offer to help me if I needed it, assuaging my fear of poverty? Instead, he appeared to be self-absorbed and shallow—even more so since his move to San Francisco.

I attributed this to him being gay.

Sadly, there was a caricature of the homosexual man as overly conceited and self-indulgent, which supported this belief. In 1985 it was easy to apply this notion to my narcissistic father, and to blame his sexual orientation, instead of his nature, for making him so selfish.

• • •

"So, I just got fired from my job," I said to Mark once he got settled on my couch with a glass of wine. He had broken up with Eileen and was happily juggling a handful of feminine prospects. We got together occasionally to hang out.

"That sucks. You weren't even there that long." I'd had the job for only six months, and I hated it, but the lack of income threw me into a panic.

"True. I saw an ad in the paper today for an administrative assistant at a recording studio equipment company." I handed him the folded *San Francisco Chronicle*, the listing for Assistant to the Vice President circled in blue ink. "I don't know if I could get it. But maybe." This job would get me back around music, and while all my experience had been with administrative work, I was no secretary. "What do you think?"

"Lis, I think you can manifest anything you want. You need to put it under a crystal or something." He fished into his pocket and pulled out a small chunk of stone and handed it to me. One end was rough and at the other was a clear, smooth point. It felt warm.

"Use this one. Cut out the ad, put all your juju into this crystal,

then place it over the ad in an ashtray. See if you don't get that job."
He made it sound easy, if not a little silly.

I twirled the rock in my hand, remembering the magic of
making wishes over a birthday cake or on the first star in the night
sky. *I wish I may, I wish I might.* I believed in wishing as a child. Some
even came true.

"Thanks. I'll try it." He looked like he swallowed the sun,
imparting his magic to me. He had shaved off his beard since I saw
him last, revealing a chiseled jaw beneath a smile filled with crooked
teeth that didn't take away from his good looks. I leaned in and
kissed his smooth cheek. My crush on him was buried under the
buddy thing we shared, so I settled for an easy affection between us.

When he left, I lit the joint that was sitting in the ashtray. Now
empty, I wiped it clean with a paper towel, then carefully cut out the
employment ad and placed it in the center. I held the crystal tightly
in my left hand, putting all my energy into it, all my hope to get this
job. I placed it in the ashtray over the ad and let out a deep breath.
Please work, I thought, knowing deep inside that believing it could
was a good start. My résumé went in the mail the next day.

Within a week I received the call to come in for an interview
at the warehouse building on Bryant Street. My interview with the
wiry, charming VP went so well that he offered me the job on the
spot. A year later, when the company went bankrupt, he gave me the
number of the president of a video production house who needed
a new assistant. As I shook Ross Scott's hand at the end of the job
interview, desperately wanting the job, I never dreamed I would be
this man's right arm for the next five years.

• • •

Most of my days were spent as Ross's gatekeeper, fielding requests
for his time, setting up travel and meetings, and typing memos for

distribution. I was his eyes on the ground when he wasn't in the building. Our steering committee met weekly and was made up of all the department heads; my role was to order lunch and take minutes. Being in the room with decision-makers both thrilled and intimidated me. Every inch of my inner high school dropout was sure my lack of education showed, like the scar that ran from my lip to my chin, a remnant from a childhood run-in with a For Sale sign on the neighbor's lawn.

After a couple years of working together, Ross grew restless in our small pond and had designs on a more powerful career in the entertainment industry. "Don't worry," he said, "Wherever I go, I'll take you with me."

By the night of the Academy Awards ceremony, we were settled into our new offices at LucasFilm. I had to pinch myself that I was among such talented people, and while I was still Ross's assistant (AKA work wife), I was also given the responsibilities of office manager. That night Sean Connery presented the first Oscar of the evening to our team.

Even though I had nothing at all to do with the hard work that went into that achievement, I partied as if I had been on set every day of shooting. It was the first of many nights toasting the winners of awards I believed I could never receive on my own merit. My role as the sidekick to a powerful man in charge felt like the closest to the top I could achieve, given the choices I'd made earlier in my life. I resigned myself to riding shotgun.

The next day we passed around the heavy gold statue, taking Polaroid photos of one another with it in front of the movie's poster. I mailed one to my mom.

"How's the job going, honey?" Dad asked over crepes and coffee one Sunday at the small cafe near his new house in the Glen Park district. I was happy to have him to myself that morning, sitting at a sunny window table under the burlap-covered ceiling.

"It's good. All the high tech is in the movies we make, that's for sure. Ross just ordered Macintosh computers for everyone and I'm researching new phone systems."

"Macintosh, huh? I've been in computers since the sixties and what's available now is beyond anything we could have imagined back then. The whole computer in a box on your desk! In the early days it took up a whole room. Remember when you girls would come to work with me and play on the keypunch machines?" He looked nostalgic for the days when he was a young star in his field.

"Yeah, I do. I loved going there with you." It had been years since I thought about keypunching at Dad's work on a Saturday, carefully typing my name, my address, and my birthday while the card in front of me filled with small rectangular holes. Then he would invite us into the chilly computer room, the mainframe a giant spaceship at the center of it, lights blinking in various colors to the loud hum of the spinning tape drives. He warned us not to touch anything without asking. We didn't dare. Then he showed us how our "work" made its way onto the massive tapes. It was magic, and my dad was the magician.

"Are you still dating your friend's brother?" he asked, pulling me out of my reverie. Dad always inquired about my love life.

"Off and on. He's kind of a flake, but we have fun when he actually shows up." Meeting Gavin at my friend Mary's wedding had launched me into a tailspin, trying to get and keep his affection. He called sporadically, usually for a spontaneous date that included lots of alcohol, some decent sex, and a longing for him to profess his love for me. He didn't, except to say what a great girl I was. Like too many guys before him, I wanted to be his girlfriend, but he wouldn't commit.

"I hear you, honey. I haven't met Prince Charming either. Slim pickings out there for a hopeful romantic like me." He glanced around the restaurant, as if maybe the man of his dreams would appear just then.

I flinched to hear Dad talk about his search for Mr. Right. "Oh! By the way, we're having a premiere screening of *Back to The Future* next week and I wondered if you'd like to go with me. I think you'll like it; a lot of it is set in the 1950s."

"You know I love anything from the fifties. Sure, it sounds like fun."

A week later, we watched Marty McFly take an unexpected trip to 1955 in Doc Brown's DeLorean time machine. Every clue to the future 1985 delighted my father.

"So clever!" he whispered when Marty saw Ronald Reagan, the current president, on the movie marquee in 1955.

Sitting in the darkened theater beside Dad, I was transported back to my childhood, when anything I did with him felt special. Going to his office or the show to see a movie was a treat, given how much he worked. So much had gone on between us for so many years that I had forgotten how much I once loved him. In that theater, I felt closer to those days than I had in a very long time.

"They really got it right," Dad said as we walked back to our cars at the end of the night. "Thanks for inviting me, honey. I had a great time. I'm sure we'll talk soon."

"Thanks for coming. I'm glad I got to see it with you." We hugged goodbye, then each carried our memory of the evening across the Golden Gate Bridge into the foggy city.

• • •

When AIDS swept through the San Francisco gay community, my fear for my father's health was tempered by the knowledge that, in a weird way, his colon surgery over a decade earlier had eliminated some of his risk. Yet it didn't make him immune. His vague but lascivious comments about his single life after leaving Robert led me to believe he was promiscuous, frequenting the bars that lined Polk Street and the Castro and all it had to offer. I prayed the surgery he'd undergone, after fighting so hard against it, would save his life twice.

In San Francisco, everyone I knew had a friend who had been diagnosed or knew someone who was sick. Dad and I didn't talk much about it, but I knew he had friends who were dying. One day, Ross and I were talking about what we could do to contribute to this cause and help bring awareness to people who were terrified to be near gay men.

"We should have a show," he said, "a rock concert here on the sound stage, and donate the proceeds to AIDS. I'm sure Huey Lewis or some Bay Area band will do it. I'll direct, and you can produce."

"Yeah! Like Mickey Rooney and Judy Garland—we have a barn, let's do a show!" My head instantly filled with the fantasy of producing a rock show, on a much grander scale than when I'd promoted the band at seventeen.

After a few weeks of talking with everyone Ross knew in the music industry, we hooked up with another group who had the same idea. Once Bill Graham got on board, and booked the Grateful Dead, it became a week-long telethon event.

"The exec producer asked me if I could be associate producer of the telecast," I said to Ross after attending a planning meeting. "What do you think? If I get Dawn up to speed to do my job until June, can I do it?" I felt like I was convincing my dad to let me go away to summer camp.

He narrowed his eyes. "I don't care what you do as long as I'm taken care of. And I'm not feeling all that taken care of right now, so yes, go, do your thing. I think you'll be great. But you better make sure your job is covered."

The following Monday started a four-month run of fourteen-hour days. My assignment was to work with a collection of talented, smart women who had mostly come from road tours with major recording artists. Like Alice in Wonderland, I dove straight down the rabbit hole, a gripping fear following behind me into every boardroom meeting.

As I took my place at gleaming conference tables with a dozen sophisticated yuppies, the feeling of being found out as an impostor trapped every idea I had in a sticky web of insecurity, one that metastasized the moment I was out in the world on my own, no longer an appendage of Ross. While others in the room spoke up, sometimes with the same ideas I had, my terror of saying something stupid kept me quietly taking notes, a job I was comfortable with.

But on the phone, I excelled. Asking boldly for people's support of their time or goods or services, impressing upon them the urgency of this cause, I booked hours of free editing time with every post-production house in San Francisco, then spent many of those hours in the dead of night watching the editor and producer create a show out of countless hours of footage. It was both exhilarating and exhausting, garnering our team commendations from the San Francisco Board of Supervisors for our community service and civic spirit.

When we gathered at the television station to watch the broadcast, we learned we had raised hundreds of thousands of dollars for AIDS research and education. After the broadcast, I watched my first production credit crawl across the screen, near the top with only a handful of names before mine. *Associate Producer*, it read. The fact that we had helped people in a community so connected to my father brought me to tears.

When Dad saw the show on TV he was thrilled. "I'm so proud of you, honey, I told all my friends to watch. Of course, I didn't sit through all those rock bands, but I watched the end and taped it!"

Post-production postpartum set in the moment I returned to my office. Ross was glad to have me back, but his expectations were high. Returning to his needs and demands, ordering office supplies, and fixing the Xerox machine were the last things I wanted to do.

On a December morning, Ross poked his head in my office. "Let's go out for lunch today. Sushi. Noon."

I had just returned from working Earthquake Relief, another Bill Graham telethon, this one supporting victims from the Loma Prieta earthquake that struck the Bay Area in October of 1989. When Bill assembled the team from our AIDS project to produce it the week of Thanksgiving, I took my vacation, since Ross wasn't as accommodating this time around. After the short walk to the restaurant, we settled at the sushi bar and he ordered two double sakes.

"I want a divorce," he said. I knew he didn't mean from his wife. "You don't love me anymore and I want someone who does. All these music projects are your passion, so go do them. I'll give you till the end of January, but then I want you out. We'll interview candidates. I'll help you find a new gig. You'll be fine. Go do what you love, Lis."

All I could do was nod as I fought back tears. Even though I was terrified, I knew he was right. He talked about contacts he had in Los Angeles and connecting with key people from the projects I had done. It was all white noise to me. He was letting me go, and even if it was for my own good, it felt like I was being dumped.

• • •

The morning after my twenty-ninth birthday I woke up with a raging hangover, and the reality that I would be out of a job soon. An interview in Los Angeles the week before had left me hopeful, but keenly aware of my limited production experience. Going down there on Ross's recommendation, to interview with a VP at Warner Brothers Records, reminded me that I was in way over my head.

When she called to tell me I didn't get the job, I was somewhat relieved, hoping it meant something better was coming my way. Still, I was freaked out about being unemployed, and there weren't any music producer ads in the classifieds to put with a crystal in an ashtray. The only work I had been offered was a short production stint with the Grateful Dead for five shows in Oakland at the end of the year. That was enough to get excited about.

On the day after Christmas, I showed up at the Oakland Coliseum production office and was put to work sewing costumes and answering phones. The week ended with the final Dead show on New Year's Eve, an event that had Bonnie Raitt opening and Bill Graham descending from the ceiling at the stroke of midnight in a chicken suit, landing on the proverbial egg of life. My job during the show was to videotape the spectacle for posterity.

Standing as still as I possibly could up on the lighting platform, I pointed the first video camera I had ever held at Bill, the egg and the pyrotechnics, zooming in and out. As we ushered in 1990, balloons fell all around me while I kept one teary eye on the lens of the camera, praying I didn't mess up. *This is it.* Ever since my days managing Tony's band as a teenager, I wanted to hang out backstage in the chaos that was the magic of a live concert, to be part of what the public never sees, and feel the pulse created when the music meets the energy of the screaming fans as they share a single heartbeat.

As the band started "Iko Iko," the place throbbed with twenty thousand ecstatic souls ushering in the dawn of a new decade. I stood in the middle of the circus that was the rock show, my pulse racing, my big dreams growing.

After it was over, the crew tore it all down. Those of us who were left at the end hung out backstage sucking nitrous oxide from balloons with the band. As my head spun with the calm euphoria of the gas, I could see the possibilities of the 1990's float like bubbles around my head. *I'll get a job in the music world. I'll fall in love and get married. Maybe I'll have a baby.* It was to be my decade of attainment, I decided, one in which my life, not just my career, would soar. As the buzz wore off, I floated back into the room and marveled at where I already found myself as I headed into my thirtieth year.

Nine

The words rush like a putrid river into the phone. "Did he really love Deena so much more than me? I'm sorry. I know this all sounds petty, but *fuck*. Really? I know they just think I'm selfish by being so upset. But the way he split the trust—feels like percentages of love, Kath. One minute I miss him so much, and the next I'm so pissed off I could spit."

Most days I go about my life hardly thinking about my sister and her power over everything that was Dad's. Then a moment comes when the wound of my father's distribution of his assets begins to fester and ooze. That's when I call a girlfriend. This time it's Kathy.

"Listen, you express the emotion for your family, Lis. They don't see that. To them, you're just too much. You talk too much, you cry too much. They're mortified by your big reactions to things. But it'll be okay. All of it."

The assurance in her voice is a comfort. I let her words sink in. She's right. I carry the emotions for my family like a heavy bucket with a wide crack across the bottom, letting the contents pour out all over everything, making a mess as I go.

"Your sister has completely shut down, right? That's how she copes. That's why she didn't cancel her trip to New Orleans when he died."

"I know she's hurting, but man, I hated her for going on vacation and leaving me with Mom. It was hard on her, I know, since she wasn't speaking to Dad that much. Last time I talked to her she wanted to stage an intervention over all the meds." My father's downward spiral of pain after a bad back surgery had permeated every day of the last several years of his life. His doctor had him on a cocktail of several opiates which he took excessively. I had come to accept that chemistry ruled his world.

"And now every time I think of the will, I literally get nauseous." The wall between my sister and me had filled with cement the moment she announced she would be keeping her plans to go away for the four days before Dad's memorial. I threw a fit, but Mom told her to go.

For much of our lives, we seemed to tag team being close to our parents, Deena and I. When we were kids, I was Dad's favorite. As adults, she was. Until recently. Mom seemed to rotate her favorite at any given time. Maybe all families are like that.

"Just remember what I told you the day he died, Lis. Everything that is said right now will be remembered for a long time."

Panic rose like ground fog as my last day of work glared up at me from the calendar on my desk. Ross kept reassuring me something would come through while he turned his attention to my replacement. He reminded me of my father sometimes.

What had started as an opportunity to grow, now felt like being abandoned for another woman with no means of support. The only hope I had was that one of the many feelers I put out would call me.

While I waited, I focused on intentionally manifesting all the things I wanted. Mark came over to make dream collages and drink wine. We littered my living room rug with dozens of pictures and words cut from magazines depicting images of music, love, peace, and travel, then we glued them to poster board to give a face to our dreams. I tacked mine on the wall, staring at it each day. "What will be, will be," I wrote in my journal, then called anyone I knew about leads for work.

. . .

"Hey, Lisa, it's Colin Benjamin," a commanding, raspy voice said. "Monica said to give you a call."

I knew Colin was a big-time production manager. When Monica and the rest of my production cohorts from Earthquake Relief left to go out on tour, I'd wished it were me.

"We're going out on tour next month, and I need an assistant. Honestly, I want Karen Kramer, but she's quit the road." His voice boomed in my ear, not hiding his disappointment. "Are you interested? Monica tells me you'd be good."

I could barely breathe. Seventeen-year-old me stepped away from making posters for Ashcraft to pinch twenty-nine-year-old me. "Yes! Yes, I'm very interested." *Be cool.*

He continued with the details that spun wildly in my head. "We head for Los Angeles on the seventeenth for a couple weeks of rehearsals, then to Pensacola for tech rehearsals until early March when we head out. We'll have a couple breaks for a few days but count on being gone for most of the year. US, Canada. Europe, and Japan. Maybe Hong Kong. The job is yours if you can be in L.A. next week. I'll call you when I know more."

The next day I splurged, spending $100 on a matched set of luggage. List after list was produced to cover all the bases while I prepared to leave my life for a year. Dad would keep my bird; Mary agreed to send my bills to hotels on the road; my passport was expedited. As excited as I was, anxiety filled my days with nagging feelings that I would miss something. I barely slept, and when I did, I dreamed of all I had to get done. It was like doing everything twice.

My last day at work was bittersweet. The art department created a huge card displaying a DeLorean tour bus circling the globe, a nod to our work on the *Back to the Future* movies. Everyone signed it like a high school yearbook, then we gathered for champagne and cake in the hallway outside the screening room. At the end of the day, Ross poked his head into my office before I left.

"Well, kiddo, it's been a trip. Go out there and kick some ass."

"Indeed, it has," I said, tearing up. "Thanks for all of it. I couldn't be doing this without you."

He gave me a hug. "You'll be great out there. Drop us a line."

"I will," I said, gathering my stuff and leaving the building for the last time.

. . .

My last weekend before heading out on tour was spent saying goodbyes, and fighting the rising anxiety of leaving my life, my home, and everyone I knew for such a long time. It felt a little like I was heading off to war. Dad came over on Saturday afternoon when I called and said I could use some company.

"Honey, I'm sure you'll do a great job," he said, over cups of coffee. "What an exciting opportunity. You've wanted to do this ever since you hung out with that band behind the barber shop. So, when Ross pulled the rug out from under you, he knew you'd land on your feet. And now you have your dream job. I've always told you to do what you love and look at you now." Birds of a feather, my dad and Ross. I suspected Colin would be the next commanding man to join the club of men I would work hard to impress.

"Thanks. As exciting as this is, I'm scared shitless that I can't cut it and they'll send me home."

"Oh, you'll be fine. I'm proud of you for even attempting something like this. You're already a success for getting the job." He looked at his watch, then drained his cup, signaling it was time to go.

After he put on his coat to leave, he hugged me tight. "Now go get 'em!"

"Any chance you can take me to the airport on Monday, Dad?" I opened the door to let him into the hall.

"Sorry, honey, I can't," he said, fishing a twenty out of his wallet, "But take a cab, on me."

He didn't get it that it wasn't about the free ride. I wanted him to see me off at the airport, to have a sendoff.

"Thanks, Dad." I stuffed the bill into my pocket.

. . .

That night, a funny feeling came over me just before Mark arrived to hang out before I left town. Our visits were always insightful and deep, an opportunity look at our dreams of love and success through different lenses. We listened to records, read tarot cards, got stoned. He would make something delicious to eat out of the five things I had in my fridge. It always felt like we were making magic.

Our shared mystical connection had drawn us into each other's lives like magnets. Even though we were platonic, it was one of the most intimate relationships in my life. We shared our deepest desires with one another, the heart of them having to do with romantic fantasies of finding The One. Like a rare bird, Mark resisted captivity while yearning for a mate. I had no delusions that mate would be me, but he modeled what the right guy might look like. More than a few of his girlfriends had become the topic of our conversation since his breakup with Eileen. We shared such a similar vision of what true love could be: not just someone to be with, but how the right person could bring us more fully into our own potential. As much as I may have fantasized about him being that man in my life, I settled for his warm hugs, and foot rubs, and a loving friendship that had been there from the very beginning.

So, I imagine it was a soft touch that lingered too long, that led to the kiss that led to the rest... When I opened my eyes the next morning, naked beside him with our heads at the foot of my bed, the memory of the previous night swam in my head, dreamlike.

"Wow, how did that happen?" he said with a smile, softly running his fingers over my shoulder. "And who knew your skin would be like velvet?" He got up, then kissed me upside down before heading into the hall to the bathroom. I lay there thinking about the night before, not remembering much about the physical act, only the glistening ease of our connection; a feeling both natural and foreign, that I couldn't quite grasp. *Wow.* Pushing away any *When Harry Met Sally* analysis was easier knowing I was leaving town for a year.

After he left, I wrote in my journal that I didn't need to agonize over whether he would call me or not, obsessing over whether we would have a future. *We'll probably end up living together in New Mexico one day,* I wrote. *Until then, I'm delighted I shared a special night with a man I know cares about me and respects me.*

And for the first time, that was enough.

• • •

The outpouring of love I had experienced throughout that week sent me to Los Angeles via cloud nine. Once I was in the production office with Colin, the coil of nerves inside me started to unwind and I buckled down to the job. Fourteen-hour days became the new routine, as I got to know the core production staff and peeked in on dance rehearsals. It was all I could do to hold in my glee and act cool.

The rest of our technical crew met us a few weeks later in Pensacola, Florida. Each department arrived—dozens of men, and four other women—to handle lighting, sound, wardrobe, and video. Like a benevolent beast, the show grew bigger each day, relentless in its pursuit of perfection. It was thrilling to watch it grow. Colin kept me under his firm tutelage.

"God, he's so tough on me," I said one night, dragging on a joint and sinking a putt into a water glass in a fellow roadie's hotel room. "I've been an assistant to powerful guys before, but he makes them look like pussies."

"Hold your ground, girl. Road Rules 101: Don't let them see your fear," Denny said, repositioning the ball and taking a shot. He missed. In just a few weeks these guys had become like brothers, each wanting me to listen to their advice, and comfortable enough to give me shit.

Paul chimed in, "Colin will test you. You need to be willing to stand up to him. He'll respect you for it. You'll fuck some things up, but you'll be all right."

"Great. That's helpful." I couldn't imagine what Colin would do if I fucked up.

· · ·

"Hi, is Colin around?" a woman said as she waltzed into the production office. She was striking, with a confidence that followed in behind her like smoke. It was a week before we were boarding the tour buses to travel to our first show in Miami, when the road life would truly begin.

"He's out on the stage," I said, picking up a walkie-talkie to call him. "Who can I say is here?"

"Karen Kramer." *Oh, no.* "You must be Collie's assistant."

"Uh, yeah, I'm Lisa." My stomach lurched as I pushed the microphone button to announce her arrival. *Holy shit.* "Hey, Colin?"

"Go for Colin," he bellowed into the quiet room.

"Karen Kramer is here to see you." The inner storm of anxiety that started the moment she said her name intensified.

Please don't be here for my job.

"Cool! I'll be right down."

I can't go home now.

She looked around and smiled, clearly comfortable in a production office. "How's the show coming?"

"Good, good. We're getting ready to head out—" Colin pulled open the door.

"Hey, K2! How are you, girl?" He scooped Karen into a hug, letting out a laugh I had never heard come out of him.

"I'm good." He motioned to her to sit in the chair beside him. Their conversation turned to people I didn't know, swapping stories about when they were out with the Stones. The ease with which she sat with this bear of a man, so cool and relaxed, was something I promised myself I'd cultivate with Colin if I could stay. *Please let me stay.* Sweat trickled down my back.

"I'm just down for the night to stay with the wardrobe crew, and to see you, Collie. I'll go back to Nashville tomorrow."

My huge sigh of relief might have stopped their conversation had they been paying any attention to me at all.

The crew buses arrived a few days later, carrying the history of legendary tours—my bunk was once occupied by Steve Perry during a Journey run—but the star and her entourage had brand new ones. Hoisting myself up the stairs of the star's bus, I introduced myself to her driver.

"Hi, I'm Lisa. Assistant Production Manager. Welcome to the tour." He smiled wide as I stepped up into the cockpit. "Hi, honey," he drawled. "My name's Jim." His Southern roots stretched his name into two syllables. Except for his ginger beard, he looked like Patrick Swayze in *Road House*, all the way down to how he pinched his cigarette between his thumb and forefinger.

I stretched out my hand to shake his, glancing into the front lounge. "You mind if I look around?"

"Why sure, darlin'." He jumped out of his seat to take my hand. There was something about him I instantly liked, despite my usual attraction to dark, brooding musicians. Jim's light brown hair surrounded a handsome face; in his hazel eyes was a look that sent a warm rush though me.

"This is a Prevost XL with a Detroit Diesel engine; a million-dollar piece of equipment, right here. It's a brand new 'en just for this tour."

His pride filled the confined space as we continued single file down the center bunk area which would accommodate an assistant, a chef, a masseuse, and security. Following him into the back lounge, I noticed the tight jeans hugging his ass, and the snakeskin cowboy boots on his feet. We stood close together in the back room of the bus that had been converted into an opulent master bedroom for the star and her boyfriend. My bus, with its slightly worn interior, would be shared by me and nine guys, plus my driver, Charlie.

Jim chattered on about the details of the bus as I shared my excitement over being on my first tour, and how anxious I was to be leaving in a couple of days for our first show.

"A newbie, huh? Well, you'll be fine. You look like a smart lady. And if you need anything, why you just come see Jimmy and I'll help ya out. I been out here on the road a long time. Seen it all." His smile widened again, letting out a throaty laugh.

"Thanks. I might take you up on that, Jimmy." His sincerity didn't mask his desire for me. I needed some air. "Well, I got to get back to the production office, so I'll see you around,"

"You will," he said with a wink. "You definitely will."

I climbed down the steps and heard the thud of the heavy door close behind me, unaware that way down the road, literally, we would have our first date. Till then, I would be too preoccupied by the many shows we had to put on before we got there.

. . .

Patience and cheerfulness proved to be my most useful tools during those first few months on the road. I got used to Colin's mercurial nature, learning what would set him off or make him smile. His stern direction, and occasional appreciation, kept me on my toes, not unlike how I felt with my father and almost every boss I had. What was it about me that had attracted exacting men, the kind who could shred your confidence with a mere look? The slightest praise evoked an even deeper desire to please. Those first shows through the Carolinas had me near tears by load-out, the tension and exhaustion pervasive across our caravan. After we got through the first important show, Madison Square Garden in New York, we had it down, making the goal each day to create a tighter show and a shorter load out.

The tedium of being in the production office all day wore on me, yet I didn't dare step foot out of it unless I had a production assistant there to answer phones. Show days could be twenty hours long. Luckily, my passion for being there sustained me when sleep was impossible. In stolen moments I called home, checking in on Mom and Gram. When I called Dad, he cheered me on to hang in there when I shared our grueling schedule.

"Those first load-outs didn't get us on the road until dawn, then we set it all up a few hours later in another city. We were all a little punch-drunk by then."

"I don't know how you do it. Even if the bottom falls out, remember I'm proud of you that you even attempted it."

"Thanks, Dad. I can do this, even though I'm exhausted. It'll get easier, at least that's what they tell me." He chuckled. It felt soothing to hear his voice, to have his approval. It occurred to me I missed my family more while untethered from daily life than I ever did in my apartment in San Francisco.

. . .

On the drive to Salt Lake City, I had the kind of nervous energy that came before a first date. Jimmy had wandered into the production office in Denver and casually asked if I wanted to get a drink in the next city.

"I'll meet you at your hotel around six," he said. Like the tour buses, the band had more luxurious hotel accommodations than we did. Since he drove the star, he stayed with them at Four Seasons and Ritz Carltons while we stayed at Hyatts and Hiltons.

Once I checked into my room, I showered and changed into the nicest thing in my suitcase—a long red tunic and a pair of blue jeans—a departure from the mostly black clothes I wore backstage. The makeup bag that had floated to the bottom of my luggage was resurrected, a relic from rehearsals in L.A., before my beauty routine had been pared down to getting a shower every couple of days. I even combed my hair.

"Whoa, Lisa has on lipstick," a fellow roadie said when I ran into him in the elevator. "Who's the lucky guy?"

"Don't worry about it," I mumbled.

When I emerged into the outside twilight, there stood a horse and carriage; Jim was bounding down the steps to greet me.

"Hi, honey," he said, taking my hand to help me up onto the seat. "We're gonna ride in style. I thought I'd been in everything with wheels, but I ain't never been in one of these." It was an unexpected romantic gesture, melting my heart a little for this country boy.

We rode through the quiet streets, holding hands, chatting about our lives. He charmed me with stories about growing up in Tennessee, his drawl like thick honey.

"I got a girl and a boy, thirteen- and ten-year-old. I miss 'em," he said. "But they're okay with their mama. How about you? Tell me about your life."

He stroked the top of my hand with his thumb while I talked about being raised in Chicago and the life I had forged in California. He listened, mesmerized. Sweet, and relaxed. When we asked the driver for the best place open for dinner on a Sunday night, he said my hotel was the only choice. We went back to my room and ordered room service.

Our make-out session on the bed after dinner normally would have ended in sex, but I knew we'd have plenty of time for that in the months ahead. Instead, we kissed slowly, his beard soft against my face, and let the contours of our bodies pull close to one another in delicious anticipation. Knowing he would pursue me, I let myself hold back, savoring the romance of the moment as he murmured in my ear his delight in holding me, each word feeling like a promise. My heart fluttered inside my chest as I imagined the possibilities.

Our next city happened to be San Francisco, where I stopped at home for a sexy dress and lingerie before going to the Four Seasons Hotel. Luckily, the girl who sublet my place wasn't there. My brief time in my own home felt awkward; the somewhat messy display of someone else's belongings in my apartment was unsettling. Still, I took my time getting ready for a proper date, drawing a hot bath, and even pulling out the curling iron. The gasp when Jimmy opened the door to his hotel room was worth the effort.

"Well, look at you, beautiful," he said, scooping me into his arms. "Where would you like to go eat?"

"North Beach. My favorite place in San Francisco." We headed out, hailed a cab, and began a memorable evening of delicious Italian food, too much red wine, and a walk through Little Italy under the sparkling lights strung above our heads. The night ended with us tangled under the covers of the king-size bed in his hotel room.

The next day we came clean to security, who had seen me

leaving his room on the hallway video camera at dawn. They busted Jimmy about it when he answered his door wearing a Cheshire Cat grin. Knowing my high-profile job would draw questions from management about my ability to stay focused while engaging in a roadie romance, we obtained Colin's blessing, then spent every night together we could. This shifted the attention of my grand adventure to one of falling in love.

· · ·

I don't think Jimmy intended to deceive me in those early weeks when we were breathlessly intoxicated with each other. He let me assume he was divorced, never stating a marital status one way or the other. I chose to let the vague details of his life back home to be enough information to forge ahead with our passion for each other. But when his wife, kids, and mother-in-law planned to come down to Atlanta to visit him, he had to admit he was merely separated by the miles his work put between him and his family.

"I've done ask for a divorce every time I go back to the house. She won't give me one. So, I stay out here on the road much as I can." He lit a cigarette, stroking his beard as he exhaled. "I'm sorry, babe. I really am."

"How could you not tell me?" I cried, shaking. Jimmy had become my fairy-tale ending, my next adventure. In the month we'd spent together, we had talked about me moving to Tennessee, and the house we could have there. His devotion to us was something I had witnessed between men and the women I envied. Never had a man I was attracted to been so enamored with me. The safe bubble of love that had formed around us burst in an instant with his admission, leaving me gasping, as if it contained the only air I could breathe. "I can't believe you lied to me."

"Honey, I never lied to ya. I just didn't tell you the whole truth.

I fell in love with you. For years, I've been asking for a divorce. We don't feel like we're married no more. She's at the house and I'm out here most all the time. The money takes care of my kids. I'm sorry. I'll fix it, I promise."

Not knowing the truth had given me permission to open my heart to this man who was so exotic in his simplicity—the opposite of my complicated father. Still, the truth didn't make me love Jimmy less; it made me anxious and bewildered about a future with him. Yet, my infatuation eclipsed my feelings of betrayal, and I agreed to see how I felt after their visit.

A couple of days later, we threw a private party at a club for the band and crew. Jim's wife showed up with him, glitzed out in full regalia, with hair that added three inches to her height. My heart pounded wildly when I saw them standing at the bar. He tried to brush her hand away every time she reached for his, but she was insistent. I ordered another vodka and shimmied up to the nearest roadie, knowing it would torture him.

I could feel Jimmy's eyes on me as I gyrated on the dance floor with the hottest guys on the crew, letting my tight black skirt slide up my bare thighs. He was seething with jealousy, knowing there was nothing he could do to stop me while his wife had her hand firmly planted in his all night. The power went straight to my head along with the vodka.

The next morning, Jim dropped his bus linens in the production office to send out with a runner to the dry cleaner's. He came looking for them in the afternoon.

"Hey, where's that bedding? I gotta make that back lounge up." He barely looked me in the eye.

"I'll check and let you know. She hasn't come back." I knew if I looked at him, I would cry. I picked up the phone, signaling he should leave.

When the production runner called in, she said she was holding

the dry-cleaning tickets until she got to meet the band. *Shit.* When I
climbed up on his bus to tell him, he was sitting in the driver's seat
looking at a map. At the front lounge table sat the woman with big
hair from the night before, and a petite older woman. On the couch
were the kids, watching a movie.

"Uh, Jimmy, there's a problem." My eyes darted toward his wife,
to get a better look at her in daylight. She was attractive, in an
overly made-up way. "Uh, oh," she said, smiling. "Hope everything's
all right." She drawled, like him. She lived in his house. These were
their kids. *Oh, my God.* I glanced at her briefly, trying to keep my
attention on Jim as I felt my heart crack in several places.

"So, the runner wants to meet the band and she's holding the
linens hostage. Colin is taking care of it, and we will have it back
shortly. We don't leave until tomorrow, so it will—"

"Hostage? That stuff costs a fortune! You better make sure I get
it back, you hear me?" He was clearly upset about more than sheets
and a comforter.

"Jimmy, be nice!" his wife chimed in. "Is he always this rude to
you?"

I looked right at her, wanting to blurt out, *No! He's usually telling
me how much he loves me, and the dirty things he wants to do to me.*

"No, he can be sweet," I said instead, and turned back toward
Jimmy, my eyes burning holes in his. "I promise I'll have the linens
by noon tomorrow. And I keep my promises."

Once we were far from Atlanta, our bubble filled up again. I let
myself breathe in his love like a swimmer coming up for air. Jimmy
brought me flowers and wrote me sweet, simple poetry about finding
the love of his life, and drew sketches of the house he wanted to build
for us in Tennessee. I plied hotel desk clerks with free concert tickets
in exchange for upgrades to opulent suites where we devoured room
service and each other. When we had shows in cities back-to-back,

with no hotel for days, he hung around the production office as much as he could get away with.

Being a mess at the end of the tour, when the married man I loved went home, seemed a given. I didn't care. The exquisite feeling of being loved so deeply left little room for shame. *Possession is nine tenths of the law.* I had him with me on the road for the summer. *I'm sure I'm going to Hell after that.*

We spent our time cautiously optimistic, living in the moment from city to city. When the show played in Chicago, we had a day off. At a barbecue with my family, Jimmy charmed my mom, who was unaware of his marital status. My sister rode on my bus as we headed up to the next show in Milwaukee, experiencing life on the road with us as we partied the night away. One night off in Philadelphia, friends from another tour got me and Jimmy free tickets to Eric Clapton's show. It felt like a real date. Each tiny moment filled me to the brim with joy.

In September, I knew we had to part ways when I would leave for Europe on the next leg of the tour, then on to another in Japan and Hong Kong. While I was gone, Jim would start a U.S. tour with a small indie band. We lived for our last days together like a terminal patient on borrowed time. Our death felt imminent, even though he talked about the future like we had one.

"I love you, and I want you smilin' all the way," he said during our last night together. I prayed we would see each other again.

· · ·

Traveling through Europe was one of the most anticipated parts of the adventure for me and proved to be the most grueling. The buses and venues were smaller, we rarely had a day off, and there was no Jimmy to play with when we did.

Days off were spent wandering around, seeing the sights. In

London, I hung out in Piccadilly Circus with my fellow roadies, getting drunk on warm beer; during our eighteen hours in Paris, I got Colin to let me borrow a runner for an hour to take me to the Eiffel Tower and past the Seine, where I snapped an entire roll of film in thirty minutes, wishing I could take a leisurely stroll or sit in a cafe instead of rushing back to the gig. In Amsterdam I went to a hash den with Sparky, staring for a long time at the menu, choosing between Maui Wowie and Thai Stick.

Still, plenty of my free time was spent moping around my narrow hotel room missing Jimmy. My desire to stay connected to him took precedence over everything. My hotel room was not only where I got some much-needed rest, but it was where he could occasionally find me. Like a Christmas gift, a fax arrived in the production office on show days with hotel information where I could reach him in the States.

"Hey, darlin', it's so good to hear your voice. Just gettin' ready to lay down. How's my honey?" We'd share our road stories of the day, profess our love, count the days until we'd be reunited. I prayed he would find a way to free himself so that could happen. Hundreds of dollars were spent on long-distance calls, especially once I got to Asia for a month run before both our gigs would end the week of Thanksgiving.

"We can buy a trailer from my brother's lot, get us some land, eventually build a house on it," he said. "Let's start a life together for real, babe. Maybe Colin'll take us both out on another tour next year. I'm not going back home. I can't. Come live with me in Nashville."

I said yes to all of it, pushing aside the small voice that said, *What the hell are you thinking?* I wired a deposit on a new single-wide mobile home from my production office in Tokyo the day of the last show. Then I flew to New York to drive with him to eastern Tennessee for a couple of days, where I met his sister, who graciously held her judgment at bay.

Our short rendezvous held an urgency beneath each moment, so eager we were to get it all in before we parted again. It felt like I was saving him from something, and maybe saving myself, too. More than being rescued from unhappiness or loneliness, it felt like I was being clutched from the jaws of my obsession with finding love, from a beast which had had a hold on me since I was a teenager pining for my father.

Free from the distraction of chasing men who let me down, I could relax knowing that Jimmy loved me enough to change his whole life to be with me, and that this part of my life was finally settled.

Ten

My inner five-year-old is still pouting over how Dad sliced up the pie of his estate. Sometimes she gets worked up into a full-blown tantrum over him bequeathing a smaller slice to me than the other adults. Torturing myself, I reread the will again and again, searching for a shred of evidence that my father thought more of me, that he had something in mind to remember him by.

I do not find it.

Every painting and antique offered to my sister or my mom feels like a sharp poke to my heart. *See, he didn't love you as much as he loved them, Lisa. You and your big mouth. It cost you his love. Remember how upset he got when you called him out? Why did you have to do that?* I replay the moments when I scalded him with my words, when I dared share a truth he didn't want to hear. Words can be a lethal weapon, especially harmful when wielded in a wounded rage. But when they expose our hearts, they bring peace. It isn't the old buffet or vintage touchier lamps I lust after; it's his words in a sentimental note that he wrote just to me, a sweet goodbye he never said.

In the end, what the will proves most is that no matter what I did he kept score.

Home. As I took in the floral couches and chocolate brown carpeting of my San Francisco apartment, I wondered if the entire year had been only a dream. It was hard to even remember who I'd been the last time I came through the door, before trekking around the world with the rock show. Before falling in love.

The rapture of being in my own bed didn't satisfy quite like I thought it would. My soft life felt a little too comfortable as I settled into leisurely days of grocery shopping and having lunch with girlfriends. It surprised me how much I missed the grueling production work, and my road family. And of course, I longed for Jimmy.

"Hey, babe, how are you?" I purred into the phone each night, curling up to the receiver. My love for him had become a pulsing thing, intensely alive. When we were together, the thrill of his devotion, his words of endearment, his touch, were all intoxicating. When we were apart, I ached with unbearable yearning.

"I'm missin' you, honey, that's how I am," he said. "But by the first of the year we'll be all set in our new life. My brother is hirin' me to move trailers, and I'll come home to your pretty face every night." As excited as I was, images of that life came in fleeting snippets, like in a dream. It was hard to picture the contents of my apartment transported to a place I'd never seen.

We didn't talk about his pending divorce, or the feelings of the woman and two children whose daddy wasn't coming home to them anymore. They felt as real to me as characters in a story. On the phone, Jimmy's reassurance that everything was fine was enough to keep me looking forward to our future. But late at night alone, a sick feeling came over me, like I was an accomplice to their pain. It swept me up in a current of guilt each time I remembered that he was still married.

How I viewed his omission of that crucial fact when we met had shape-shifted during our months together. From betrayal to uncomfortable truth to temporary inconvenience, the further I fell in love with him the lesser the indictment became. Shame surfaced in the quiet hours, when the long night of missing his warmth next to me forced me to think about him across the country filing papers and breaking hearts.

My willingness to participate in the unraveling of a family made me wonder if any future we built together would be on solid ground. Would I be punished someday for sleeping with another woman's husband? Regardless of not knowing the truth in the beginning, I continued our affair even after meeting her. Burned into my mind was the possibility that one day he would leave me the same way.

Pushing those thoughts away, I began to pack up my California life, once again choosing to move to an unfamiliar place.

. . .

The day Jimmy arrived in San Francisco to move me to Nashville, I awoke to a pale sky of mauve and country blue, the colors of every room I'd seen during my short visit to Tennessee. I looked around my apartment, packed and ready to go to our new home, and felt wistful about leaving California, a place I loved. To soften the blow, I came to believe that the call to come to the coast nearly a decade before had been a path to Jimmy, and that's what I told my family when I shared the news.

"I'm moving to Nashville with him," I told my father. "I know he's the one." Telling him felt easier than telling Mom. His past impulsiveness gave me permission for my own.

"Is his divorce final soon?" Dad asked with concern in his voice.

"It will be," I said. "She wants it over now, too." The clatter of dishes being bussed filled the air between us while I doctored my coffee. Since I'd shared the truth of Jim's marital status with my father early on, he knew I felt uncomfortable until the divorce was final. He didn't judge, most likely because of how he had left his marriage to my mother to be with someone else.

"He loves me, Dad." The words echoed my father's certainty over Robert years before. Years that had softened my disdain for his choices.

His eyes held a dozen questions about what I would be leaving behind in the life I had crafted so diligently, in the beautiful place I loved so much. To say I hadn't pondered them myself would be a lie. Concerns over how I would continue my career, make new friends, and navigate a city I didn't know rang loudly through my head each night when I collapsed into bed after packing my life into cardboard boxes. I pushed aside the voice inside that whispered a warning about relinquishing too much of my independence—and too much of my money—to this relationship, like ignoring the flight attendants when they go over the emergency card. *Nothing bad will happen.*

Dad nodded. "Well, as long as you're happy." He asked how my mother was taking the news, though he likely knew.

"Mom is excited for me but thinks I'm jumping in a little fast. She likes that Jimmy stopped in to see her when he went through Chicago on the Alchemy tour, and that he and Deena went out for a beer." Tears threatened as I felt the full weight of the coming changes. "Mom's glad I'm settling down with someone." I lit a cigarette, feeling the first calming drag of smoke push down the tears. I skipped the part where I'd assured my mother that Jim's divorce was a "technicality," just simple paperwork to be filed.

"I look forward to meeting him on Sunday. I just hope he can handle you. You're a strong woman, not some quiet little country girl." We laughed easily at his joke, but underneath I could hear his concern.   The sun streamed onto our favorite window table as we finished our coffee. I felt the twinge of loss that living far away from him would bring. We had come such a long way since that night on Polk Street, when he had just arrived in San Francisco.

As Jimmy strolled through the airport gate and into my arms, he had tears in his eyes. After longing to be loved without trying so hard, I barely knew how to take his love in without feeling like the other shoe would drop. This would take some practice and a faith still fragile from watching him leave his family.

The following night, all my dearest friends gathered to celebrate my thirtieth birthday and my departure from California. Jimmy looked handsome as he met the people who meant so much to me, secretly telling most of them that he had an engagement ring stashed at my mom's house, to surprise me with on Christmas Eve.

My dearest girlfriends were all there, along with Ross and a few of the men I had loved, or tried to, over the years. The Greek bar owner, a bad-boy fling that never amounted to much more than a dozen late-night booty calls and a discount for this party; Brad, a musician I had been friends with for years, another good looker I'd crushed on in vain; and of course, Mark. He arrived with a large gift box and his new girlfriend, a redhead who seemed aloof, and the opposite of his type.

Opening the box labeled Survival Kit, I carefully unwrapped each item, and read the tiny note he had attached to it: a collection of David Letterman Top Ten lists for *when you need a laugh*; a nature calendar for *when you need to remember the beauty of California*; a horoscope guide for the coming year for *when you need advice*; and a book, *Warrior of the Heart*, for *when you need to navigate love's challenges*.

"Aww, Mark. This is so thoughtful," I said with a lump in my throat.

His face glowed with pride. "You're welcome, sweetie. Go be happy." I glanced at his girlfriend. She looked slightly suspicious, as if perhaps she'd underestimated the relationship between her man and his friend.

For a millisecond, I wondered what could have been had that one night we spent together before the tour led to more nights like that. Just then, Jimmy looked over at me, beaming with love, and I pushed away any thought of sharing my life with someone else.

. . .

"I hope you can handle her," my father said to Jimmy at dinner the night before we left town, echoing what he had already said to me. Dad was cordial, although I could see doubt written all over his face once he took in this handsome hillbilly, with his mullet haircut and thick accent.

"Well, I reckon I can, Don. She's a firecracker, and a real smart lady. Smarter'en me, that's for sure. All I know is I love her like crazy. I'll take good care of her, I promise you." His sincerity was clear, though I don't think Dad was as concerned about a protector for his daughter as he was about a man who could be a stimulating mate for the long haul.

He loves me, Daddy, I wanted to say when I saw him cringe over Jimmy's grammar. It was clear my genius father saw this redneck's good looks as his primary redeeming quality, assuming it was what had attracted me to him. He wasn't all wrong. I hoped he could see how funny and sweet Jimmy was, with a devotion to me I thrived on.

Dad quizzed him with a few more questions about where we would live, and his plans for coming off the road unless we got another tour together.

"I hope we can go out on the road together next year with Colin," Jim said, "Till then, I'll be working with my brother moving mobile homes and setting 'em up."

"Well, that sounds good." Dad turned to me. "You both seem to know what you want, and I know you always land on your feet." He lifted his glass in a toast. "Cheers. I hope you're happy in your new life together."

My father seemed satisfied, but I could feel his apprehension.

Whatever misgivings he had about Jimmy's ability to make me happy he kept to himself, but I knew they were there, and I understood them.

Jimmy was the only one oblivious to how mismatched we were.

• • •

Crisscrossing the continent for months, incubated in the bubble of the tour, we had spent our nights ensconced in hotel rooms across North America, wrapped in fine linens and enjoying room service. We shared lavish meals in upscale restaurants, paid for by per diem. All summer we'd woven a fantasy of domestic bliss, one that was held together with chemistry and longing—and called it love. There was nothing domestic about life on the road, and I was about to find out what living with him would really be like.

We arrived at Countryside Estates in Antioch, Tennessee at nearly midnight, after a three-day drive across the country. Our new home stood in the pouring rain among dozens just like it—prefabricated rectangles measuring 14' x 70' in a neat row, bare trees surrounding the perimeter. The trailer park, on the outskirts of Nashville, was a maze of winding paved streets with Hawaiian names like Honolulu Road and Hilo Court. Jim and his brother had moved our trailer onto a lot on Waikiki Drive, setting it on footers that would need to be skirted with aluminum siding in the coming weeks; then Jimmy could build a porch. There was nothing tropical about the place except the rain.

We unpacked half the truck to get to the bed, slogging it above our heads through the mud and into our manufactured home, which came partially furnished with a couch, chair, coffee table, dinette set, and assorted floral picture frames, all in shades of mauve and country blue. I didn't love it, but it was a place to land, and it had a nice master suite with a big corner tub.

Exhausted and giddy, we started a bath, only to find that our small hot water heater held enough to fill it halfway. None of this dampened our excitement.

As happy as I was, that first night's sleep in our new home was restless, and for the first time I dreamed of Jimmy's ex and the kids. They were all on the way over to our place. Panic-stricken, I hitchhiked in pickup trucks to get away, feeling lost as I traveled down unfamiliar roads in the cold and snow. When I woke up, the ping of rain on the roof soothed me, and I curled closer to Jimmy, watching him sleep.

A rush of tears came when I thought of the anticipation of this moment, not only for the past months, but during all the years I had wondered who I would spend my life with. With each failed romance I'd had, along with the dozens of crushes that never materialized into more than a one-night stand or unrequited infatuation, I had painted a picture of a life with the man of my dreams.

None of it looked like this.

. . .

"No! It's our first Christmas Eve together!" I cried, literally biting my tongue to keep from berating Jimmy for wanting to drive up from Tennessee by himself instead of flying with me.

"Honey, the roads are too bad heading north to make it through," he said from a pay phone at the Kentucky border. "So, I reckon I oughta head east to Mama and Daddy's. I'm so sorry." I'd flown into Chicago the day before, excited about sharing the holiday with him and my family. He could only get away from work for a few days, even though his brother was his boss. "I promise we'll make it up at home, but this weather is gonna get worse before it gets better. I'll call you later from Mama's so you can open your gift."

When he called several hours later, I opened the small velvet box he had left behind with my mom weeks before. Nestled inside was a solitary marquise diamond ring set in gold, its matching thin wedding band beside it. "Oh, babe, it's beautiful," I said, waiting for the question that went with it.

"Darlin', you deserve the best of everything. I wish I was there to give it to you myself. We'll finish our Christmas back at home. I'm just excited your mama got to see you open it. She's been hidin' it for me."

From where I stood against the kitchen sink near the wall phone, I could see my mother sitting on her couch, beaming. The importance to him of sharing the moment with my family carried a tender sincerity, yet I was disappointed not to have him there to put it on my finger in an intimate proposal.

"It's beautiful. I love it. Thank you." It was hard not to be bewildered by my expectations. In all my dreams of a romantic engagement, I was in the same room with my betrothed, a declaration of undying love and devotion pouring from his heart.

I put the ring on my finger and called myself engaged.

• • •

"Jimmy's a good guy. I hope you'll be really happy," my sister said while we shared a pizza in her small living room the night after Christmas. "He was so cute when he took me with him to pick out your ring." Deena was the last person I imagined picking out jewelry for me, yet it was sweet that he wanted her along. "Then Ma spent half an hour finding a place to hide it. She ended up putting it at the bottom of her clothes hamper."

"That's funny. It's nice that you guys were part of it. I just wish he was here to put it on my finger, you know?" She nodded and pulled another slice onto her plate. "So, what about you, Deen? Any romantic prospects?" I took a bite of my pizza and watched her eyes dart away from mine.

"Yeah, well, kinda." Deena had only had one boyfriend that I knew of: a nice Jewish guy Mom called the rabbi. They dated for a few months after she finished college. Unlike me, she was spared the boy-crazy gene, and I'd wondered for years if my tomboy sister preferred girls.

"Her name is Cassie." She paused, still looking down at her pizza. "I've been meaning to tell you, I mean, you probably know, but I'm gay." She looked relieved. "Mom and Dad don't know, so please keep it to yourself. Obviously, Dad will be fine, but I'm not ready to tell Ma. And I can't have a secret with him and not tell her." Ever the good daughter, Deena.

"Well, your secret is safe with me. Though I'm not sure they haven't thought about it. I know I have." We talked easily about how she had come to the conclusion that her desire for women was something she couldn't change.

"I really tried to fight it. I wanted to get married and have a bunch of kids, ya know? But this is just who I am."

My thoughts went back to finding out about Dad and my initial disapproval. It felt vastly different learning this about my young, single sister. My anger at him had been about the effect of his homosexuality on my life, all the lying and pretending he did at our expense. As my anger softened over time it became utterly clear that Dad was difficult for reasons that had nothing to do with being gay. My sister's choice of partners didn't have anything to do with me. I was happy for her.

"I'm glad you told me, Deen. So, tell me about Cassie. What's she like?"

My sister's eyes lit up as she described her girlfriend as a free-spirited artist. "You guys would get along great. You want to meet her? We can go to the bar and have a drink with her."

"Sure." I gave her a hug, making note of her confidence in sharing this news with her big sister, and how good it felt. We cleared away our dishes and headed to meet Cassie.

The only thing more surprising than finding out my sister was gay was finding out there was a lesbian bar in the neighborhood strip mall, wedged between Just Tires and Sally Beauty Supply. We entered through the door in the center of a windowless storefront.

"So, this place is a gay bar? I always thought it might be a strip club." She laughed and we took two seats at the bar. I could feel eyes on me in a way I never had before; it made me uneasy being checked out by women. I tried to ignore my discomfort while Deena introduced me to her friends over the loud, thumping music.

"Cass, this is my sister, Lisa." Deena was more relaxed than I had ever seen her with her boyfriend. She was attentive to Cassie, who had choppy blonde hair and offered a wide smile. *They look cute together*, I thought. *What a trip.*

In revealing her life to me, my sister was sharing a part of herself none of us knew; it was like seeing Dad in the Castro in San Francisco. Being a confidant to my only sibling felt good that night, like we were friends—even though we had nothing much in common beyond the same parents.

Eleven

"Deena should be here with us," I'd said several times to my mother during the long weekend between my father's death and his memorial. Sometimes with disdain, others with sorrow. Each time, Mom defended her. Four days felt like forty.

"Lisa, I told her to go, so stop it!" she yelled when I went on another rant about Deena keeping her trip to New Orleans. "She's not having fun, believe me." Mom and I were both on edge after too many days together under one roof.

"I don't care! She should be here!" Despite the distance I put between me and my family, there was a primal urge to experience this loss with my only sibling, for us to experience the immediate grief of losing Dad together. To comfort each other. Or at least drink together.

After all these weeks, my outrage over how my sister handled our father's death is still aflame with discord, sitting heavy on my heart right beside deep compassion for all of us. Each time this tender spot gets pressed, I shriek with the pain of her detachment.

I know she is equally appalled by me.

Domesticity fit me like rubber gloves, loose and awkward. Sometimes while dusting a framed picture of myself in Holland or Tokyo I would sigh sharply, stunned to have landed in a trailer park in Tennessee. But at night when Jimmy slid into a bubble bath with me, and snuggled under cool sheets, it all made sense. That part was easy. We made love with fervor, as I embodied a woman fully in her skin. Sex had been a portal to love for me, often not very satisfying. My wish that one day love and sex would be delivered in the same package felt like it finally came true with Jimmy.

The hard part was the combining of lives, not flesh. Trying to find a comfortable rhythm in our new household took some adjustment. So many of my daily routines had been absent during the year on the road, things like grocery shopping and laundry. Now I took care of those things for both of us. Finding a balance between me and our relationship was an unexpected challenge. Jimmy came from a world where women catered to their men; I had a gay dad who cooked and cleaned as much as Mom did. Jim didn't expect me to be like his mother, but he did expect me to be a domestic wife, to take care of the house while he made the money. My reality didn't match romantic fantasies of sharing my life with a man every day— an idyllic blend of the rom-coms I loved and my parents' ease with each other when I was a child.

I had spent years chasing men, scurrying around doing all I could to win their love. Now that I had a man who wasn't going anywhere, I resented his expectations, lacking patience and compromise. Still, I busied myself with the house, running errands up and down country roads, and making a good supper.

There wasn't enough money to go around, and Jimmy was stressed about the demands of his ex-wife. The divorce was final now, and his child support and alimony ate up more than half his pay. I missed working. It was startling to find out our love bubble wasn't going to sustain me any more than his salary would support us and his kids. With another tour a year off, I needed to look for a job when unemployment ran out. In the meantime, I faced surgery to remove a uterine tumor that was growing quickly.

"What if I can't have kids, Jimmy?" I whispered as we lay in bed one night after I scheduled the surgery. Even though I wasn't sure I ever wanted a child, possibly losing the choice made me cry. A couple of times we had talked about the idea of having a baby, a theoretical notion that fell into the *if it happens, it happens* category even though I was using birth control.

He stroked his beard in the dark. "Well, babe, I got my two and didn't plan on more. We have them to love. And each other. It'll be all right either way."

On one hand this offered relief that if I wouldn't be able to give us a child, or didn't want one, he would be fine with the family he brought with him. On the other hand, I wanted him to want a family with me.

• • •

I hated the trailer park. In the light of day, it was hard to ignore the loud, crass neighbors twenty feet away, the scores of screaming kids. Skirting the bottom of the trailer was an expense we couldn't afford, so our home appeared to be floating above ground, ready to take off in a twister. Building the porch would have to wait, too. I was sure there were some kind of critters living beneath us.

Going from living in the most beautiful city in the country to living in a mobile home park in the South was like trading in a brand-new Mercedes for the old beat-up Chevy your uncle drove into the ground. Jimmy looked for land where we could move the trailer, and instead found a log house for sale by owner, sitting on six acres off a country road twenty-five miles outside of Nashville. We worked out a monthly payment, rented out the trailer, and moved in on Valentine's Day.

Decorating the two spare bedrooms in our new house for Jimmy's kids was weird and wonderful. Jim's mama gave us his Granny's bedroom set, so my old brass bed got adorned with colorful pillows and a soft throw for his daughter, Chrissie. We bought a twin bed for his son, Jason, in anticipation of their first visit.

The few moments spent on the bus with them while we were on tour felt like eons ago, though it was less than a year. When Jimmy pulled up the driveway after going up to Knoxville to get them, I said a silent prayer that they would like me. It seemed a fourteen-year-old girl would be easy enough to connect with, but I hadn't been with a ten-year-old boy since I was in fifth grade. As it turned out, Jim's daughter was much more leery of me than her friendly brother was; by the end of the weekend he and I had become fast friends, baking cookies and playing cards.

Chrissie clung to her daddy, snuggled up to him on the couch any time he sat down. Her possessiveness felt big enough to include her mother's, and I was sure by the way she looked at me that her mom had fed her more of our story than was wise. I could see her sizing me up, the other woman, the one who didn't look or sound anything like her or her mother. A Yankee, by way of California. An interloper, like Terry had been when I was her age.

Seeing myself in her, I wondered how it would have felt if my dad were straight, how it would have been to meet my father's fiancé, a woman who seemed to be the opposite of my mother. Would it have been a deeper betrayal of Mom to be traded in for a different model instead of coming out to be true to himself? Would I have competed with his new wife like Chrissie did with me, cleaving to Dad's side to stake my territory in a way I never did around his boyfriend after that first bowling date? Would I have been as upset as I was when he left us for a man?

At what point are parents allowed to choose something for themselves without being the villain if their kids disapprove? Especially when it impacts their lives in huge ways. The actions people take that blow up a family gain a different perspective when you are the grown-up taking those actions. Becoming involved while Jimmy was married complicated matters, especially for his kids who didn't want their world to change. Seeing them up close made my part in changing their world more real.

"I'll sit with you," Chrissie said to her younger cousin as we slid into a booth for lunch at the mall with Jim's sister-in-law, Mimi, and her daughter. "I can't remember the last time I saw y'all. It must have been last Christmas at Mamaw's." Chrissie shot me a look that cast me as an outsider.

"Why, I guess it has been that long," Mimi said. Everything about her teased hair and meticulous eye makeup reminded me of Chrissie's mom—and how different she was from me. "I'm glad we could see you finally. So what color are you girls gonna get?" The conversation shifted to nail polish.

"I think I want neon orange." Chrissie smiled at me, and I smiled back. It was easy to have empathy for this teenage girl, who chattered on for the rest of the day as we got manicures and went shopping. She was trying not to like me, but I gave her every reason to give me a chance. My need for her approval was strong enough to loosen my purse strings even though funds were low. By the end of the weekend a silent truce had been declared, yet I wondered what she would report back to her mother.

• • •

When I started job-hunting, I learned Nashville was a cliquish town unimpressed with my West Coast credentials. Once I'd exhausted my search for a gig in entertainment, I landed a job as an event planner. It didn't pay much but it was something. After too many squabbles with his brother over pay, Jimmy went back on the road. Loneliness settled in quickly. My successful surgery had activated a maternal longing I'd never experienced, which felt like a sure sign I was supposed to be a mother. Keeping that desire to myself, I turned my attention to a prerequisite we had barely talked about.

"Babe, I want to get married," I said when Jim was home for a couple of days on break from the country music tour he was on. We were sitting at the kitchen table, the smell of bacon still hanging in the air. "I feel like this ring doesn't mean anything. We've been engaged for six months and haven't set a wedding date."

He looked at me startled, as if the concept of marrying me was a novel idea, then back down at his half-eaten breakfast. "I didn't think it mattered much. We barely have enough for the bills let alone a weddin'."

Some part of me crumbled inside to learn that it didn't matter much to him, making it even more important to me. More than wanting to be married to him, I wanted him to want to marry me.

"Well, it does matter," I said. "We can set a date." Searching my mind for what I always thought my wedding day would look like, I came up short, only remembering being seven years old in Laura Hegland's backyard wearing her mother's tattered bridal gown as we took turns marrying Davy Jones. "We can have it here at home; it doesn't have to be fancy. Maybe in the fall, outside at dusk."

He pulled out his tour itinerary and looked at the coming months. "I have a four-day break at the end of August. The longest one till Thanksgivin'. I reckon I can be home that Wednesday evening. If we want any kind of honeymoon, we'll have to get married on that Thursday."

"Okay. Let's do it."

"Who gets married on a Thursday?" my mother said when I called her to share the news.

"I know, but Jimmy's tour goes for the rest of the year. It's the only break that gives us a couple days for a honeymoon. We booked a room at Fall Creek Falls for the weekend. I hope you and Deena will come."

"Of course, we'll come. It's your wedding! I'm happy for you, Lis." I knew she was, having shared with me enough times how good it was that I had "settled down."

When I called my dad with the news, I didn't actually invite him to the ceremony, assuming he wouldn't take off work. "How exciting! It's about time you guys set a date," he said. "Your mother and I will have a reception of some sort for the two of you up here. I'll talk to her. Maybe a luncheon at Tom's." The thought of all of us celebrating me and Jimmy in the private banquet room with the pink swirl wallpaper brought unexpected tears to my eyes.

"That would be really nice. Jim's tour has a weekend off in September. We could come up to Chicago then," I said, touched that my new husband could meet the rest of my family.

Most of Jimmy's clan had agreed to come to the ceremony, including his kids who were unfazed by the news. Jim asked his son to be his best man and I asked his daughter to be a bridesmaid with my sister, who would be my maid of honor. "I can do your hair," Chrissie said. "You can't just wear it straight. We need to curl it and put it up."

I would have let her cut it all off just to have her be part of our wedding.

. . .

When the big day came, our mothers met for the first time, amplifying the contrast between our two families. My urban Italian mother struggled to understand Jim's Appalachian mama's accent, and we rolled our eyes at her discontent over us serving liquor. Luckily, my new mother-in-law didn't see me smuggle the Jack Daniels Lynchburg Lemonades into the bedroom while I got ready. As we were setting up the tables in the screen porch three hours before our outdoor ceremony, the heavens opened up and released a torrential rain that forced us to move it into our living room. When I thought all had gone wrong, Jimmy's ex called Jason to tell him my beloved bird, who I'd given to him for his birthday, had mysteriously flown away. I was near tears.

"C'mon. Let's go outside," my mother said while the eye of the wedding hurricane seemed to pass over for a moment. We shared a smoke on the porch swing, watching as the rain fell in sheets across the freshly mowed lawn.

"It's good luck to have rain on your wedding day," she said, exhaling as she handed the cigarette back to me.

"Well, then I'd say we'll have a fabulous marriage." I took the last drag, then flicked the butt into the soggy grass. I could see Jim's sister through the window taking video of us and wondered if I looked as tense as I felt. She waved, then came out with the camera still rolling.

"It's the blushin' bride on her weddin' day." She interviewed us about the festivities, then asked, "So what is the best thing about marryin' my brother?"

"His last name," I blurted, not sure where it came from, "I'm only doing it for the name." My mother laughed. The name we had both inherited from my father was one that always had to be spelled. Jim had an easy, common name.

"It is a good name!" Belinda was smiling and the spitting image of Jim, with Southern girl big hair. "You best get dressed then. Let's get you two hitched!"

Within a few hours we walked down the stairs from the loft into our living room, which now included a few more guests: our landlords and people from my office. Chrissie and my sister went down the steps before me and stood in front of the windows beside Jimmy and Jason. Between them stood our officiant, Doc, a local guy Jim knew who had married Steve Earle and his girlfriend in an airport when they were on tour together.

My dress was a long homemade ivory satin skirt with a cream lace top I tied at the waist with a satin ribbon. Nestled in burgundy tulle were dried flowers I had made into a bouquet that included roses Jimmy had given me for my thirtieth birthday. Inside my grandmother's prayer book I carried a picture of my father. His idea. "So I can walk you down the aisle," he said.

I never felt more beautiful than when Jimmy, dressed in a dark paisley shirt and black pants, took my hand and we faced each other to share our vows. Despite any misgivings I'd had in quiet moments about spending the rest of my life with a man so different from me, I meant every word of those vows. I already knew I would need to lean on them during hard times. *For richer or poorer. For better or worse.* As we were declared husband and wife, destiny seemed to wrap itself around us.

A quick getaway to a rundown motel in the mountains proved to be a disappointing start to our wedded bliss, beginning with being too tired to make love on our wedding night and ending with my eyes swollen shut by an allergic reaction to the horses we rented and rode in the rain. The best part was the bottle of Dom Perignon waiting in our room, sent from my California girlfriends. I drank it alone since Jimmy preferred beer.

When we returned home, he went back out on the road. A few weeks later we met in Chicago for a reception hosted by my parents at Tom's Steakhouse. Dad, handsome and elegant, toasted our nuptials to a room full of extended family.

"To the bride and groom! I hope you'll be happy together for a long, long time!" Mom's eyes shone bright as she lifted her glass to us. Deena brought her girlfriend Cassie, and while she didn't introduce her as her date to our aunts and uncles, I was glad she brought her to meet the family. Jimmy was comfortable with all of them now, laughing easily with my mother and sister. With Dad he was a bit more reserved, but friendly. His conservative upbringing made him uncomfortable around gay men, though decades of rock-and-roll tours had made him more open-minded. We didn't discuss it, and when they talked it was mostly about me.

"Gram, what do you think of my husband?" I said, hoping she would get to know him better over holiday visits. She was getting further into her eighties, and I wondered if maybe I would get to introduce her to another great-grandchild someday.

"He sure is nice lookin'," she said. "And he has that sparkle in his eye for you. I hope he takes good care of you." She brushed my hair from my brow with a scarlet fingertip. "I'm just so glad to see you happy."

My gratitude to all of them for celebrating us brimmed over. It was a joyful party, unencumbered by wedding day jitters and preparation. In the pictures taken in front of the pink swirl wallpaper our clothes are the same as on our wedding day, but we look more relaxed. And my hair is not nearly as big.

. . .

Our married life revolved around work, chasing money, and what little time we had together, sometimes sharing that time with his kids. I was bored and lonely when Jim was gone, and jealous when he came home with stories from the road. Everything about my own life felt small.

I kept thinking about having a baby.

Before the surgery, I was not the kind of woman who waited her whole life to become a mother, but instead was a somewhat selfish free spirit who was afraid of losing herself to a bundle of needs. But seeing Jimmy as a father swelled in me a need to sit at the table he occupied with his ex-wife and their kids, the table reserved for a *family*. It was as if they were members of a club I could not join as a mere stepmother. So, despite the inner voice in my head that said I might not completely fit in, I was excited to join that club.

After Thanksgiving, enchanted by his sister Belinda's baby boy while they stayed with us for the holiday, Jimmy said, "Throw them damn pills away." By Christmastime, my period was late, and suddenly, another adventure was upon me.

• • •

"I do the best I can, and your lip ain't gonna make the money come any faster!" Jimmy yelled, as I ranted over the bills we couldn't pay.

"Look, I thought we'd be going back out on tour together! This is not what I had in mind. So, no. I'm not going to keep quiet!" As if I could. At thirty-one, the thought of getting pregnant in twenty minutes never crossed my mind, yet here I was, barefoot and pregnant at home alone while Jimmy traipsed around the country with the rock stars I dreamed of touring with.

"Hey, we moved back to town so you wouldn't be so lonely out there in the woods. Gave up our house for you." We had left the log cabin when we didn't qualify for a home loan because of Jimmy's credit, along with his name still on his ex's house.

"We couldn't get a mortgage! Don't blame losing that property on me. It was a lot to take care of by myself anyway. I have a job I don't like, I'm four months pregnant, and you're gone all the fucking time. From where I stand, you have it made."

A crimson fury rose up his neck and across his face. "Well, you just don't know how to be a good wife, is all! You need to support your man to do what he needs to do. You probably won't be a good mama, neither. You and your opinion about every damn thing."

"Yeah, well, you don't have to listen to my shit anymore," I said, storming out of the room, "I need to get away for a while." *Dad may have been right. Maybe this guy can't handle me.*

I cashed in my frequent flyer miles and the next day fled Tennessee to visit my girlfriends in California. Within twenty-four hours of arriving, pollen, dog dander, and the stress of my fight with my husband sent me to the emergency room in Marin County with a severe asthma attack. Without strong meds the doctors couldn't get it under control and put me in the ICU.

Terror for my baby's life made it even harder to breathe. The prospect of losing this little being inside me spawned a certainty I hadn't yet felt about my unborn child. I wanted this baby more than anything.

With our fight instantly forgotten, Jimmy was desperate to be there with me, but we were too broke to buy a plane ticket. My mother was beside herself worrying about me and the baby, but she wouldn't be coming out until my delivery date.

My salvation came, as it often did, in the company of women, the fierce durability of their friendship the force that guided me through my roughest days. Nan and Monica tag teamed, sitting with me in my room for hours, bringing me graham crackers to crumble into milk—my pregnancy craving. It was Nan who saw the first glimpse of my child with me on the ultrasound. She called it Little Bit.

My girlfriends did their best to keep my spirits up and distract me from my fear, as well as from the deep abandonment I felt when my father, who lived fifteen miles away in San Francisco, didn't come to see me right away.

"I'm scared, Dad. It's so hard being here without having Jimmy or Mom. Will you come?" I had called him the day I was admitted, certain he would be there for something so serious.

"Well, honey, I'm sure the doctors are doing all they can. I just can't imagine the traffic on the Golden Gate Bridge after work. I'll come and see you Saturday if you're still there." Utterly bereft and speechless, I was unable to get enough air to scream, *You asshole. You selfish asshole.*

Wounds that had scabbed over got picked off clean. They oozed with the anguish of knowing I was not important enough to go to any trouble for, to warrant a day off work, or an hour in traffic. And apparently neither was his grandchild, who I was struggling to keep alive inside me.

On Saturday he showed up when I was in a regular room being discharged the next day.

"Well, honey, you look pretty good, all things considered," he said. My rage throbbed inside my chest, threatening to steal my breath. If I told him how I felt, how incredibly selfish I thought he was, I was afraid I'd start screaming and never stop.

"The worst of it was earlier in the week," I said, unable to look him in the eye. "When I was in the ICU." *Don't you get it? I was here all alone, without my husband or my mother. I was scared for my baby's life, not to mention my own. When you were so sick, we ran to the hospital for you.*

"Good thing that didn't last long," he said, already looking at the clock.

A deep, vile hate filled my heart for him that day, pushing out all the love I had fought so hard to foster. I prayed my unborn child would never feel that way about me.

Twelve

Anger is hard to express when it is tied up in grief. It can be difficult to tell the two apart. Dad giving his power, and the lion's share of his estate, to the agreeable daughter he could count on, shines a spotlight on the difficult daughter who fought with him to be seen and heard while risking his rejection. Being the one who is reliving the details of her life in search for clues to explain why her father rebuffed her makes me hurt and angry. But being mad at my dead father doesn't seem right. So, I stay mad at my sister since she is an easy target.

We should be getting drunk together, my lament in those first couple of days after Dad's death, played over and over in my head. *Isn't that what siblings do when their parent dies suddenly?* Deena's absence had felt like a missing limb in those first days after he died.

I'm still mad that while she cried into her cocktail in New Orleans with her best friend, I was in Mom's back room writing Dad's eulogy, drinking a stiff belt of vodka I poured into my half-empty club soda can from a bottle I'd hidden in the basement. Sneaking alcohol behind my mother's back was better than listening to her judgment, because no matter what age I am, I revert to sixteen when under her roof.

I'm mad about that, too.

In my sixth month of pregnancy, Mom threw a shower for me over Mother's Day weekend, when the Midwest air was sweet with the scent of lilacs. I was feeling good during this part of my journey toward motherhood, after suffering in the first trimester with morning sickness and loneliness, then the hospital stint in California with an asthma attack. The shower would provide most of what the baby needed, which was a blessing since we were on the verge of bankruptcy.

That same weekend my father was in town for his annual visit with Grandma for Mother's Day. He and Mom invited me to join them for dinner. I accepted their invitation, choosing to put aside my hurt feelings over Dad not visiting me in the ICU. When we arrived, he was already there, seated at a table for four.

"Well, hello ladies," he said, standing up to give us both hugs. There was such an easy friendship between my parents now, as if they had only ever been friends. It seemed impossible to imagine the kind of forgiveness my mother had to muster for that to happen.

"Hi, Dad," I said, sitting across from him and Mom. They both lit cigarettes. The strong smell didn't make me nauseous like it had months before. I missed smoking since giving it up for the baby.

"So, Peg, you look like you've lost weight, and boy, Lisa, you seemed to pick it up!" He laughed, finding humor in his observation.

"I've been on Jenny Craig," Mom said, looking rather svelte in leggings and a long blouse.

"And I'm pregnant." I was already annoyed, and absentmindedly rubbed my belly.

"You look nice, Peg. I hope you can keep it off."

My feelings still didn't seem to matter to him. *Here we go again.* I buried my head in the menu even though I never ordered anything but the filet mignon. *Breathe.*

Mom continued talking about her weight loss, and how my aunt had joined the program, too. "She lost about fifteen pounds. She looks good."

"Well, I never knew Marge to be heavy," he said, "I'm sure my brother would have told me if she gained weight." *Really?* I thought. *The brother you hardly ever speak to?* I couldn't hold back any longer. His comments had touched a raw nerve.

"Maybe he loves her unconditionally. Maybe he didn't even notice her weight." I glared at my father, his petty judgments hovering like around him, like insects.

He slammed his fist on the table. "That's enough!" The water in the glasses sloshed from side to side. I held his gaze. "I've been to therapy, and I know I'm a good person. I won't stand for any more of this from you, Lisa." Mom sat quietly, eating her salad, unwilling to take my side.

"Fine." I got up and gathered my things. "I'll be at Gram's, Ma." I stormed out, sobbing.

• • •

"It's all going to be okay, Little Bit. Mommy is new to this, but we'll figure it out together." Lying in bed watching my belly undulate with his constant movement, I talked to my son about the world he was about to enter and how loved he already was. My surprise that we were having a boy was made sweeter when I thought of my stepson and how close we had become. It was a relief that Chrissie would remain her father's only daughter.

"We're gonna have so much fun. Just wait till you see the trees, and ladybugs, and play baseball. You're going to have such a good life." Each night I prayed I could make that true.

The hot, humid month of August stretched out before me like a desolate highway as I waited at home alone for my child to be born. Some days, euphoria swept through me with the relief of a cool breeze, bringing with it a certainty that this was the best next step on my path; on others, a sense of terror filled me as I imagined what my life would look like once this new little one entered my days and nights. During a manic week of nesting, I sat on the floor reading old journals I had pulled from the closet, weeping for the young woman who'd written them, her entries both hopeful and pitiful as she gave so much of herself away in the pursuit of love.

"I don't ever want you to read what a mess your mom was, Little Bit," I said to my belly as I shed fresh tears on the pages already smudged by the wine-fueled cries of a woman stood up for a date, or rejected, or worst of all, ignored.

I was horrified that my unborn child might one day come across them. The thought of him discovering his mother's insecurity, and how much she'd suffered over love, sickened me. I hefted myself up off the floor and went in search of a box. Once the most shameful volumes of my past were hidden inside, I sealed the box and put it in the trunk of my car. The next day I pitched it into a Dumpster behind the Piggly Wiggly.

Each night I prayed Jimmy would be home when I went into labor. In the later months of my pregnancy, things between us were loving and sweet each time he had a few days at the house, every reunion joyful and passionate. Jimmy kept promising to try to come off the road again, but he wasn't really skilled at anything else. Driving a tractor-trailer had him home more, but the trade-off was less income and more financial risk. I resented that there was little left for us after he paid his ex. This finally pushed us to file bankruptcy, ruining the perfect credit score my father had insisted I learn to maintain—along with health insurance which we didn't have either.

The shame of both was heavier to carry than the baby growing inside me. The weight of failure.

My hospitalization in California had cost me my event planner job, so I took a part-time gig at UPS answering customer service calls. The pay was next to nothing, but it got me out of the house during those long months alone while I awaited my baby's arrival.

A few weeks before my due date, my sister and her new love interest, Shannon, came to visit. They seemed happy, holed up in the guest room much of their visit when they weren't playing Tennessee tourists. In the time we did spend together she said she would be coming out to Mom before the baby was born.

"It will be a good time to tell her since she'll have her new grandchild to focus on," she said. Mom wasn't likely to be upset. I often wondered if she had her own suspicions that Deena was gay, the way I had, though we never talked about it. I was sure she would be fine.

"Great! You send her to me after you drop the bomb," I teased. "Actually, that's not a bad idea," I added, not believing it would be a shock or an issue. As they drove off, I felt a little closer to my sister for having had a glimpse into her personal life, and I felt even further apart for having lives that couldn't be more different.

. . .

Zachary, due on our first anniversary, was born in the dead of the night in a hospital outside Nashville. My water had broken after Jimmy and I shared a sliver of wedding cake we'd saved and taken out of the freezer that morning. "It must have triggered labor," I said to the doctor when I called her at midnight. She laughed. "I didn't think anyone actually ate those."

All the books I had read, and movies I had watched, could not have prepared me for the process of delivering a baby with a man who acted like one by my side. Jimmy had made it to only one of the birthing classes I had taken, another bone of contention I had with him because he was gone most of my pregnancy.

"Honey, I don't know if I can make it through the labor still standin'," he said as I lay in a hospital bed for twelve hours, with little change beyond increased contractions. "My other two was both cesareans and I was in the waitin' room for them. I'll try, babe, but I can't make no promises."

"You will stay in this room with me, goddamn it," I insisted through gritted teeth. "I have to make it through this labor doing the hard part, so you will stay. I don't have my mother here, only you."

"Yeah, well, my mama and daddy ain't here neither, and that's a first. Never been a grandbaby come to this world that they weren't there." He cried, real tears, upset that none of his family members had made the four-hour drive down for our child's debut. Only his brother's wife, Mimi, and her kids had stopped in for a few minutes. I wasn't up for much company.

"Please get over it, and just hold my hand, okay?" *You big baby.*

My gaze fixated on a Dr Pepper can left under a chair by one of the kids; a focal point during hour after hour of searing pain that ripped through me. At one point an orderly tried to put it in the trash. "Leave it!" I screamed. By midnight, I was delirious with exhaustion.

At 3:20 a.m., my doctor was coaxing my son from me and I was pushing like hell. As he emerged, cord draped around his tiny neck, a crash cart was brought in, trapping Jimmy beside me.

"Looks like you're staying," I said to my husband, squeezing his hand hard, and pushing harder. The doctor untangled my son and he let out his first scream. In an instant, I felt tremendous relief, and a rush of cold I had never known, as they slipped the epidural tube from my back. After a brief look at my baby, they whisked him away and tended to my uncontrollable shaking, a reaction to the medication.

An hour later, my son was swaddled on my lap as I sat up in bed, feeling better than I thought I could after twenty-seven hours of labor. Jimmy was asleep in the chair beside us, seemingly more exhausted than I was. Carefully, I unwrapped this new little person, marveling at his tiny fingers and toes, counting each one.

"Welcome to the world, Little Bit," I whispered, wrapping him back up and placing him in the bassinet beside my bed, before calling the nurse to help me take a shower.

We went home that evening, since my long labor had eaten up the allotted time we were allowed in the prepaid birthing package the hospital offered to self-pay couples. The hospital wasn't thrilled by my choice, but without insurance it would have cost us hundreds of dollars we didn't have to stay overnight. As I bundled Zachary into his car seat, I imagined all the women who gave birth to their babies in third world countries, or in fields, or at home. It felt like a natural thing to take him home.

Those first days blurred together while my body made the adjustment from expectant mother to a nursing one. The extreme changes my body was experiencing were nothing compared to the emotional shifts. A deep abiding love for this little creature, mixed with frustration at myself for not knowing what he needed each time he wailed, bumped into my annoyance with Jimmy for having to leave so soon, and my intense need for him to comfort me.

Mom showed up on day three and took the edge off everything. Her delight in seeing her new grandchild touched my heart with exquisite love for them both. She was competent and sure where I was uneasy and tentative. Yet she helped with food and the house, letting me tend to the baby unless I asked for her help.

"Ma, my boobs feel like bowling balls," I complained, trying over and over with the breast pump. The baby had some trouble latching on in the beginning but was getting the hang of it. My engorged breasts were in pain as my milk came in with a vengeance.

"I'm sorry, Lis, but we used bottles when you were born. They gave me pills to dry up my milk. I'll help change diapers and wash dishes, but I can't help with that one." I was determined to feed him what I believed was the healthiest, most natural thing to give him. It was also always ready, and free.

Mom and Jimmy had an easy camaraderie. The house hummed with the hustle and bustle of a new family for those first ten days of Zac's life, then panic set in as Jim left to go on the road and Mom prepared to go home.

On the day Zac was born, Mom had called Dad to let him know his grandson had arrived. I had it in my mind that this news would prompt a call from Dad in the days after the baby's birth. It didn't. Our argument at dinner, when I stormed out and went to Gram's, had not been resolved and I hadn't spoken to him since. Like other times we fought, he was waiting for me to apologize. This time I refused, believing that what I said to him was true.

"It's devastating to not have my son acknowledged by his grandfather," I sobbed to my mom. "I'm so hurt that I don't even want his name in the birth announcement for the newspaper." It was childish of me, and maybe I should have set aside my fury and reached out to him, but it felt like another way in which my father put his feelings ahead of mine and I wanted to hurt him back.

· · ·

If I felt alone being pregnant before he was born, Zac's birth had me feeling overwhelmed and even more alone once he arrived. As mesmerized as I was by this beautiful creature, he came with a tremendous amount of work for a new mom by herself. With my family hundreds of miles away, and my husband on the road, I grew resentful that Jimmy was living the life I dreamed of while I was at home alone with a new baby.

Postpartum depression masked itself as loneliness. The baby's needs were plenty while mine went unmet. I barely even knew what they were. For weeks at a time, it was just me and the baby on our own in a constant loop of feeding, diapers, cleaning up, and crying. Many of the tears were mine.

"Please, Zac, please," I begged my son as he wailed each night at suppertime after I nursed him. He would not be soothed until I walked miles back and forth across our living room, patting his back and cooing to him.

"Shhh, shhh. It's okay, it's okay." Pacing for at least an hour until he settled enough to lay him down in the bassinet, I wanted to scream the whole time, cursing his daddy in my head, furious I had to do this alone. In moments of exasperation, I wanted to scream at my baby, too. In the mornings Jimmy called from his hotel to check on us, a few beers in after a long drive. It usually started with his tale of the night before.

"I just run Kansas City to Dallas, and I'm beat. Nearly five hundred mile with those yahoos hollerin' all night, watchin' movies in the front lounge. My bus is trashed." I imagined him laying across the bed at a Hilton, the phone tucked under his ear as he took a swig from a bottle of Budweiser, a cigarette burning in the nightstand ashtray. "How y'all doing? You two have a good day yesterday?"

"It was okay; he was fussy again. He's as cute as ever but screams his head off every night at six. I just can't get him to settle down in the evening. The most he has slept at a time was three hours for the past few days. I'm so exhausted, Jimmy."

"Aww, honey. I'll be coming home in a few weeks, and when I do, I can't wait to get ahold of you. I'll make you feel better. The coast should be clear by then." *Are you kidding me? You should see me now. And I smell like puke.*

"Jimmy, that is the last thing on my mind. My God, you don't get it, do you? You have it easy—you drive around the country, sleep in hotels, eat good food. You know what I ate yesterday? A piece of cold toast. Zachary puked on me twice, and I am still wearing the shirt from the second time because wiping it off was easier than finding another clean shirt. Then I slept on the couch with the bassinet beside me because, honestly, I'm afraid I won't wake up if I get in the bed. Even if he's screaming. I haven't had a shower in days. There is a pile of bills to pay and the check hasn't come yet. And all you can talk about is wanting to fuck? Jesus."

My resentment was a red stain, indelible and dark, saturating the pristine cocoon that was our sweet beginning. It didn't matter how much he loved me. After months of this kind of conversation, he should have known that all I wanted was to soak in a hot bath and have a nice night out.

"Sorry, honey. I miss you, is all. The check oughta be there shortly. And you and Zac'll be fine. Just having a few bad days is all. Call your mama. I gotta lay down. We roll to New Orleans tonight. Love y'all."

"Okay. Talk to you tomorrow. Love you, too." The words felt automatic and false, barely masking my deep disappointment in the life I found myself in—even though I had signed up for all of it.

• • •

The choices we make to marry and have children are colored by the people we choose to have them with. In my case, instead of the abundant Crayola 64-count box of crayons I lusted for in my childhood, the one with a sharpener burrowed into a box containing Teal and Burnt Sienna, now my world was filled in by the value pack of ten basic colors, a limited palette with which to paint my life as a new wife and mother. Choosing to marry Jimmy felt less vibrant than I had imagined married life to be. But then, I hadn't really imagined it much; only the romance leading up to it.

The vision of my life as a 64-color masterpiece didn't always include a child, either. The love I felt for my newborn son was diluted by frustration with the amount of care he needed that I alone had to provide. New mothers aren't supposed to be alone with their babies for days on end, week after week, with such a narrow prism through which to view the world. Yet, there we were—just Zachary and me.

My naps on the couch between reruns of *Mary Tyler Moore* and *Cheers* left me like a zombie during my endless cycle of laundry, dishes, and caring for my baby's every need. Those first months felt like one long, exhausting day.

As desperately as I wanted my husband with us, when he came home for a few days I grew indifferent after the first few hours he was there. I longed for the old days when Jimmy's return from the road had us falling in love again. Once the baby arrived, Jimmy felt like an intruder who knew nothing about our world and brought another set of needs to satisfy, instead of bringing relief.

Yet, alongside my numbing fatigue were moments with my baby that carried an almost holy quality. In the bubble of our endless hours together, I memorized every inch of him, all his expressions, each cry. An invisible thread tethered us in a way I knew could not be broken. Eventually, a rhythm to our life emerged, shrinking my resentment to a manageable size. As a result, my previously exciting life faded as my infant son's burgeoning one became my reason for being, turning my teal dreams to an ordinary blue.

In the fall, I visited Chicago to see my family and basked in my mother's joy in her grandchild. I slept for hours and took long showers. My sister loved being an auntie, spoiling her nephew with toys and clothes, spending as much time with him as she could. I promised to come back with Jimmy for Christmas. In early December, Karen Kramer, who I ran into at a concert while I was pregnant, called and offered me a part-time job at her artist management company. The opportunity to converse with adults and be back in the world I loved was a much-needed gift, and I could work from home making money we desperately needed. I gratefully took the job.

As Christmas approached, I longed for the sound of my father's voice. We had not spoken in six months. One Sunday morning while Zac cooed on my lap, I picked up the phone to make the apology I knew had to come from me.

"I'm sorry I hurt your feelings, Dad," I said, hardly remembering what had set him off.

"You know that's not good enough." His stern words were clipped, snippy. *Please don't be an asshole. I said I was sorry.* It was clear my apology had to be for what I actually said.

"I'm sorry I insulted you. I was wrong." It was painful making up contrition, but I hated that we hadn't spoken since Zachary was born, that my dad didn't care or was too hard-headed to let it go. "I know you're a good person."

"Well, all right, then." Satisfied that I was wrong, and he was right, his voice softened. "So, when is that little guy coming to meet his grandfather?"

I knew better than to expect an apology from him for not acknowledging his grandchild's birth. As always, something settled in me just to reconnect with him. We had buried the hatchet once again, in a shallow grave where I couldn't see it. But I knew it was there.

In the spring, I took Zachary to see my dad in San Francisco. Our trip was short and sweet, including visits with my girlfriends who oohed and ahhed over the baby. It was hard to believe a year had passed since they were visiting me in the hospital.

One night, a friend watched Zac while a group of us went to hear Dad sing at the piano bar. As he belted out tunes from *Anything Goes*, I remembered him onstage in Oak Park when I was a kid, when my adoration of him was still intact. It occurred to me I was now as old as he was then—early thirties—yet while his life seemed to get bigger as he aged, mine was getting smaller. Having martinis with my friends was now a rare treat. It reminded me of a world in California that I'd left behind and sorely missed.

I had given up a lot to become a wife and mother.

Sitting on that bar stool, savoring the tang of vodka and olive while my father sang show tunes, I thought about how my current life could not have been more different. Yet, I was still me. Trapped inside an exhausted mother of a seven-month-old was the free-spirited gypsy who had landed on the shores of California with stars in her eyes. Those eyes were fatigued and cynical now. I wasn't sure how I could have ever left the life I'd so intentionally crafted.

As much as I loved being out with them, my friends reminded me of a life I didn't dare think of very often, a time when I traveled, and partied, and did challenging work. They took exciting posts in faraway places without another little person to consider. Their decisions were much bigger than mashed peas or carrots.

As I fished out the plump olive at the bottom of my glass, it occurred to me that even more than getting married, having Zachary had changed everything.

Thirteen

My father was an OCD narcissistic gay genius who was generous, hardworking, and romantic but lacked any kind of empathy. These words are scrawled in a notebook I'm opening for the first time since I wrote Dad's eulogy and obituary.

When I sat down to draft these remembrances of my father, I hadn't realized that writing them would feel like taking a quiz I could fail. Turning the pages in the notebook takes me back to being holed up in my mother's back room sorting through memories and photos of Dad, with Mom poking her head in to offer details she remembered, and me sneaking more vodka from the basement.

The prayer card that was handed out at Dad's memorial sits in front of me on my desk now. The photo looking back at me is from Zac's high school graduation. I chose it for the wide smile on my father's face, proud and joyful. He looks healthy. Since he wasn't a prayerful man, on the back are quotes Dad carried in his wallet for this very purpose.

The first quote is from *The Thorn Birds*, when Barbara Stanwyck admonishes a vengeful God for inflicting old age on our bodies, while leaving the mind still wanting. My father's many desires come into clearer focus now that the broken body that contained them is gone. He wanted attention, and to be admired—which is really just a desire to be loved—and to not have any kind of pain whatsoever. A tall order for someone over seventy. Most of all, my father wanted to be right in a way that often needed you to be wrong.

The second quote is his own: "*If I go through life never deliberately hurting anyone, if there's really a God and heaven, then I'll be entitled to the rewards. — Don Haute, my whole life I don't/didn't believe in God, but always like/liked to cover all my bases. I did my best to live up to the above statement. I hope I succeeded.*"

Deliberately being the operative word.

Whatever I thought I would love about an everyday life with an everyday man escaped me. Of course, that man wasn't around every day. I didn't dare think about what it would be like to share the daily joys and challenges of my son's early life with my husband, tag-teaming through the daily grind, then falling into bed at night together, where we'd share pillow-talk about the future, and make exhausted love once in a while, like the couples on TV shows I didn't even like. *Is that really what I wanted?*

After packing and schlepping through three household moves in as many years, mostly by myself with a child to take care of, I felt more and more like a single mom charged with doing all the domestic heavy lifting. When Jimmy came home on breaks, he wanted more of my attention than I wanted to give, expecting home-cooked meals and lots of sex. I wanted romance, and freedom from the tedium of mothering a toddler. Catering to his needs was just more work for me.

Relief finally came when Jimmy announced on the phone one morning that I could get a break. "I'm driving Foreigner this summer, after I finish the Eagles. We have a ten-day leg in California, and they said the wives can join us. Come on out with me if you want to, if your mama'll keep Zac."

"Oh, my God! Of course, I want to. She and Deena would be thrilled to have him." My head spun with the prospect of being free for ten days, out on tour with a band I loved, and time alone with my husband. The thought of freedom felt like a life preserver thrown into my arms, pulling me back to who I was.

Six weeks later my sister gathered my babbling son in her arms at gate B3 as I connected through O'Hare. I knew he would be in safe hands as I headed to my beloved San Francisco, and Jimmy.

Being back on the bus and in hotel rooms with my man woke up the part of myself that had been knocked unconscious by two years of nearly solo motherhood. We relaxed easily into the life where we had fallen in love, giddy with freedom and passion.

After a few one-night gigs, we settled in for a string of several shows at a small resort venue on Clear Lake in Northern California. We stayed in a collection of cottages surrounding a picnic space nestled in the woods that lined the edge of the water. On a day off, Jimmy begged me to take a motorcycle ride through the foothills with him when the band got some loaners from the Harley shop nearby. I was nervous on the back of a bike so it was not my idea of a good time, but I went. Later, when we were all gathered for a cookout, I was happy to be back with the crew and the band, sitting on a picnic table passing a joint around as burgers sizzled on the barbecue. Jimmy shot me dirty looks, though he knew I hadn't smoked at all since before I was pregnant. I ignored him.

The cocoon of life on the road felt like a familiar embrace—laughing and cooking with people I had met only a few days before but who now felt like family. When the lead singer came down with a boombox, leading us in a rousing chorus of Beatles tunes, I sang my heart out with everyone else while Jimmy and the other good 'ole boy drivers kept to themselves, drinking beers and talking trucks.

"Let's go on upstairs, honey," Jim said as dusk settled over the group. I had a nice buzz on for all kinds of reasons, not least of all the excitement of hanging out with the band and talking about their music.

"I'm good. I want to stay down here with everybody." *Are you kidding me? I have a chance to party with my teen idols and you want me to leave? No way.*

"I said I want to go upstairs. We have a long drive tomorrow. C'mon, let's go." I stood my ground, not caring that it would make him angry.

"No, I'm staying down here, Jimmy." I knew he wouldn't make a scene. *Fuck you if you think you can control me.* He went up alone. By the time I crept into the room near midnight, he was asleep. The next morning, I caught hell.

"You embarrassed the shit outta me, Lisa. My wife hanging out with the musos while her husband goes up to bed alone. Goddamn it! That ain't right."

"What's not right is trying to tell me what to do! You got me to ride on the back of that bike all day—which I hated—but I did it for you! My God. This world is where you met me, Jimmy! Don't give me any shit for wanting to have a little fun while I'm free of raising our son for five minutes. Who do you think you are?"

"I am your husband! And you are a wife and a mama now. You best well act like one!"

"Yeah, well, you don't own me! Fuck. You can't even let me have a good time. I don't need your permission."

His face contorted with anger and disgust as I raged against his archaic view of marriage and motherhood, keeping to myself the revelation that despite the love I knew we still had for each other, we could never really be what each of us wanted in a partner.

• • •

The discontentment in my marriage grew more ferocious as time marched on, but I kept telling myself that I had to make it work, that I owed it to my son to be a family. So, I scrimped and saved enough for us to put a down payment on a house, even after the bankruptcy.

Zac grew like a weed, becoming a complete source of joy as his little personality bloomed. We had hit a sort of stride, my son and I, and by the time he was three, I could see glimpses of the smart, funny man he would grow up to be. He loved the preschool he went to three days a week when I returned to work part time at Karen's office. Jimmy was like a phantom, drifting in and out on rare occasions, touring on a grueling schedule that had him gone for months at a time.

"I'm not happy, Jimmy," I said during one of his breaks. We were making up the nine bunks on his bus with the clean sheets. "You're never here, and when you are, all you want is for me to take care of you and what you need. Like washing sheets for this damn bus. I take care of Zac day in and day out. I take care of the house and the bills. And who takes care of me, Jim? Nobody. Ever." Tears burned hot behind my eyes while I tucked the elastic corner around the edge of an upper bunk mattress.

"Well, honey, I thought I was takin' care of you. This is how I make a livin'. I'm sorry. I am working my ass off out there to send you a paycheck. I am faithful to you." I looked into his eyes as they filled with tears. "What more do you want?"

Oh, Jimmy. I don't know. You're a good man, you are. Guilt mingled with my screaming need to be understood. Guilt for wanting more than what I signed up for when I said yes to this life with him. *It's me, not you.*

I could hardly breathe and moved to the front of the bus beside an open window, each memory of our beginning moving through my mind like fish I couldn't quite hook into. The romance of our months on tour together blurred with moments of laughing and playing under the covers while Zachary conspired to make the connection that would bring him to this world. *What if he's the only reason we're together?*

Our life had become all work and no play. I saw the simple man Jimmy was, and the simple woman he wanted me to be. He seemed to think the instant Zac was born I would lose all desire to do anything else but care for my child, and him. Maybe I thought that a little, too, believing that each facet of my complex personality would fade in the light of motherhood. That I could be happy in an ordinary life.

It was one thing to give up a big career, to have an occasional glass of wine, and try like hell to suppress my envy over Jimmy's cross-country adventures. It was another to give up every dream I'd had before getting married and becoming a mother. As much as I wanted to be satisfied with a simple life, simple was the last thing I could be. It scared me that I might carry the ghosts of those dreams inside me forever, like the throbbing ache of a tooth starting to abscess, choosing to live with the kind of pain you knew you could handle right now but would soon hurt like a motherfucker.

"I don't know what I want, Jim. It seems like I talked myself into a life that really doesn't fit me, and it makes me cranky and mean. Sometimes even with Zac." Shame rushed in as my words reverberated in the small space, admitting to how short my fuse could be, hating how much I raised my voice out of frustration and exhaustion. "And with you gone all the time I feel like a single parent already." The truth revealed itself with each word, becoming clearer with each syllable. *I don't want to hurt you, but I can't help it.* I looked out the window at the house that had begun to feel like a prison.

"I think I want a divorce."

• • •

By Halloween I had drawn up papers with a lawyer. Jimmy reluctantly agreed to split up since he was unwilling to do much to save us, including couples' counseling. His hurt and upset had turned to a cold dismissal of me, which from afar suited me just fine. Zac and I went to Chicago for Thanksgiving while Jimmy spent it with his family in Tennessee.

A light snow fell as I pulled into the parking lot of the Dearhead Bar to get a drink after Christmas shopping, taking advantage of my mother's offer to babysit. Since Zac and I had arrived, I could tell my decision to move back to Chicago when my divorce was final would be good for my mother and my son. And much needed relief for me.

The bar was already crowded as I slid onto a stool and ordered a drink. Out of the corner of my eye, I saw a familiar face.

"Hey, there!" It was Tony, my teenage crush from the band behind the barber shop.

"Hey, you," I said when he sat down beside me. "I hoped you would come down." The cryptic message I'd left on his mother's answering machine, the only number I had for him, asked her to relay that I was in town and would be at the Dearhead at 6:00 p.m. *Why did I call him, of all people?*

He motioned to the bartender to take his order. *Man, he looks good.* His hair, still a dark, shaggy brown, fell slightly over his left eye; his biceps stretched the short sleeves of his black T-shirt. The years had been kind to him. "Yeah, it's good to see you. So, what have you been up to since we talked last? You were out on the road."

Over the years we had kept in touch. I had called once from a hotel room after a few glasses of wine, mostly to brag that I was doing what I thought we would do together with his band and happened to catch him at his mom's. "Well, after the tour I ran off to Tennessee with a roadie, got married, had a baby, and now I'm going through the inevitable divorce." I laughed a little too loudly, taking a long sip of my vodka soda.

It felt a little daunting to be sitting so close, our knees touching.

"My son, Zachary, is three now. So, I'm thinking of moving back up here in March to be close to my family. How about you?"

The last time we talked he said he was married, with a set of twins. "I've been separated the last few months, so I moved back in at my mom's. That's how I got your message. It was my wife's idea, to separate, I mean. Mostly over money—not having enough of it. I miss my kids so much, since I just get them every other weekend. Mostly, I work on my music, and I'm a security guard a few nights a week."

He was in nearly the same place he'd been when I met him twenty years before—only then he drove a cab part time and didn't have a couple of young kids to support. His eyes still lit up when he talked about music. Those nights of sitting on the floor of the old studio watching him play guitar while rolling joints and listening to Eric Clapton felt like yesterday. Two drinks in, I was seventeen again. *I loved my life then. That's why I called him.*

We talked easily about the limbo we found ourselves in as the air between us crackled with possibility. "How long are you in town?" he said.

"I go back on Sunday." *How do I see him again?* It was startling how attracted I was to him, and I chalked it up to how long it had been since I'd had sex. But it was more than that. I knew he wanted me, too.

He ordered us another drink, and a couple of hours later he was kissing me goodnight before I got into my mother's car to drive back to her house. The muscle memory of his lips on mine so many years before made kissing someone other than my husband faintly familiar.

Jimmy's ginger beard was soft and didn't bother me when we kissed, something we hadn't done like we meant it for quite some time. Tony's silky face with just the hint of stubble reminded me that I loved the sexy kid glove softness of a clean-shaven man.

"Can we meet for lunch before you leave?" he said, pulling me in for a hug.

Yes. Oh, yes.

To say I left my marriage for an affair with an old flame would not be fair. I left Jimmy because I was wildly unhappy and had drawn up divorce papers before encountering Tony again. But to say I moved, *ran* really, back to Chicago ridiculously fast because I fell hard for Tony would be the truth. When the possibility of a new man's love showed up, it was enough to start me packing everything I owned to be near him.

With the decision to leave my marriage behind me, I felt free; with a toddler in tow, I felt scared. As much as I wanted to regain control of my life, I knew I had to consider my son's life in every decision. Moving near my family was a no-brainer, and a new love interest was the extra tasty bait to seal the deal.

The spark that was reignited with Tony gave me hope for not only romance, but for a new beginning. A chance to get it right for both me and my son. My fantasies of instantly becoming each other's soulmates had me drafting the letter to Oprah in my head. *Then, after twenty years, we found each other again, while I was home for the holidays. We were going through a divorce at the same exact time and fell back in love instantly! It was destiny.* We would be featured on a show about childhood sweethearts finding each other decades later. I would buy something fabulous to wear.

Tony represented an instant family: Just add water and stir.

. . .

"I'll be back up there for Christmas," I promised during one of our daily marathon phone calls. Since I had returned to Tennessee, talking to Tony each afternoon while Zac napped felt like an invisible rope gently tugging me northward.

"Oh, yeah? Good. I can give you the present I've been working on for your birthday."

My hunch that it might be a song turned my insides to molten chocolate.

The weeks flew by as I threw myself into imagining a brand-new life while putting up the tree and taking Zac to see Santa. United Airlines ran a special on flights, and I made March reservations to fly my sister and Shannon down to help move us to Chicago. I had started making plans. Each morning when Jimmy called to check in, I kept it brief. When I mentioned that we needed to finish the paperwork when he came home, he changed the subject.

On my thirty-fifth birthday, Karen came by with a bottle of Dom Perignon. We toasted the upcoming new year, her new marriage, and my divorce.

"May yours be better than mine!" I said as our glasses touched. "And may I get it right someday, too. Maybe with Tony, who knows?"

Any deep emotional wound I was inflicting on myself by jumping headlong into the abyss with a financially unstable man who was grieving the loss of his wife and kids was far from my mind. The wounds I inflicted upon Jimmy would heal with a third wife, then a fourth. As for the wounds we inflicted on our son, time would tell.

It was Christmas Eve when I called to tell Jimmy I was moving back to Illinois sooner than I had expected. Standing in my mother's kitchen, I nervously dialed his parents' house.

"Merry Christmas!" his sister drawled into the phone when she answered on the third ring.

"Hey, Belinda, Merry Christmas. Can I speak to Jimmy, please?"

"Sure, hang on," she said, "Wyatt, honey, go fetch Uncle Jimmy for me, Aunt Lisa's on the phone."

I listened to the sound of small feet running across my in-laws' tile floor, remembering another Christmas Eve when we'd gotten engaged through these very phones. We were so in love then, hungry for a life together, the future laid out in front of us like a grand banquet. Now, I felt nauseous. Even though Jim knew I had gone to a lawyer and drafted a separation agreement, he didn't seem to take it very seriously. As he picked up the receiver, I knew he would not expect my announcement.

"Hi honey, Merry Christmas," he said.

"Hey." All my courage evaporated with that one word, but I knew I couldn't stay married to a man who saw me as only his wife and Zac's mama.

"Remember when I said I might want to move back to Chicago when the divorce is final?" My mouth went dry as I pushed out the words before he could answer. "I've decided to move back now."

The line was silent until I heard him light a cigarette. "Well, baby, there's no guarantee there will be a divorce. I ain't signed them papers yet. It's Christmas. Can't we talk about this later? How's Zacman?"

"He's fine. He loves it here with my family." *And we don't miss you.* "Really, Jim, I need you to know this is what I'm doing when I get back. I'm looking for a little apartment for us while I'm here."

"What do you mean, an apartment? Why don't y'all just stay up there at your mama's till I'm off this tour. Maybe I can come off the road again." He rattled on about buying a truck, being home more. I knew we couldn't afford any of it.

"Jimmy, no. We tried all that. Even with me working it's tight with what your ex gets. Plus, daycare. And it's not just about any of that. I'm not happy, Jimmy. I don't want to be married anymore."

He started to cry. I knew he didn't understand. "Honey, we made promises. We have a child. That little guy needs his daddy."

"Don't you think I know that? You haven't been with us most of his life! I will never keep him from seeing you." I started to cry, too.

"But we can change it!" I knew he would promise me anything. Promises he couldn't keep. Ones I didn't even want him to make. His words roared through my head.

"No! Jimmy, we can't. I want to be near my family, my mom. She has only one grandchild. I want him to know her."

"We can move up there!" His voice raised in desperation.

"Now you're talking crazy. You wouldn't be happy here. We've talked about all this. You weren't happy either when we decided to file papers and move on. It's been months since we agreed our marriage is over. Now you want to move to Chicago? C'mon. That's crazy. Let me go. Please. Say you'll sign the papers."

"No, I can't say that right now. I ain't gonna let you go that easy, Lisa. Merry Christmas." He hung up.

As I stood staring down at the receiver in my hand, I wondered exactly how this would all unfold. I pressed down on the switch hook to get a dial tone and punched in Tony's number, desperate for reassurance and commiseration.

• • •

Nothing Jimmy could say the next night, when he called me drunk and hysterical, could change my mind about being his wife.

"If I can't have you, I don't want to be on this Earth," he slurred. "When I got home from Mama's Christmas dinner, I done drank all the beer I had in this house and took some Tylenol PMs. I just want to sleep and never wake up. I can't live without you, babe."

I snapped. "Goddamn it, Jimmy! Fuck you for thinking this is gonna win me back. You have three children you need to think about and not just your damn self. How dare you think this kind of stunt will win me back." Fury blinded me, burning away any shred of sympathy I had for him. "I'm gonna call your brother to come over right now to check on you. You better not do anything else foolish. Do you hear me? Please try to throw up." Pity and disgust tag teamed as I considered how becoming a widow would change the situation, pushing aside the speck of relief that played in the shadows.

"Baby, please don't leave me. I love you so much."

"Jimmy, you are Zachary's daddy and I will always care about you. And about Chrissie and Jason. But I can't stay in this marriage anymore. It's killing my spirit."

"What does that even mean, Lisa?"

That he had to ask me was enough to be sure I had to leave.

• • •

I had already decided I would move with my son to Illinois in the days between Christmas and New Year's. It was simple: Tony would fly back with me on Zac's airline ticket, and we would pack my stuff in a U-Haul and drive back. Jimmy was leaving out on tour, so I would be able to get out without him pressuring me to stay.

Before we left, Mom and I went to see a tiny attic apartment nearby for $500 a month, with two small bedrooms and a faint scent of curry wafting from the landlady's place downstairs. The linoleum was peeling in a few places, but it was clean. "What do you think, Ma?"

"You're going to do what you want anyway, Lis, so what I think doesn't matter. You know you and Zac are welcome to live at my house for a while." Winter light pooled on the kitchen floor through a window overlooking a tree-lined street.

She was right. Her opinion didn't hold much weight, especially since I knew she would have said anything to get her grandchild nearby. And we both knew there was no way in hell I wanted to live with my mother.

"I'll take it," I said, writing a check for $200, postdating it for the first of the month. I would pay the rest from my stash of hundred-dollar bills I had squirreled away from my paychecks.

We had a place to live. I'd find a job. It would be okay.

Fourteen

I suppose if the man who spent nearly a decade as a devoted partner to my father were a woman, he would have become my stepmother. I've been heartbroken for Benny since he moved back to Pennsylvania just weeks after my father's death, shattered by a sudden life alone. He took little from Dad's house, cherishing most the rose containing a handful of his beloved's ashes. My weekly calls to check in on him feel odd, given his place in my life had been only as an appendage to Dad.

In those first days after my father's death I went to visit Benny, knowing he was grieving by himself. He seemed hollowed out by his sadness, as if the wind could blow through him. We sat together on the floral couch Dad had had for decades.

"You know, I'm shocked he left me anything." He stamped out his cigarette in an ashtray I had seen my father hold hundreds of times. "I can only imagine how you must feel. I could tell by the look on your face when you read the will that it seemed like your dad favored your sister." His sincerity rang like a tiny bell only I would ever hear. "But he really appreciated how often he talked with you these past couple years. Especially the last few months."

"Thank you." I blinked back the tears that sprung up often in those first few days, grateful for this man who had witnessed my attention to my father in his last years. "You deserve something, Benny. You took care of him. It was just shocking to see those numbers, you know, and all that stuff with everyone else's name next to it. It all felt like percentages of love, and that he loved me the least."

He nodded, letting me voice my feelings without judgment while dozens of my father's clocks ticked in the silence that followed; Dad's energy still lingered in the air, clinging to the couch cushions like the smoke from Benny's cigarette.

Tony held my hand as we waited to board our flight to Nashville. *What the hell am I doing?* I watched a gentle snow fall outside the window where our plane was being deiced. *How can I be moving back to Chicago? I hate it here.*

As we passed into the jetway, the gate agent barely glanced at the boarding pass Tony handed to her, which calmed my nerves. I followed him onto the plane and settled into the middle seat beside him.

When Karen picked us up from the airport, the awkwardness of bringing Tony to my house felt like a heavy cloak I kept trying to push off me. With Jimmy gone on tour he would never know, yet it still made me uncomfortable. When we arrived, I turned on several lights and the Christmas tree. Everything looked slightly different, yet I couldn't put my finger on why. It just didn't feel like mine anymore.

"You make a beautiful home, Lis," Tony said, pulling me into a hug. I let him hold me while I tried to catch my breath, feeling the full weight of leaving. I had worked so hard to buy our house after the bankruptcy. It didn't matter that it was my husband's financial issues that led to our demise. Guilt by association was enough to destroy my credit, too, making starting over even harder while carrying the shame of knowing I had failed my family's code of financial responsibility.

"Thanks. I'll miss this house." The glow of the white lights sparkled in the reflection of the window. "But I'll have another one someday."

"Okay, so what happened here?" Karen said, pointing to a fist-sized hole in the living room wall.

"Shit." I remembered Jim's drunken fit a few nights before. "Jesus. I can't wait to get out of here." I shared my plan with Karen to pack what I was taking the next day, then rent a truck to drive back by New Year's Eve.

"Girl, you seem to always help me pack when I move. This time we have to haul ass."

She laughed. "We may as well get started. We can get some boxes in the morning, but tonight we can throw things in garbage bags. Where are they?"

"I'll get them." I flipped on the light as I walked into the kitchen. On the counter was a piece of yellow legal paper and a hundred-dollar bill

"Honey, I hate to do this, but I don't know any other way to make you give us another chance . . ."

The words blurred on the page as angry tears stung my eyes. *Shit.*

"You need to listen to me. I been thinking about us, and little Zacman, and I just can't let y'all go. You can try to leave me, but I don't think you will get very far. You would be best to stay put and work this out. You know it's best for our boy."

I ran to the bookcase to find my cash, knowing before I thumbed through the pages of my mother's copy of *Little Women* that the money would be gone.

"That son of a bitch took my money!" I screamed, "He took my money! Goddamn it!"

Karen and Tony stood silent as I ranted and raved, tearing through the house to see what other damage he had done. Everything seemed okay, except for a pile of photos upstairs on the bed; any picture of me with another man had been torn apart.

"Sweetie, you have to calm down—" Karen said as the phone rang.

"Hello?" I said, grabbing it as I tried to catch my breath.

"Hi, honey—" Rage roared through my head.

"You asshole! How dare you take my money! Do you really think this is the way to keep me here?"

"Babe, calm down. I will be at the house shortly and we can talk about this."

"The house? You should be in Birmingham by now." My eyes darted around, as if looking for exits. *How could he still be in Nashville? He was supposed to be three states away by now.* Karen and Tony just watched me, unable to do anything while I unraveled.

"My bus broke down, so I been in town fixin' it. I don't got to be nowhere till Tuesday. I'll catch up with the band in Kansas City."

"I don't believe you, or give a shit where you go, but it is not going to be to this house. You're a liar, and a thief! I have nothing to say to you, Jimmy."

"We need to talk, Lisa. You can't just say you're leaving and up and go. That's why I took that money you been stashing behind my back. I figured you can't get far on a hundred dollars."

"Watch me!" His challenge was all I needed to try to get my head straight. "You stole money I earned. I mean it, do not come here." My mind raced at what I would do with Tony, how we could get out of Dodge with Jimmy in town, what I would do for money. "I'll meet you at Shoney's and we can talk there."

How will I get out of here? I felt like an outlaw. All I wanted was to pack up and get back to my son.

"All right. You gather yourself and meet me there in an hour. But I will be staying in my own bed tonight." He hung up.

Karen pulled me into a hug as gulping sobs shook me. Making the plans to go home to get all our stuff and come back to Chicago felt a whole lot easier while talking about it in my mother's kitchen. The reality of dismantling a family I had once really wanted, leaving a house I fought like hell to buy, and gathering a lifetime's worth of belongings in a day and a half hit me like an avalanche, suffocating me, burying me alive in my decisions.

Tony quietly watching as my world crumbled made me feel exposed, guilty. Even though he was not the reason for leaving my marriage, he was now a part of its collapse.

"I'm not staying here with that man tonight, Karen. I don't trust he won't do something stupid."

"Okay, you head on over to see him, and I'll take Tony to the office. Y'all can stay there tonight since my cats will give you an asthma attack. Everything will be all right. Tomorrow you can decide what you want to do, and we'll do it." As always, her level-headed ability to solve any problem calmed me down.

"All right, I will. Thank you." I was unsure of how I could ever live without her nearby. "I love you, girl."

"Love you, too. Now, take a deep breath and go talk to Jimmy."

. . .

"Welcome to Shoney's," the hostess said over the din of clinking dishes and conversation. I ignored her and walked over to where Jimmy was seated in a booth, absentmindedly stroking his beard like he always did when he was worried. It took everything I had not to punch him.

"Hey," I said as I slid in across from him.

"Hi, honey." He looked like shit. I probably did, too, and didn't care. "I been thinking about everything, and I know we can work this out. Maybe we need to see a therapist or something. I don't want to lose you and Zac."

His words didn't pierce my rage. "It's too late for all that, Jim.

Over a year ago I begged you to get counseling with me and you went out and bought a Harley. Remember that? Without even telling me."

"I know, but that was before I got my head on straight, Lisa. I didn't know you'd really leave me."

"Well, I really am. You wanted a divorce, too. Remember?"

He looked bone-tired, in that way people do when there has been a sudden death in the family, a combination of shock and grief. Pitying him, for a split second I thought maybe we should try to work it out. I felt so sorry for him; but pity was not love. I just didn't love him anymore, and maybe I had only ever loved the idea of him, of someone loving me so much.

"You stole my own money from me to trap me! Did you think that was going to win me over, or just intimidate me to stay with you? You get the house, for God's sake. It's in the papers you didn't bother to sign. Did you even read them?"

"Please see a counselor with me tomorrow," he said. "Just once. If he says we don't have a chance, then I will let you go."

This kind of desperation had surfaced in him before, when he had truck issues that cost way more money than we had while he was pulling trailers for his brother, when he spent our last $200 to a phony loan company. This kind of despair sent him back out on a tour bus. Our life together had never been easy, as hard as we tried, yet impulse buying, like his motorcycle, made it impossible to ever get ahead. I couldn't wait for this to be over.

"Okay." I agreed knowing it didn't work that way, that one session would not solve our problems and a therapist wasn't going to make this decision for us. Yet, it felt like it was my one shot at freedom. He said he would find us an appointment and we could meet. My announcement that I was staying at Karen's brought resistance, but he didn't have a choice.

In the morning I called him for the address of a therapist he found, and he said to be there at eleven. Tony and I had slept on couches at the office, barely saying much of anything. My desire to fall into his arms was so strong, yet it felt like further treason against my marriage. Even though we had made out like teenagers in my mother's car over Christmas, we had not consummated our rekindled love. I knew it wasn't going to be until we were safely back in Chicago, on the other side of this nightmare. Until then, he felt more like the "family friend" I would say he was when I told Jimmy he came down to help me drive the truck back.

I arrived on time and took a seat in the office of a middle-aged man who specialized in family therapy. His office was neat and compact, and we made awkward small talk while waiting for Jimmy. When he was ten minutes late, I knew he wasn't coming.

"I think we should call him," I said, embarrassed and angry that I had driven thirty miles for this shit.

The therapist dialed our number on a speaker phone, and my husband answered on the second ring.

"Jimmy, where are you?" I shrieked. John gestured to me to calm down.

"Jim, this is Ray Harrison. You set up this appointment for you and your wife, and she's right here. Why aren't you, Jim?" He was reassuring, like he was talking to a jumper on a bridge.

"Well, Ray, I'm sorry about that. I just don't trust her no more. I love her, just don't trust her. So, I am here at the house making sure she didn't just go and take off on me whilst I was up there with you." I bit my tongue to keep from screaming for him to *fuck off*. It was a setup from the beginning. He never meant to show up.

"Jim, Lisa tells me you took all the money the two of you had as a way to keep her with you. Do you think that is a good way to show love and respect?"

I imagined Jimmy stroking his beard, leaning against the kitchen counter looking at the letter still laying where he left it, smoking one cigarette after another, pinching the filter between his thumb and forefinger before grinding one out and lighting another. I had pocketed the hundred-dollar bill.

"Ray, you don't understand. I love this lady. I work hard out there running those miles to give her and Zachary a home. I ain't done nothin' wrong against her. Please tell her we can work it out."

"Jimmy, don't. We can't work it out. I don't want to do this anymore. Please—" I glanced at Ray to save me, to say something to my husband to help him understand it was too late for me, that I didn't want to be married to him anymore.

"I'm sorry, I can't do that, Jimmy. Lisa says her mind is made up, and you can't force her to stay with you by trapping her. Not showing up for this appointment doesn't help this situation. It appears that if what she wants is a divorce, you need to accept that." His words were kind and measured, the voice of reason. I prayed they got through to Jimmy, who seemed to be listening.

"I know... I know." His voice cracked as he broke down. "I don't want to force you, Lisa. If you need to go, go. I'll sign the papers. But you better know you are breaking my heart in a million pieces, and our little boy's, too."

. . .

The civility with which Jim and I spent the next forty-eight hours was a miracle. We rented a U-Haul; agreed which furniture I would take and what I would leave behind, which was most of the big stuff; we signed divorce papers he had drawn up with his brother's lawyer. All while keeping our conversation to a minimum. It was a suspended truce, the kind that lets you navigate hard things, like feuding siblings planning a funeral.

Karen came loaded up with boxes and trash bags. We packed everything I was taking while Jimmy sat upstairs in our bedroom, crying. By the end of the day the truck was full, my car was loaded on the trailer, and all I had left were the clothes in my closet.

"I'll be back in an hour with Tony. It will be okay," she said before pulling out of my driveway. "You're almost outta here, girl."

"I know," I said, not really sure things would ever be okay.

With an armload of trash bags, I went upstairs to the master bedroom where Jimmy had holed up all day. He was sitting on the edge of the bed, a second-hand king I'd found in the want ads, which would be left behind along with the matching dresser and most everything else in the room. His back was to me, his head down, hands in his lap.

Remembering he had a pistol in the house, something I was vehemently against, my heart raced as I entered the room. He kept it on a high shelf in his closet, unloaded, with a box of bullets on another shelf. In a flash, I imagined a desperate, grief-stricken man turning his pain against the cause of it, the callous wife who was stealing his life from him. He shoots her once... *I love you so much...* twice... *I can't live without you...* then turns the gun on himself, orphaning their three-year-old son.

Snapping out of my gruesome reverie, I hurried to my closet and shoved all I could into each bag, as my heartbeat thundered in my ears, accompanied only by my husband's quiet sobs. *Oh, God. What could I possibly say to him? I am a horrible person.* Without uttering a word, I tumbled the bags down the stairs like boulders in an avalanche, then hoisted them into the back of the truck. When I was done, I sat on my front porch for the last time.

The dark green shutters against the white siding were striking, making the well-worn facade look more elegant than it actually was. After touring a dozen houses, I knew this would be my next home. It took every cent and all my powers of persuasion to get the loan. The house needed a new roof that we couldn't afford, but it was on a cul-de-sac where Zac rode his first bike and trick-or-treated as a Dalmatian puppy. Me and my little boy had made memories there, most of which didn't include Jimmy.

We had lived in the house not quite a year. Now, I was leaving like a fugitive.

I lit a cigarette as dusk faded around me and pulled my jacket tight against the chill. The smell of a fireplace across the street reminded me that people were still celebrating the holidays, an anomaly that seemed impossible. *Had Christmas really been just a few days ago?* Saying goodbye to the first house I would ever buy was harder than I thought it would be. We had no equity in it, so I walked away with nothing. Jimmy said he wanted to stay, though I knew he would end up back in East Tennessee before long. We would have to shuttle Zac back and forth to see his dad. I just couldn't imagine at that moment how it would work.

Karen pulled up with Tony hunched down in her passenger seat.

"You ready, girl?" she asked, looking up at the master bedroom light in the second-floor window. "You okay?"

"I'm all right. He's a mess. I just want to get—"

The front door flung open and out stormed Jimmy. "So, who is the liar now? Huh? Mimi done gone through our phone bills and you been talking to some guy up in Illinois for weeks now! For hours on end, every day, burning up the phone lines, probably hatching your great escape from me. You whore! Saying you're leavin' cuz I ain't never here when you're leaving me for another man!" He stood in stocking feet in the middle of the yard, waving a piece of paper.

"Jimmy, stop it! You don't know what you're talking about. But if it's easier for you to believe I left you for another guy, then fine! I don't give a shit what you think. I'm leaving you for ME!" My screaming rang through the cul-de-sac, into the burgeoning darkness.

"I bet that's him!" He pointed to Tony, who was opening the

passenger door of the truck. "Who the fuck are you, man? Are you fucking my wife?" Tony silently disappeared into the passenger door of the truck before Jimmy could get to him.

"He's a friend, and it's none of your business anyway!" I tried to lower my voice, calm down, but I wanted to fight, to let out all the rage I'd felt in a marriage that made me feel small. "It didn't have to be like this, you know. You are making this so much worse than it needs to be, Jimmy. Just let me go." Some part of me knew I had set him up to make a scene, rushing my departure with a new love interest in tow, trying to pass him off as a friend. But Jimmy wasn't supposed to be here, standing in the front yard watching me leave.

"Fine. Go. You ain't nothin' but a whore. Get the fuck outta here!" he screamed from the porch. I hugged Karen and climbed up into the truck. Lights across the street went on; neighbors peeked from behind their curtains. Humiliation and relief filled my heart as I put the truck in gear and inched into the street, driving into the night.

Fifteen

"I could use a hug," Mom says on the phone. "Your sister is so busy I hardly see her. She mostly just texts me. Come and help us rent the vacant apartment." She and Deena are overseeing Dad's rundown six-flat building until it sells. I can help rent it from home, but in my mother's voice is a plea for some company.

"Okay, I'll come this weekend if I can use Dad's miles." She tells me to go ahead and book the flight without my sister's permission. I will likely catch a bunch of shit for this, but I don't care. It's also likely that when Deena gets mad that I didn't ask her, Mom will deny that she told me to book it, adding to the string of little white lies that follow her like toilet paper on the heel of her shoe. She will believe her own story, too, and in time it won't matter.

I book a United flight for Saturday morning and place an ad on Craigslist for the vacant apartment, stating I will be showing it on Sunday.

When Tony and I arrived with the truck in Chicago, a collection of my sister's friends helped me move my stuff up the narrow, winding stairway that led to our attic apartment, sans the queen box spring which wouldn't make the turn. My mattress would have to live on the floor of my tiny bedroom, creating a tacky dorm-room feel. Zac's room was smaller but had enough space for his little bed and all his toys.

The first night of passion I shared with Tony was at the Holiday Inn after ringing in the New Year at FitzGerald's nightclub. The stress of the past few months had whittled me down to a size I had never been, and I felt beautiful as Tony kissed me at midnight, ushering in a new beginning. In our room at the hotel, he sat naked on the bed with his acoustic guitar and serenaded me with the song he wrote for my thirty-fifth birthday, "Where Do We Go From Here?" His words implored us to explore the answer, which I assumed was to live happily ever after. It was like I was living *in* a love song, my primary model for what romance should be.

After that, he stayed most nights with us. His patience with Zachary melted my heart, and he watched him while I found a job. What a cozy trio we made, me and my son wrapped in love with this sublime man who loved being a father to his own kids.

"Don't you think you're moving too fast with this guy?" my mother said on a snowy day in late February, when Tony moved in his clothes and recording equipment and we added his name to the mailbox. "You're not even divorced yet, for God's sake."

The hair on the back of my neck went up. "No, Ma, it's fine. I would have been divorced by now if Jimmy hadn't been an asshole about Dad." In the original divorce papers, it stated that my son couldn't be alone with his grandfather, another below-the-belt tactic Jim used to hurt me. I refused to agree, insisting the papers be revised.

"Tony and I kind of picked up where we left off when we were young." This was true, but not exactly. Being with Tony after twenty years was like starting with a familiar stranger. An erotic, safe place to begin again, especially with a young boy to take care of who my new man adored. "Can't I just be happy? Or would you prefer I respectfully date, like you did when you divorced Dad?"

She sighed. "Of course, I want you to be happy. You just need to think about Zac, too. You need to put him first."

"I have! He's been my complete focus his whole life. He still is, but I want a life, too. Tony's great with him. He's good for both of us. You'll see."

By the time he moved in, I had started working as a marketing assistant for a corporate office, not exactly my dream job but it paid the bills. Long days chained to a desk while my boss barked orders was a far cry from working a few days a week for Karen in Nashville, or running around the world with the rock show. The wake-up call of single motherhood was like being doused in ice water, then thrown in a meat locker. For all the ways I felt like a single mom while married to Jimmy, the truth was I knew he was out making money, and I wasn't completely alone.

Trudging through the snow to get Zachary to daycare, fighting traffic to get to work, grocery shopping, cooking, and doing laundry was eased by my boyfriend. He picked up Zac from daycare, he picked up the toys that littered the living room, he picked up something to make for dinner. He picked up the slack. *This is how it feels to have a wife,* I thought. A spouse, even. I loved it. I loved him. And I especially loved the way he treated my son.

At the end of each day, I came in the door to Zac's squeals of delight as I scooped him up and covered his face with kisses, inhaling his warm love.

"Tell me about your day, sweet pea!" His eyes lit up as he shared each small wonder and discovery he'd had while we were apart. After spending most of a thousand days and nights in captivity with my child, the delicious return to each other after being out in the world separately cleaved us in a new and special way.

I loved missing him.

Following the smell of something savory gurgling on the stove, we would head down the hall and find Tony playing guitar on the foot of my bed, Zac's toys strewn at his feet.

"Good day?" I asked with a kiss, then he handed me his headphones, smiling.

"Have a listen. I've been working on a new song. Dinner'll be ready in half an hour. C'mon buddy, let's go play Candy Land while your mom takes a little rest." They would disappear while I laid on the floor for ten minutes, listening to the haunted melodies of my beloved before joining their game. It was heaven.

The harsh winter was warmed by the joyful bubble I lived in with my two favorite guys. Tony was sweet and thoughtful, leaving beautiful cards for me on the kitchen table when he arrived home at dawn after his security shift. Then he slid naked into bed with me, bringing with him the outside chill.

"Mmm, you're so warm," he said, his hand sliding over my skin. "Come here."

We made slow, quiet love while the sun came up through the frosted windows, sharing a passion that felt both familiar and new.

Sex with Jimmy had become a wifely chore in those last couple of years. When he was on the road it was all he talked about during our phone calls; when he was home it was all he wanted to do. At first, it had been the one place in our marriage where we were compatible, yet eventually my resentment over how little he understood me killed the passion.

As Tony and I thrived, Zac thrived, too. My easygoing kid was happy, and entertained Tony's ten-year-old twins when they were with us every other weekend. In moments, it felt like we were a real family, all of us nestled under blankets with a huge bowl of popcorn passed between us, six little feet pressed against us as we watched the latest Disney video.

It was as exquisite a contentment as I have ever known, like starring in my own single-mom-gets-the-hot-guy-devoted-to-her-kid chick flick. And so unexpected that it landed me back in Chicago with my teenage crush.

My life with Jimmy had dissolved so completely, so quickly, that I wondered if I had ever really loved him. Again, I thought perhaps I had only loved how much he loved me, and how that love brought me Zachary. By moving so quickly from one life to the other, the edges of my perception became blurred; instead of grieving my marriage, it was almost as if Jimmy never existed.

Until he reared his ugly head.

"Lisa, I didn't agree to no child support until those divorce papers are final in July, you can read it for yourself," he said, as I demanded he send me some money.

"He's your son! You need to help support him, Jim." I had barely read the temporary agreement we signed when I left, so desperate I was to be free. "Have you forgotten how much of your child support I paid? Plenty."

"Don't you forget it was you who wanted this divorce, not me. I coulda kept you here. I only let you move because of your mama."

"Look, we went bankrupt keeping up with the alimony and child support we paid your ex-wife. We paid her every cent she was due, so how dare you think you don't have to help support Zac!" I was beyond pissed off, feeling like he was trying to get away with something, to punish me.

My income was just about enough to get by, and after his own child support and bills, Tony could barely contribute grocery money. I told myself I would be paying the rent and utilities anyway, so the help I received with Zac and housekeeping was enough. But Jimmy was not getting off that easy when it came to his son. Round and round we'd go, with him hanging up angry and me wondering how I could have ever married him.

But as much as I wished he would disappear from my life, I thought Zac's life would be better with his father in it. Maybe it was because of the wounds I carried from feeling like my own dad abandoned me, and maybe it was because deep down I didn't fully trust my fairy tale. As delirious as I was over Tony, I knew that as my son got older, he would want his real father in his life.

• • •

The picture from that Easter in 1996 was taken by Tony. It shows Mom, Deena, Zac, Gram and Uncle Ed, and a sliver of my right cheek; we're gathered around a table I put up in the living room. It was the first time I ever hosted my family for a holiday, so I took great care in presenting a spiral honey ham with all the trimmings. Aside from Zac spiking a fever with the onset of a cold, the day was free of the tension I often associated with family gatherings.

I hardly noticed that Tony was quiet most of the day. His culinary skills kept him in the kitchen all morning, and through dinner my loud Italian family kept the conversation lively. Once they were gone, and I settled Zac in bed, I found Tony in the kitchen doing dishes.

"Uh, we need to talk, Lis," he said, his back to me as he rinsed a sudsy plate under running water. For a moment, time stopped, though the sound of the clock ticking on the wall echoed through the room. When he turned around, I could see in his face he was leaving me. *Poof.* In a single moment I felt my world topple like a house of cards.

He said he missed his kids, that he wanted to see if his wife would take him back. He said he wasn't really happy with me because he missed her and the kids.

"I can't do this," he said. "I love you. But I love them more." He said he would be moving back to his mom's in the morning.

"Please. Please. Give us a chance. Please. I love you. We're so good together." I begged him not to go, pleaded. *I can't lose you.* He stared at me with sadness as I shamelessly groveled, carrying my desperation into bed with us where I asked him to make love with me one more time. He woodenly obliged. As I clung to him sobbing afterwards, he gently disengaged and went to sleep on the couch.

I woke up alone and nauseous, sickened by my unabashed request for what was no more than a mercy fuck. I had to get Zac up and ready for preschool and somehow go to work. Tony was already gone when I looked for him in the kitchen, hoping it was all a bad dream. The note he left said he would get his things while I was at work, yanking me back to the stark reality that the love of my life was leaving me, and there was nothing I could say to change his mind.

"You'll be okay, Lis. Focus on Zac, and eventually you'll meet someone else," Deena said, the most unexpected person to come to my emotional rescue. She was the only person who could meet me when I fled from my desk at noon in a fit of uncontrollable sobs, the pain in my chest feeling like my heart was literally broken. We met at the hospital where she worked, and she sat with me on a bench until I calmed down. My sister as a soothing presence was unfamiliar, yet it was so comforting to be with her.

"But I love him so much." Another sob overtook me, shaking me from the inside out. While she had nothing against Tony, I knew what she and Mom thought of my impulsiveness and how it affected my son. The thought of telling Zac he was gone made me cry more. Tony's departure would be yet another adjustment I would place on my son's tiny shoulders. I never said Tony would be with us forever, even though I had been sure of it.

"I know I have to move on—but we were going to get married!" My cries came in waves, violent and howling. "Maybe she won't take him back, maybe he'll change his mind—"

"Seriously, you don't want him that way, Lis. C'mon." Deena sounded level-headed and reasonable. The opposite of how I felt.

"I don't care. I just want him back." The thought of another man's touch, kiss, *smell*, was unthinkable. Only he could fill the hole inside me that had finally felt full.

Deena reminded me that I was still married to someone else, a fact I had tucked into some corner of my mind, shielded from my life with Tony. In less than six months my new life had settled into my bones, and Jimmy and the house in Tennessee felt like ghosts, remnants of something real. Now, Tony would be a ghost, too.

. . .

My family helped me see that my impetuous romance was likely God's way of getting me back to the old neighborhood. I hated that they were right and turned my attention to juggling a full-time job with single motherhood.

Most nights, after Zac was asleep, I licked my wounds in a hot bath with a glass of cheap wine, letting the tears flow. In these quiet moments I finally felt the full weight of my failed marriage. It seemed clearly my own fault for confusing passion with partnership, for believing a man's love would sustain me.

Yet our union created my adorable little boy whose whole world revolved around me.

Sometimes, when he crawled into my bed after a scary dream, I held him tight, yielding to his unguarded heart and the intoxicating scent of innocence, and told myself his love was enough.

As the weather warmed, my father came for his annual visit to see my grandmother for Mother's Day. I invited him over for coffee.

"Well, you sure have grown, Zachary," he said, pulling his grandson onto his lap.

"I'm almost four!" A light breeze came through the open kitchen window, sending the smell of fresh cut grass into the room as I poured us each a second cup. Zac squirmed off his lap. "I'm gonna go make you something, Grandfather." He trotted off to his room.

"How are you doing these days, honey? Your mother said you've been doing better." The idea that my parents talked about my mental state made me uneasy.

"I'm okay. I should have seen it coming. He really missed his kids. Maybe she won't take him back, but I'm not holding my breath." My calls to Tony had not been returned. Almost worse than being without him was wondering if he got what he wanted, while hoping that maybe he didn't.

"Well, you know how things went when I moved in with Robert in San Francisco. That turned out quite poorly, but I survived." The memory of us sitting at Robert's table on Polk Street felt like it happened in another lifetime.

"Yeah, breakups suck but they don't kill you. It feels like I'm going through two at the same time, it's weird. My divorce is just now hitting me, too. Thank God, I have Zac to focus on." As if on cue, he came bounding into the room and climbed back onto Dad's lap.

"It's a tower!" he said, standing his Lego creation in front of him on the table.

"Wow!" My dad's praise brought a huge smile to my son's face. *How sweet they are together.* Seeing the man I came from with the little man who came from me filled my heart with love. Yet it still wasn't enough to seal the crevice left by the man who broke it.

. . .

Right after my divorce was finalized in late July, I looked up from my sadness to see Nick, a handsome, funny, blue-collar guy who was installing our A/C unit at work. Suddenly, I wasn't sad anymore.

Apparently, the attention of a good-looking man was still a

narcotic for me. The initial glance, the flirtation, the drinks. I loved all of it. That rush of dopamine when you wanted someone you liked to kiss you, and then he *did*, lit me up like sparklers in the dark. Once I tasted it again, the craving was irresistible.

If I could have identified the moment when I became so obsessive in relationships with men, maybe I would have been able to stop it. Instead, it crept up on me slowly, then *BAM*, I let the need for the sound of his voice on the phone, or his silhouette at my door, soothe some anxious place inside of me while I waited for him. The way I had waited for Dad. It was a familiar sense that I wasn't complete without reassurance that I mattered to him.

Nick called incessantly or he didn't call at all. He was equally charming and unreliable, a good guy and a bad boy, the deadliest combination for a single mother. Good with Zac, he was gentle and protective, a sober pillar of responsibility when he was with my son, having raised two boys of his own. Mom loved his polite nature and sense of humor.

Then on nights when we were alone, he had a crazy side.

"Babe, come over and get a bump of this, you'll like it." He snorted a thick line of coke off a framed photo he'd removed from the wall of his apartment. As he slid a straw across the glass to draw the white powder into his nose, I cringed, content to stick with my Merlot. I wasn't a prude about drugs, but I didn't like them.

He'd be manic, we'd have great sex, and for that brief moment I let go of everything and just let my body take over. Letting go of who I was supposed to be, not needing to know my next career move, or how to pay for everything, or what my mother thought. An exquisite feeling that was enough to put up with his bullshit, especially since my mother and son loved him.

When I had a sitter for Zac, Nick would escort my mother down the carpeted ramp of the opulent theater where I had landed a job as a marketing director soon after we met. Mom beamed on the arm of this good-looking man as he sat beside her in the fifth row to see David Copperfield or The Wizard of Oz. Offering her those nights on the town was a perk that helped justify the insane hours I worked.

"He's so wonderful," my mother gushed.

She was unaware of the drugs and the way he lied to me, often disappearing on a binge to return remorseful days later. It was a charade I put up with for two years because he fit in my life somehow, certainly more than the idea of dating did. Until wondering which version of him would show up was too exhausting to continue.

Sixteen

"Lisa, you've got to get over this. Your father did what he did." We're in my mother's car on the way to her doctor's appointment. I'm driving. And bitching. About my sister's chilly demeanor, among other things. As predicted, she threw a fit over how I'd used Dad's miles without her permission. "So, he put your sister in charge, and split your inheritance with your son. So, what? You should be nothing but grateful. I didn't get anything from my parents. Your father and I helped pay my father's debts when he died. And I never expected anything from your dad."

In classic Peg fashion, this isn't entirely true. When Dad helped to buy her townhouse, it wasn't a loan, but rather an advance on her share of his estate. I don't begrudge my mother Dad's support; I appreciate that he loved her and wanted to take care of her. It's the notion that his love for Mom and my sister somehow meant more to him. Being singled out for something special left to them made them special to him, the opposite of being at the bottom of his list. Being back in town magnifies these feelings.

"Yeah, well, he didn't split his inheritance from Grandma Haute with us, so it doesn't feel like that was his intention. We all know my son has been less than grateful for Dad's money in the past, and Dad gave him more flack than anybody about wasting it. And putting Deena in charge of Zac's money till he's thirty? Geez."

Even if he meant to just split my slice with my son, the thought of my sister doling his portion out to him makes me cringe. "You know, Ma, it's more than all that. It's all the secrets; that you guys don't trust me."

She silently looks straight ahead, and I can feel her exhaustion deplete the oxygen in the car. I open the window, wishing I still smoked for the first time in forever.

When Zac started Kindergarten, Mom suggested she sell her house and we buy a duplex together. I thought about what having my mother close by all the time would look like. Free babysitting! Shared utilities! A backyard! It also meant I would be subjected to her scrutiny.

After a few weeks of looking at homes, we stumbled upon a huge house nestled on a quiet street with a playground on the corner. Mom wandered from room to room with the vision of an architect, imagining ways to split up the space into two homes.

The idea of having so much space for Zac and me to spread out, to own a house again, and to have Mom right there to help with her grandson was more than I could have hoped for, regardless of the small voice in my head that warned me of the cost of having her so close.

"I give it a year," my sister said half-kiddingly when we shared the news. "If you two don't kill each other first." The family was taking bets, certain my mother and I would butt heads living under one roof.

"We'll be fine." I said. "There will be a door between us. It'll be great for Zac."

We moved in at Halloween. By a month later, we were bickering over the Christmas decorations. "Ma, I'm really busy, and it's not even December. I'll do it next week," I said, defying her insistence that we decorate the day after Thanksgiving.

Her answer echoed the hundreds of times I'd resisted her instructions in my youth. "C'mon, get moving, let's just get it over with." Her favorite marching orders.

While Zac was on a rare visit with his father after Christmas, I ended my relationship with Nick. Even though he could be good to me, I knew he wasn't good *for* me. We drank too much, we ate too much, we fought too much. I had gained twenty-five pounds, and a bad attitude in our last year together. When I stopped recognizing myself, I knew it was over—even though it would hurt my mother and son to break Nick's heart.

Once again, detaching from an unfulfilling relationship freed me to turn my attention on myself and Zac. After weekend trips with my son to the zoo, and the movies, and McDonald's Playland, a girl needed some grownup time. Having Mom close meant I was free to go out more. But freedom wasn't free. Mom seemed happy to watch Zac for me when she was available, while I had happy hour with girlfriends after work or went to aerobics class. When I had a date, the price was her opinion. Those same watchful eyes that I wanted to avoid when I moved out at eighteen could now see my every move. Yet, without Mom there would not likely be much freedom at all.

"You had to work, and Grandma wouldn't let me leave the driveway all day. It's Saturday!" Zac's eyes filled with tears. "I think your job is more important to you than me, Mommy." I held my own tears back, vowing to try to be home more. Within six months, I found a corporate project manager job with regular hours and good benefits, sacrificing work I loved for my five-year-old son.

Shedding more than just Nick's bullshit after our split, by summertime I'd lost all the weight I had gained, and then some. Feeling good in my skin was exciting, and I found a nimble and curious playmate, a decade younger than me, with whom I shared an intellectually stimulating connection over the cube wall we shared at work. Sometimes I went to Juan's apartment late in the evening after my son was sound asleep and my mom was in her robe watching TV. Her permission to go out was granted begrudgingly.

"You can go, but do you have to stay out so late?" she said. "Why do you have to stay out until all hours on a weeknight? For God's sake."

"Ma, please. Does Zac even wake up at all after I put him to bed?" She shook her head, letting out a disapproving sigh.

"See? He's fine. I'll be close by. What difference does it make what time I come home?"

"The difference is that you're a mother." *Yeah, I know. But I'm not you.*

"Well, Ma," I said, shrugging off her judgment, "being a mother isn't the only thing I am."

My mother had been a different kind of divorcée in her thirties, a glowing example of single parent respectability. She had an active social life after her divorce from Dad that was supported by my grandmother, who watched us when Mom went out, often with her girlfriends.

She met Harry at Parents Without Partners, and got dressed up on Saturday nights, carefully applying her makeup before sliding her feet into pumps. He would pick her up in his lime green Torino to go out for a nice dinner, then dancing at the Willowbrook ballroom. She would be home at a reasonable hour. Like Cinderella. If they went back to his house to fool around before she came home, none of us knew it.

The one and only time he spent the night with her at our house was when my sister and I were both on sleepovers in our teens. My friend had to bring me home earlier than expected the next morning, and I panicked when I saw Harry's car in front of the house. "Oh, my God, my Mom would die if I walked in right now! Go! Don't stop!" I waved her to keep going. "Take me to Denny's." I filled up on pancakes while waiting to call home at nine.

"Where are you?" my mother said, the sounds in the background tipping her off that I was at a restaurant. "I'm at Denny's, and I need a ride. I was home at 6:30 this morning, and saw Harry's car, so I came here."

"Oh." Her Italian-Catholic guilt wafted through the phone like a lasagna in the oven. "Please, don't you dare tell your grandmother." *God forbid.*

"I won't," I promised, not sure why it was such a big deal. With a brand-new driver's permit in my hand, that promise bought me a lot of extra driving time, and I never told Gram. I respected Mom's right to privacy even if I didn't agree she needed it. And so began our stark contrast when it came to motherhood and sex. My mom was a good girl who believed that if you had kids, you didn't let a man spend the night unless you were married to him.

Each day, my child's needs came first as a small ember of discontent burned quietly deep inside me. I focused on the tiny daily joys of raising him. His first school play, an A on a spelling test, his arms wrapped around my neck in a hug. Fits of giggles. His growing curiosity. In moments, I wished I could be satisfied with devoted motherhood and a mediocre job. It would have been so much easier than always yearning for something *more*. Being a single mom had led me back to a place I didn't like to live, and to abandon a career I had worked very hard for. I didn't have a man around to help me raise my son, and we lived under the same roof as my mother.

Giving up sex was not an option.

It didn't occur to me yet that I was more like my father than I realized when I struck up an affair with the hot, young guy at work. In his mid-thirties, Dad met Terry and whirled like a dervish in the throes of passion with a much younger man. My pleas for his attention paled in comparison to the joy he found in finally being free to be himself after years of hiding. Of course, as a child, I wouldn't have known that. I was oblivious to my parents as individuals with desires completely detached from their children. Even as an adolescent it was hard for me to see my father separate from that role.

If parenthood for fathers is like a uniform you are required to wear daily, for mothers it is like a second skin, fused to your being. My role in my son's life required so much more of me than fatherhood had demanded of Dad, yet my ache for some separateness from that role inched me toward better understanding of him—yet not enough to keep my mouth shut when I reverted right back to being that hurt adolescent girl.

"That's enough, Lisa!" my mother yelled at me as I tangled with my father in her kitchen in an argument over not coming over to say hello. Dad had moved back to Illinois when he retired, and my parents had breakfast together every Friday.

"Why do you always side with him, Ma? For God's sake, I live under the same roof!" I turned back to the source of my fury. "This is not the first time you came up to Mom's and didn't even knock on my door to say hi. Jesus, Dad! But then you couldn't drive over the fucking bridge when I was in the hospital when I was pregnant. I mean, really—"

"Stop it. I don't ever want to hear another word about that goddamn bridge!" He was shaking with anger, and though I knew he wouldn't, he looked like he might hit me.

"You two always side with each other and never with your *daughter*. I just think it's shitty that you don't even think to come and see me, Dad." My chest tightened as my tears turned to heaving sobs, and I stomped back to my side of the house and slammed the door.

At times, searing envy consumed me every time my mother was the object of my dad's affection, a childish jealousy born of my bewilderment over their abiding friendship. It was hard to understand how my mother would still care so much about a man who lied to her for years. I could understand being civil to an ex with whom you shared kids, but nothing about siding with them over your child made sense. Now that he was back in town, his favoritism toward her was in my face when he made his weekly visits.

As usual, my sister took his return to town—like most things—in stride, not seeming to be bothered much by either of our parents, staying busy with her life and her work. I didn't see her often, except when she picked up Zac for an outing, one of his favorite things to do. His "DeeDee" had become an essential part of his life, a buddy who took him on adventures and sleepovers at the lake house she shared with Shannon on weekends. Deena taught him to ski, on water and snow, and took him to festivals. She built him a jungle gym in our backyard, and every year they went downtown to the car show. She offered him expensive life experiences that I couldn't provide on my own, and I was grateful for their closeness, although sometimes I struggled with wishing I had her disposable income and freedom. I made only just enough to cover the bills, especially since Jimmy was inconsistent with child support.

We were all back within five miles of where we'd begun. It was astonishing that the choices I made had landed me in the same suburban life I came from, the one I'd fled as a young woman. All my big plans, world travel, and the spectacular career I had blurred in the background of the picture that was my life now, and clearly in the foreground was my family flock and me—the black sheep.

. . .

As my fortieth birthday approached, I treated myself to a trip to California. It had been a hard year, particularly when we lost my beloved Gram after several years of declining health. Her frail body diminished slowly, yet she wore her crimson fingertips till the end, always lighting up when I painted them for her while she shared the stories of her youth I loved to hear. It became harder and harder to watch her suffer, and when God called her home, my sadness mixed with relief that she was at peace.

She was on my mind as I was driving from the airport across the Golden Gate Bridge and the rolling hills of Marin County rose to meet me. My long weekend in the heat of Indian summer would offer time with my tribe and a chance to relax, to unwind the tight knot my life had become in the decade since I'd lived there. Monica graciously hosted me, and I slept like a baby on crisp white sheets in her guest room, listening to the rain falling softly outside the open window. Each morning I hiked alone, embracing the strength I gathered when my attention was unencumbered by a man at the center of it. The months of reading about spirituality, and journaling about the kind of life I wanted for myself and my son, felt concretized by the time alone. At night, delicious meals were prepared with the women who formed a sisterhood I had left behind when I married Jimmy. It felt like home, and I was happy.

"Seemed like the only choice," I said, when describing my exit from the world of music and film that connected us. "The mommy guilt of long hours and being stressed out all the time was too much. So, now I peddle junk mail for Domino's and Walgreens, and the productions I attend are in the school gym."

"Sounds pretty good compared to living out of a suitcase half the time." Monica poured herself another glass of wine and curled up in a chair. "Not to mention dealing with equipment hell out on the road."

"The suitcase in your guest room is the first one I packed in a long time. I missed it."

They chattered on about upcoming gigs and itineraries. My life seemed terribly bourgeois compared to the lives of these women who still toured the world and produced TV, all childless. Alongside my gratitude for being Zac's mom lay a melancholy for the world I had left, making itself known with each glass of wine. It was easy to soak up their stories like a sponge, vicariously living the global life I used to have.

"I fucking love you guys," I said, late in the evening while nestled in the corner of Mon's couch. "I wouldn't even have the life I do without you guys."

They had led me to Jimmy, and all that came after, down my twisty road back to Illinois and my life as the single mom of an eight-year-old. "It just seems like so long ago that my life was here," I said, barely able to remember a time when these women were my colleagues. Then I slipped off to sleep.

We put together a dinner party for Saturday night that included Monica, Nancy, Cathy and her husband, and Mark and his wife. By Saturday morning, those plans unraveled as Mon and Nancy boarded a plane for a last-minute video shoot, Cathy called to cancel due to sick kids, and an email from Mark said he would be coming alone. My party would be dinner for two.

Whatever part of me that wanted to conjure up an evening alone with Mark did so without my conscious knowledge, since I specifically included his wife in my invitation. Still, I dressed carefully, feeling sexy in slim black leggings and a silky, loose blouse. When I opened the door to find him standing there, I knew I was in trouble.

"Hey, Lis," he said, a slow, appreciative smile spreading over his face. "It's been a long time." We stood smiling at each other. "You look so...*hot*." He looked startled, and I laughed, not sure he meant to say that out loud.

"I've been working out," I said, openly flirting with him for the first time ever, it seemed. It felt exciting, and a little dangerous, when he hugged me for a second longer than expected. He smelled like amber and soap. Then he handed me the bottle of wine he brought.

"What a *thing* that it's just the two of us, isn't it?" he said, walking into the cozy room. "Like the Universe had other plans or something." Handsome and fit, he was a graying version of his younger self, but with short hair. In his eyes was the naked appreciation I'd only seen directed at other girls. It made me giddy. He followed me outside to the patio once I opened the wine, where we swapped stories about our lives under the bougainvillea.

"I wish I could say it was a phase, but I just don't feel romantic towards her," he said about his wife. "Rarely did." It sounded clichéd, but he had said the same thing on the phone during one of the few calls we'd had over the years. "I love our family, and the horse thing we started with Savannah sustains us, but I'm just not in love with her." His eyes were moist as he continued talking about his six-year-old daughter, and his unwillingness to leave her mother. "So, I put my passion into the music I play and count down the days till I can be free."

He patted my thigh. "So, how about you? Why do you think true love's been eluding you?" I could feel the heat of his warm hand through the fabric.

"I've put up with too much crap for a little romance," I admitted, "except I don't want to settle for a little, even though I keep doing it. I want the whole shebang, you know? For Zac, too." It felt good to be honest about weaving fantasies about the men in my life, how easily I fell for them.

I changed the subject. "Let's cook! Make something fabulous."

We moved into the kitchen and started dinner. He sautéed chicken and steamed vegetables while I opened another bottle of wine and changed the music. Memories of hanging out in my San Francisco apartment poured in, only now he put his finger to my lips to sample the sauce he made with lemons and cream. My fingertips grazed his arm to reach for the towel. Eros filled the space between us as the pasta bubbled on the stove.

After dinner, we danced to Van Morrison in the dim stove light, our arms entwined around one another, holding on. He kissed me, a slow tentative kiss that sealed the unspoken deal that I would fall in love with him, if only for the night. Maybe he would fall, too.

My moral compass spun wildly as I took off my clothes and joined him in the hot tub under a dark sky. We kissed deeply in the warm swirling water as a steady, cold rain fell on our heads, mingling with the rising steam.

His hands caressed each inch of me he could reach. I couldn't get close enough, as if pulling him inside me would be the key that unlocked the mystery of why love had disappointed me over and over. Because none of them were him.

"Oh boy, I want to—" I whispered, pulling back slightly. "It's just not—" I pulled away completely.

"Shh. I know. I know." He reached to take my hands into his. The rain had stopped. "I can't either."

On the flight home I wrote him a letter in my journal, remembering the night that I didn't want to end. It felt more like a beginning. While the plane glided through the clouds, his band's CD poured into my ears, and I was living inside the songs. *I'll be your lover; I'll be your friend; I'll be your nothing at all...*

Knowing he would never read my words, I let my love spill all over the page while wondering what we would do with all the feelings we had stirred up in one another. Longing made my heart ache. I was certain the cosmos wasn't quite through with us yet. *The magic between us seems to be evaporating already, like the steam that rose off our skin in the rain.*

Mostly, I cried buckets knowing I wouldn't see him again for a very long time.

The day after I got home, Mark sent an email saying he needed to stay away. *Don't contact me. Please. It's too much.* It felt abrupt, yet not surprising, that he would have to pull all the way back. Like ripping off a Band-Aid, he left me with the sting of no say in the matter.

Holding Zac close in the comfort of my daily life was a balm that brought me back to reality, to third-grade homework, and to my boring job. The night with Mark, and my thoughts of what could have been, faded with his silence. By the time the holidays rolled around, I was sailing into another love affair that was over by the following summer.

Like the rest, I had thought perhaps he was The One. Like the rest, he was a distraction from looking within at what I wasn't doing to make myself happy. Like the rest, his love was validation that I was lovable—until he took it away.

$$\bullet \ \bullet \ \bullet$$

For several years, Jimmy had barely paid any attention to his son between their infrequent visits, which had been reduced to every couple of years. We met halfway at a truck stop in Indianapolis to drop Zac back and forth, an awkward exchange with a man who felt like a stranger now. When he came home from these visits, Zac was full of mixed emotions, excited to see his mom but missing his dad after the recent contact.

"I wish we could all live together, Mom," he said as I tucked him back into his own bed. His distress tugged at my heart. As much as I wished his dad would pay more attention to him, when he did, the disappointment later was rough. It was hard to know what to say to him.

"I know, but it's okay. I love you, and Daddy and Sandy love you, too." My son had just met his father's fourth wife. "You had fun there, right? Sandy's nice?" He nodded. "Good. It'll be okay, sweetie."

His hug reminded me how very much I had missed him, and I prayed this time Jim would call more often, while knowing he wouldn't.

In autumn of 2001, three weeks after 9/11, I was laid off from my job. The chance to get off the treadmill of a corporate career I didn't love was liberating once the terror wore off. After succumbing to pressure to get a regular job, to focus on Zac, I had assumed I'd stay in a marketing job forever. After the initial shock, receiving a modest unemployment check gave me a little time to figure out a new game plan.

My mother stood on the sidelines watching the clock.

"You better get a job soon, kid. We can't lose this house," she said, giving voice to her fear.

"I will, Ma. It'll be okay. I just need time to figure out what I want to do. Don't worry. I have a little money saved."

"What's there to figure out? Send out your résumé. You'll find something."

To her, that was the logical choice. Yet the concept of thinking about what I might rather be doing gnawed at me. What would it be like to do meaningful work, to think about what I was good at, and apply myself to it? Giving up the entertainment work I was passionate about had been a trade-off that benefited my family. Sudden unemployment could be a chance to explore other things I might love to do. It felt like a sign there could be a new career out there for me.

Even though I was one of many who lost their jobs after the tragedy of 9/11, my layoff felt shameful. There were lots of us thrown off balance by a sudden loss of security, all vying for mid-level jobs that seemed to be the ones phased out first.

"Oh, you'll find something, honey," Dad said, echoing my mom and offering the same encouragement he always did when I was between jobs. "You're a smart girl."

"But what if I don't want to do just *something*?" My mind flipped through the many heated discussions I'd had with my supervisors in the corporate world. It occurred to me that maybe I could change what I did for a living entirely.

"Well, what would you like to do? As I've always said, it helps if you love your work. It's too bad what you loved to do required so much of your time."

"I know. But I can't go back to that world. At least I have a little time to figure it out."

. . .

My ancient knee-jerk reaction was to call a date who stood me up for a dinner I'd spent the afternoon preparing. This time, when a guy I had gone out with a few times didn't show up, I wrote in my journal about how much of my time I wasted on men.

The events of 9/11 have left us all feeling scared and uncertain, an uneasy feeling I am so well acquainted with I'm not sure if the knot in my chest is from being stood up or the fear of annihilation. How awful it is that they can feel like the same thing. It's fucked up that my date could do this to me, especially since I have the house to myself with Zac at Deena's. The refrigerator hums while I contemplate a car accident or worse, reasons why he couldn't get here. But I know better. He's blowing me off.

I encouraged my frustration to push my anxiety out of the way. *Get mad instead of hurt for a change. Give pride a turn, for God's sake! Why do you stay in this pattern of worry and forgiveness when you know he is just another selfish asshole?*

While contemplating this obvious and painful question about undeserving men taking up my time, my thoughts, and my body, I poured myself a glass of merlot and plunged the VHS of *Someone Like You* into the VCR. Misery loves company.

Later in bed, I wondered what I could have achieved in my life if

I had given over my energy to education or personal growth instead of chasing love, then reached for one of the inspirational books on my nightstand. The books had become a sanctuary of hope, encouraging me to look deeper and stretch further into who I wanted to be. Marianne Williamson looked back at me from the cover of *A Return to Love*. When I opened the book to a random page, the message that caught my eye taunted me: *We receive what we request.*

You get what you ask for. Of course.

I closed the book and picked up *Illusions*, the book Mark and I discussed endlessly during the San Francisco days. Its well-worn familiarity reminded me that our problems often come bearing gifts. The dog-eared pages of this slim volume implored, *What do you really want?*

Really? Anything? To never have to work in an office cubicle again. And True Love without suffering.

That starts with loving yourself, a voice in my head whispered.

Despite my wish to remain free of the dreaded cubicle, on Monday my résumé went out to the few mid-level jobs I could find in the *Tribune* newspaper job section. Most required a degree now that the market was saturated by the unemployed, a degree I didn't have. All week I applied to entry-level jobs which I didn't get because I was overqualified. With savings and unemployment to keep us afloat, it was a secret relief not to get hired, allowing me time to explore writing, and the shiny new information highway that was the Internet.

Seventeen

The stench of stale smoke permeates my father's home, lingering long after his last breath. I sit at his desk where he inhaled thousands of cigarettes in the final years of his life, searching online for God knows what. Between the outlines of where pictures used to hang, nicotine stains drip down the walls as a gooey reminder of the many hours he spent in this chair. A profound sadness comes over me.

While I knew his health had been deteriorating over time, I had no idea that he'd slid into an oblivion that allowed his place to become so gross. It's impossible to believe this was the same man who made me comb the fringe on the Oriental rug.

Flicking on the computer, I wait while the whirring drive spins to life and the desktop fills with files. Dad was meticulous about paperwork, so finding the lease he used for his tenants should be easy. Searching under L for Lease I come up empty handed for a file by that name. I do, however, see a file named Lisa. *I knew it!* Finally, the letter from my father I have been praying he left behind for me.

What began as a fun flirtation with a handsome Canadian man escalated into a full-blown romance when, after a month of email banter on an online dating site, he decided to drive five hundred miles from Toronto to take me to dinner.

All my concerns over what to do next were soothed by this mysterious stranger who wrote thoughtful letters about life and its complexities. Even his name seemed to come straight out of a fairy tale: *Liam Alexander*.

From the moment I saw him sitting at the bar through the frosty windows where we met for dinner, until Zachary was begging him three days later to stay at our house after an evening of bowling, I felt myself falling head over heels for this lovely man who seemed to have come out of nowhere.

"Could you stay here tonight, Liam? Please, Mom? Does he have to go back to the hotel? We have a guest room, you know." My son's eagerness to have a man around squeezed my heart; it had been months since I'd had a boyfriend. If it wasn't a good idea to bring someone new around, you wouldn't know it from my son's reaction. We had included him in most of Liam's visit, with trips to the park and out to eat. They were pals now.

"Sure, buddy, I can do that, if it's okay with your mom." Liam winked in my direction. "Can we make pancakes in the morning?" he said. Zac nodded enthusiastically. *Could it really be this easy?* I wondered. *Probably not. He lives in another country.* Yet I couldn't resist their smiling faces and said yes.

Sneaking into the guest room in the middle of the night, I slipped out of my robe and into bed with Liam, feeling both dangerous and safe. We made love furtively, my head spinning at the audacity of it all. Somehow, in a matter of days, we had hopscotched over all the preliminaries, landing in a comfortable place tinged by magic. He felt like he was mine already—a crazy and ridiculous anomaly, against everything I knew was reasonable. His departure the next day was bittersweet, and we didn't say anything out loud about the future.

"Let me know you got home safe," I said, already counting the ten hours before he would be calling. My face was nestled against his chest, memorizing his scent.

"I will. Be good." He kissed me once more and climbed into his old Buick Regal. I watched him back out of the driveway and felt the familiar nausea of romantic uncertainty.

. . .

The next day, Zac and I went down to Nashville for a few days to spend some time with Karen over spring break. We also planned to stay a night with Jimmy's brother and his wife, Mimi. After her betrayal during the divorce, I chose to find common ground in my son, calling a truce for his sake so he could know his aunt and uncle. I agreed to bring him for a visit while we were down there.

In the warm glow of her country kitchen, I told Mimi all about this man I had just met, and the wonder with which our romance seemed to be blossoming. "Oh, honey," she drawled. "How exciting!" Her eyes were wide with the vicarious thrill of a woman married twenty years to a man she now barely tolerates. "He sounds just wonderful! I hope y'all can make this thing work with living in two different countries and all." Hope seemed too small a word for what that might require.

Time with Karen nourished me. Zac delighted in the nature surrounding her house. Liam sent a short letter asking for patience.

I am away for the next 6 days, and I am not thrilled by this fact. We both have a lot to say to each other. Time will be quick, and we can save our thoughts for just awhile longer and then we can fill in all the blanks. You are someone very special. The world is a nicer place because of smiles like yours. Thinking of you (way too much)

Liam Alexander

Late that night, under a blanket of stars, I wrote a long, dramatic letter to him in my journal, saying everything I didn't dare say out loud, weighing the obstacles against the possibilities taking root in my heart. Karen cautioned me to take it easy as I spun round and round.

"I love being a couple, and I do well on my own, but I just hate being in between. This is definitely in between." She nodded, then reminded me that marriage isn't always so great either, sharing the issues she and her husband were going through.

When Zac and I returned home, a week passed with no word from Liam.

"I'm obsessing over our time together," I told Karen on the phone. "It was so good. I don't want to believe he is just an asshole like most of the guys I've dated."

"Well, sweetie, he could be." She knew better than to tell me anything but the truth. "Look, patience isn't exactly your strong suit. Give him a chance, he'll call."

It must be the distance that has Liam taking a step back. Or maybe that I have a kid. But he's so good with him, I wrote that night, scrawling rationalizations for not hearing from him, forging them like armor against bad news. I ignored the inner whisper of my recovering love junkie who warned me to see the hole before I fell head over heels into it. Since I wasn't working, it was easy to fantasize about frequent visits back and forth across the border, ending with him eventually moving down to the States.

Against my better judgment, I left messages and emails. *I'd like to hear that all is fine and that you have just been occupied so as not to worry.* Then I checked my computer every couple hours for anything from him. All I received after a week was a note that simply said: *Please be patient.* Distraught and a little angry that he left me hanging, I was desperate to hear his voice. *How could he create all this closeness, then disappear?*

He must be married.

Each day I woke up in the T-shirt I shamelessly asked to keep, praying it would be the day he called, then busied myself with Zac and job hunting. That weekend I carried a heavy oak dresser while helping a friend move and saw a Canadian penny on the ground. I almost dropped my end to retrieve it, certain it was a sign that we were Meant to Be, regardless of Liam's silence.

Of course, I knew it was best to hang on to the irritated woman inside me, the one who needed to let the fantasy go and focus on her next career and her son, the one who was learning that depending on another person to define how you feel about yourself is a setup for heartache. But instead, I clung to his request for patience like a life raft, ignoring the books stacked up on my nightstand. My journal filled up with hope for his call, peppered with new pleas to myself to not make a man's love so essential to my well-being, combating the enemy that was my insecurity.

Just when I'd begun to think it was destined to be a brief, meaningful affair, the flowers arrived.

Thank you for waiting. Love, Liam the card read, attached to a fragrant bouquet of lilies and mums tied with a pink ribbon. I immediately called and left an ecstatic message of thanks, my despair draining away.

"He sent flowers!" I gushed to my girlfriend who was over for coffee when they arrived. After the endless days of doubt, waiting for his call, the picture she took of me sitting beside his gift radiated joy.

"I'm sure he'll call tonight," she said before leaving to get her kids, "Let me know what he says."

As I was about to leave to pick up Zac from school, I quickly checked my email, and found the one that would change everything.

Hello Lisa,

I met a pretty face with bright beautiful eyes. Mirror to the soul they say. What harm would there be to tell this lady how she made my heart flicker just looking at her soul? What harm could there be to allow myself to know such a beauty, even if life in all its cruelty has brought her to me at a time when I can't imagine a future?

Now the harm is apparent. She is nicer, prettier, and in all ways better than I thought, and I had high expectations. And she likes me back!

Please know what I want is what's best for you, almost more than what is best for me. I'm not writing to say goodbye. You are all the things you made me think you would be. Even more.

My eyes misted over. *He's married.* I thought. *I knew it.* Another unhappy guy who steps out on his wife with me. Goddamn it.

I wanted to tell you things in person, but I couldn't. I have an illness which will not be going away. I'm alive today, able to laugh, cry, and even fall in love with a beautiful lady from the USA, all the while having cancer.

Cancer. The word slapped my face. *No!*

I like you too much to want you to have anything less than a million years with the guy you love and who loves you back. I like you enough to want to step back and leave you to the best life you can possibly have, even if that life turns out to be one without me at the center.

The thought of him leaving me was nearly as horrible as the thought of him dying.

I've missed you, a lot. Regardless of the news, I know you missed me, too. I'll call tonight.

Liam Alexander

I drove the five blocks to my son's school in a catatonic state. When I arrived, I could hardly walk to the door to get him, and instead sat down on the curb and sobbed until the bell rang. Gathering myself together as the kids came barging out the doors, I waved to Zac as he ran towards me, then hugged him close.

"Are you crying, Mom? What's the matter?" he asked, noticing my eyes were puffy and damp.

"I just got some bad news, sweetie, that's all. But everything will be fine." *If only that could be true.*

My heart broke wide open that day. Liam and I talked for hours through the night, hanging on to every word like life preservers. Mine saving him from death, his saving me from heartache. We made ridiculous promises to each other that felt as natural as breathing. Within a week I was on a plane to Toronto, rushing to his side armed with the love I thought could save him.

The visit was a bittersweet mix of tender moments and uncomfortable silences. On the drive from the airport to his house I tried to be upbeat, the girl he met in Chicago and fell in love with.

"We only have a few days, but I was hoping we could go to Niagara Falls. Maybe check out a few wineries. We go through the wine country to get there, don't we?" My chatter filled the car. He offered a weak smile.

"Sure, sweetheart. Let's see how I feel tomorrow." Now that I knew, his health would dictate most conversations, each outing. He admitted he hadn't worked in months and was collecting disability. That he'd been treated for kidney cancer before the lymphoma showed up. It felt like in our initial visit he may have extended himself a bit further than he was able to maintain in the real world, his world, the one filled with prognosis, CAT scans, and fear.

It seemed impossible to walk away from someone I had grown to care about just because he had cancer, regardless of the newness of our relationship.

The next morning the sky was steel gray, and a cool breeze swept around us as we arrived at Niagara Falls. "You want to go out on the Maid of the Mist?" he asked. "We'll get wet!"

The wind felt like an invitation to an uncomfortable afternoon. "No, that's okay. Let's just take a walk." The grounds were welcoming spring, a carpet of tulips and daffodils taking over the lawns. We walked hand in hand as the thundering sound of the falls reminded me of the power of nature, of things we can't control. On the way home we stopped at one of the tiny wineries that dot the Ontario landscape. As we tasted the best pinot noir I'd ever had, he looked tired and was quiet, as he had been most of the day. My usual cajoling evoked a few laughs, but it wasn't like it had been in Chicago. We made love during the night, and he clung to me like a child when we were spent, our bodies glistening with sweat and desperation. I thought he might weep.

In only a few short days I had to leave for home, my anxiety mounting as we approached the airport. I tried to talk about difficult things.

"Do you think we can we get through this together?" I said, the words heavy in my mouth.

"I don't know." His face was stoic as he looked straight ahead out the windshield.

"Well, no matter what, I'm gonna help you fight this, Liam. I'd rather have ten beautiful years with the right guy than thirty mediocre years with the wrong one."

He took my hand and squeezed it. It felt like I had nothing—and everything—to lose. *But where would we live? I can't move to Canada. I* thought. *And what about Zac—how does this affect him? Of course, this affects him.* I had so many questions that I knew we couldn't answer, so I stayed silent the rest of the drive. When he kissed me goodbye at the customs gate, I knew I had made a promise that would be very hard to keep. Our relationship had the same prognosis the doctors had been giving him about his illness: Watch and wait.

. . .

Returning home reminded me of the priorities in my life and how important it was to stay true to them. My life was taking care of Zachary and finding a job. In the short term, unemployment was keeping me afloat, and I loved how Zac thrived with the extra time with me. We did homework together, played board games, and cooked. We snuggled on the couch and watched *Hercules* dozens of times, learning each line by heart. When a rom-com about a single mom and her son mirrored us so closely, I was delusional enough to believe Liam could be my George Clooney and sweep me and my son off our feet.

Without a job, I was a better mom, more patient and fun. Yet, I needed to work, dreading the thought of going back to the corporate world. I sought out career workshops to help me find a new path, knowing I would die in another cubicle and couldn't return to the grueling hours of the backstage life I loved. All I wanted was to do something meaningful, maybe write, but writing wouldn't pay the bills. If I were to stay out of a corporate office, I needed to figure out a new direction.

Liam continued to be at the forefront of my thoughts. Most of my phone calls were either with him, dreaming of a future we weren't sure was even possible, or talking about him to my girlfriends. In my spare time I searched the internet for a cure for non-Hodgkin's lymphoma.

In late May, I planned another trip up to see him, this time for a week. My mother, who wasn't thrilled about the first visit, was exasperated that I was pursuing this relationship.

"Lis, c'mon. The guy is sick. He has *cancer*," she said it like a death sentence. "But more than that, he lives in another country. How can you think this will work?"

"I just have to try. We have this incredible connection, Ma. I can't explain—"

"You always have a connection! This guy has problems, Lisa. Think about your son, for once." I resented her thinking I never thought of Zac. My devotion to my son's care was a daily responsibility I'd taken seriously for nearly a decade. He loved being with my mother and sister, and would be fine with them, especially since they couldn't get enough of him. I knew I was taking a chance, but I deserved to make decisions for myself, too.

"The doctors say Liam could live for years," I said, angry that she couldn't understand my desire to be a good mother—and to be in love.

"If you don't want to watch Zac, I'll wait till school is out and take him with me." It was a bluff. I had no intention of taking him to Canada yet, but it made my point. She agreed to let me go.

The trip was darker than the first visit. Liam was distant, withdrawing into a depression he no longer felt the need to hide. His irritability over small things put me on eggshells, afraid of upsetting him. In between, his sweet appreciation of my love made up for it.

"You're the best girl," he said. Because I was. Who else would sign up for such a sad beginning? The obstacles we faced crashed into each other with every attempt to piece together a future I could imagine. Rethinking the whole thing made sense, even to me, but how does one rethink love? Considering his health as a reason to walk away felt cruel. As easily as I could lose him to cancer, he could lose me to any number of fate's unfair, untimely events. We are all dying someday. It was unthinkable to lose our love to fear.

My dream was that I would save him, and he would love me forever for it.

"I can't wait to see you, sweetheart. I have an idea for a summer holiday. How about if I buy us a camper? We can have a grand adventure!" It filled me with love to hear joy in his voice.

"A camper? Really?" Being a hotel lover, I would not have picked camping as my first choice.

"Yeah, I found one in your area on eBay. It's old and needs a little TLC, but it has a good engine. I need a project, I think.

We could go to the beaches on the Atlantic if Zac goes to his dad's this summer. I'll fly down so I can drive it back."

I bristled at the mention of my son's dad and the thought of dealing with Jimmy. But it could be fun to camp with Zac on the way to Tennessee.

"Okay! Let's talk about when you get down here. I'll see what Jimmy's plans are for Zac." After several months together, mostly from opposite sides of the border tethered by a phone line, we agreed to surrender to the ambiguity of the future and take things a day at a time. As hard as this was for a planner like me, who hated feeling insecure, it took the pressure off the challenge of how he could move down to the States.

He arrived in the warm sunshine of a June day, bringing gifts for Zac and me. We went to see the camper, an old Toyota chassis under a big box shell that housed a loft bed, a dinette, a tiny kitchen, and a bathroom. He was thrilled, and paid cash for it, rattling on to the seller about the summer holiday he had in mind for us.

When I cautioned him not to get ahead of himself, he objected. "Why can't we plan a trip? I just want time alone with you, baby."

"I know. I haven't reached Jimmy yet, so I left a message with Mimi. Karen would love to have Zac stay with her, but I have to figure it all out." My desire not to upset him made me choose my words carefully. "But I'm sure we can go."

"Zac gets more of your full attention than any child I've ever seen. He'll be fine."

"He's been a trouper while I've spent time up at your place, Liam. I've never been gone from him as much as this year." I hated his little comments about my devotion to my son. In moments when Zac interrupted our conversation, or snuggled beside me on the couch, I caught a whiff of Liam's displeasure.

"Well, it wouldn't kill his father to take some responsibly for his son for a change."

I couldn't argue with him on that.

The next day, we started a remodeling project in my kitchen—to put a door where a window was—and I could tell he was on edge.

"What the fuck are you doing?" he screamed. "I asked for the other screwdriver. Don't you know the difference?" He looked like he hated me.

"Sorry! My mistake." I flinched at his outburst. That morning he had felt new lumps emerging on his abdomen, which was a sign his illness might be progressing. With little patience for his limitations, he had started complaining more about his discomfort. *It's the cancer talking* became an easy excuse for his nastiness.

Yet, between countless hours working on the kitchen door, with him alternating between Jekyll and Hyde, we cheered at Zac's baseball games and took him bowling. We cooked, and laughed, and sat at my mother's kitchen counter where he told funny stories, coaxing her approval with his charm. We made love and plans, scheduling our camping trip for the end of summer, crossing our fingers that Zac would have a visit with his father for his allotted two weeks. By the time Liam left for home, the kitchen project was finished, and he nervously headed north for more scans.

"It'll be okay," I said each night on the phone. Sometimes I almost believed it.

After a few weeks I couldn't stand being apart, wanting to go up there for a month to see him through new tests, and the results from his scans. We hoped the news would be that his disease had not progressed. Since Zac was out of school, my intention was to take him along this time.

"Just let him stay here and go to day camp. How can you drag him up there with all that is going on with Liam? Do you really think that's fair to Zac?" My mother knew that guilt was her most effective weapon.

"I hate to leave him, Ma. He and Liam get along well, and we could have a good time up there, just the three of us. It will be an adventure. Have some fun, be normal."

"Seriously, do you think it will be fun for Zac to deal with tests and doctor appointments? C'mon, nothing about this is normal. Just let him stay here with us and his friends. He'll be fine."

I had never been away from my son for longer than a week, and the thought of a month apart was unsettling. Torn between my devotion to Zachary, and my attachment to the man who now consumed much of my head and heart, I decided it was best for all of us if I went alone. By the end of the month, I would have more answers about our future together.

"I guess you're right. He loves camp. It would free me up to go to Liam's appointments with him. Okay, he can stay here with you."

• • •

Arriving for several weeks at Liam's in Canada felt like moving in. Without my return date looming by week's end, I settled into what life together might look like. His house was a remodeling work-in-progress that had screeched to a halt when he was diagnosed, along with his relationship with his girlfriend, who had bailed on him when he got sick. He talked about her a lot. Each time he did I cringed, trying to ignore it as a touchstone to his life before cancer. Before me.

When I arrived, he was moving slowly as he carried my suitcase up the large plank ladder that stood where a new staircase would eventually be. I pulled together a meal from what I found in the fridge, and we settled in for the evening. In the morning we had the first of several appointments at the Sunnybrook Health Centre, this time to see his psychotherapist.

All the horror stories of substandard medical care in Canada were dispelled when we arrived at the glass state-of-the-art facility and headed to room 230. I held Liam's hand as we sat in mint green faux leather chairs, trying to pretend we were there for strep throat or a knee injury. The dozens of cancer pamphlets screamed at me that this serious illness was now a part of my life, too. In a few minutes they called his name, and we followed the nurse to the doctor's office.

"Hi, I'm Dr. Bryant. But please call me Dean," said a bald man with a pleasant voice who extended his hand to me. "You must be Lisa. Liam has shared a lot about you."

"How are you doing, Liam?" he said as we sat down across from him.

"I'm okay. Better." He took my hand and smiled. "Being with Lisa makes me feel better."

Liam talked about his depression since the diagnosis. How he felt suicidal after Veronica walked out on him. "I thought my life was over." He smiled in my direction. "Then I met Lisa."

A warm feeling swept through me—*I am saving his life*—followed immediately by a gnawing sense of dread. *What a big job.*

They talked about his meds, anti-depressants, and sleeping pills, and how they were helping. Dean shared how concerned he was that Liam keep a positive attitude, then turned to me.

"Now that Liam has shared his diagnosis with you, how do you feel, Lisa? The fact that you are here says a lot." I took Liam's hand.

"I just want him to stay well. He says there is a chance he can be healthy for a long time. They could find a cure by then." It was the prayer that we had been sharing. The fear that he could die in a couple of years, I kept to myself. "What about clinical trials in the States? I've been reading—"

"Well, be careful about what you read on the internet. Some of the information is not applicable or the trials are well underway. Being Canadian, his chances of getting in are slim to none. I'm sorry, but I find it best to tell the truth. At this point, watch and wait is the best protocol we can offer."

Liam looked at the floor, withdrawing. I wondered what the laws were in the U.S. for fiancé visas. Dean picked up on my desperation.

"You two are at the early stages of your relationship. This illness is just a part of that. I suggest you take your time to get to know each other. Spend time away from cancer. Go on dates. Have fun."

Liam offered a weak smile. "That's a good idea."

Like a dog whistle I could hear Dean's veiled warning that I was taking on too much, jumping in with both feet with this man I had known for less than six months. *We're only dating.* I told myself. *He's right, I don't have to save him.* But if I didn't, I could lose him in the very worst way.

The scans showed his disease had progressed slightly, though not enough for treatment. More watching and waiting. The month together flew by, alternating between seeing his friends, having dinners, and doctor appointments. We felt like a normal couple, except when we were poring over his scans and internet articles on lymphoma. His occasional outbursts of anger flared up like ignited newsprint that quickly turns to ash. They became another symptom I got used to, like his fatigue and nausea.

It felt good when I got back home to my life with Zac.

• • •

"I'll be down next week and Moby will be ready," Liam said, referring to the old Toyota camper. He had worked tirelessly on it to prepare for our summer trip by replacing each rusted screw that held it together and installing a new fridge. The getaway meant so much to him, as if it would be his last holiday. I was glad for a getaway together, too. Over a month had passed since my trip up north, which had been colored heavily by Liam's condition.

I prayed for a light-hearted visit, without either of my loves being jealous of the other. As the summer was coming to a close, I just wanted to have some fun.

Eighteen

Once I open the Lisa file, a quote from Shakespeare in italics fills the top of the screen.

How sharper than the serpent's tooth it is to have a thankless child. . .

My eyes flood as I keep reading. It is devastating in its meanness; Dad going on and on. *You don't like us very much, and I suppose we don't really like you either.*

"You fucking asshole," I say aloud, hoping he can hear me in the ether. "All the years I tried so hard to love you!" My voice grows shrill as it echoes through the empty house. "You wanted me to be some perfect little daughter who never called you on your shit. Well, guess what? I'm not fucking perfect! Neither were you!" I slump back in his chair, sobbing. Anger and pain and grief and shame coarse through me while I grasp for the truth between his words and my memory. "I loved you so goddamn much, and you didn't even like me."

The letter appears to have been written several years ago. Wracking my brain, I deduce it was shortly after an argument we had about Easter dinner in which I yelled at him for always sending an invitation to us through my mother, one of those patronizing things he did that pissed me off. One of those things I made a big deal over because it wasn't about the invitation; it was about not being special enough to receive a direct call from him. Clearly his letter is about more than that, too. He has poured years of disappointment in me onto one single page, each word throbbing with disdain.

Stunned, I look around for a flash drive so I can save it but can't find one. It feels important for me to keep the words he didn't mean enough to send, words that at the time may have been a little true; words that had been forgotten by the time we truly accepted each other. And then he died.

The temperature was near one hundred degrees when Liam pulled the camper out of my driveway. We were headed south for a night of camping with Zac before dropping him with Karen for a visit in the country. Jimmy had not agreed to visitation with his son since he and his wife were actually living in a camper on his brother's mobile home lot, according to Mimi.

"Mom, why isn't there any air *conditioning*? It's so *hot*," Zac whined a few minutes into our four-hour drive.

"Because the camper is old and there isn't any. I'm sorry, honey. Sit next to the fan by the window and let's play a game. You'll be fine. C'mon." I shot him a glance that said *please, don't complain.*

"There was no air conditioning when your mom and I were children, and we lived through it," Liam said from the driver's seat, not hiding his annoyance. "You kids think everything has to be comfortable all the time." Zac rolled his eyes. Tension and humidity hung around us like a heavy, damp blanket. Liam often accused me of spoiling Zac when I put his needs in front of ours. This, like so many things, made him angry. Staying quiet was my best defense.

Once at the campground, we settled in. Liam insisted we take a walk, an unpleasant trek that had both my son and me nearly in tears. He hated the heat; I hated him moaning about it. Dinner was a tense negotiation, with Liam berating me for no reason. As night fell, Zac and I made a fire while Liam went to bed early.

"Mom, Liam's mean sometimes. Not to me so much, but to you."

His face glowed in the firelight, more mature than the cherub he had been when he was small. He would be ten years old in a couple of weeks, not a little boy anymore. A decade of my life had been spent being his mother, and I could barely remember when he wasn't at the center of it.

The teeter-totter of being a mother and being a woman had been a constant series of ups and downs. Turning my attention from either one for more than a short time made me feel awful. While the little man of my dreams filled my heart with sweet adoration and love, the grown-up woman in me still wanted a lover, a partner. Someone who cherished me like Jimmy, had the spiritual chemistry I shared with Mark, and who would be a good dad to Zac. *Blender man*, I called this phantom who lived only in my imagination. At the core, my series of romantic pursuits all aimed at one thing: for me to love and be loved without conditions.

It seemed every relationship I'd had with a man had been on his terms. Blaming Liam's unkind behavior on his illness was simpler than admitting he was selfish, which made it easier to allow his mistreatment. Especially since it wasn't constant. We believe what we want to believe when we're in the misty dawn of new romance.

The long stuffy drive had brought out the crabbiness in all of us. Liam wasn't abusive to my son; he just wasn't as indulgent as he'd been during the first few visits. It was clear they both liked having me to themselves.

"I know Liam gets upset, sweetie. I'm not sure he realizes it. You're not afraid of him, are you?" He shook his head, absentmindedly stroking my arm the way he always did when he was tired.

"No, I just hate when he talks mean. The rest of the time he's pretty nice, I guess. He's really funny." *I hate it, too.* I thought. *But I'm not ready to tell you he's sick, and it's mostly the cancer talking when he's mean.*

"I don't like when he talks mean, either. He's just tired. Let's hope he'll be in a better mood tomorrow, okay? We'll be to Aunt Karen's before you know it."

He nodded as I scooped him up in a hug, inhaling his familiar scent mixed with campfire and sweat. "I'm sure gonna miss you, Zacman. But you'll have so much fun there. We'll talk every day."

His wide smile set the world right again.

"Let's go to bed, okay? So we can wake up and go see Aunt Karen and her kitties. Fill our cups with water so we can douse the fire." He nodded and helped me clean up. A cool breeze finally filled the camper as he settled into his bunk.

"Sleep fast! Love you, sweetie." I kissed his warm cheek.

"Love you, Mom." He smiled and closed his sleepy eyes.

I crawled up into the bed above the cab, hoping not to wake Liam. Lying there for a long time, listening as my son's breathing settled deeper into sleep, I prayed this trip would be good for both of us.

By noon the next day, hugs and itineraries were exchanged with my best friend before Liam and I left for our two-week beach adventure. Just knowing Zac was safe and happy, I could breathe easy.

· · ·

"Left, right, or forward?" Liam asked as I navigated a map with a flashlight. We had just spent a couple of peaceful days in Chattanooga, camping beside a lake where Liam paddled around in his blowup boat while I sat in the sun, reading. For a while it felt like we were just a normal couple on vacation. Now we were outside Charleston, South Carolina, looking for the KOA Holiday campground, and Mr. Hyde was behind the wheel.

"Well, it looks like we take 4 East, then 24 East—" Panic clenched my stomach as I scanned the map trying to get my bearings.

"Left, right, or forward?" he screamed, gripping the steering wheel with force.

"I think—" For the first time, I was afraid of him.

"Left! Right! Forward! Pick one."

I blinked back tears, losing my place on the map.

"Right." *Please be right,* I thought. "Turn right, up ahead." *He's tired. It's the cancer talking,* I told myself. Luckily, after the turn, a sign for 24E appeared like a gift from the gods.

I reminded myself that much of the time he was loving and funny, generous with his affection. We had lunch in quaint rural towns, played in the surf at seaside enclaves. While exploring the history and beauty of Charleston, I absorbed as much joy as I could, praying for no more tirades.

About a week into our trip, I got a call that my grandmother Haute, Dad's mom, had passed away. It was just shy of her ninetieth birthday, and as sad as it was to hear the news, she had been slowly deteriorating for quite some time. Liam and I had gone to see her at the nursing home just before we left, when a small voice told me she may not make it until I returned home. I wasn't as close to her as I was to Gram, yet I was happy I had seen her to say goodbye.

"She didn't want a funeral, so we will just have a luncheon on Friday for her, at Tom's Steakhouse," Dad said.

"That's only a couple days from now, and Zac's in Tennessee." I carefully weighed the consequences of cutting this trip short for Liam against disappointing my father. The fear of the hell I would go through by upsetting Liam pulsed in my head. "I'm sorry, Dad. I'd like to be there, but I don't think we can get back in time." Getting on a plane had occurred to me. *What if he offers to fly me home?* But he didn't.

"Well," he said, his voice dripping with disapproval, "okay, then." Clearly, he thought I should drop everything and be there for him.

The memory of being pregnant and scared in the hospital flashed through my mind. Maybe deep down this was a way for me to hurt him back, even if I didn't do it intentionally. Being there to honor my grandmother was a given had I been home. But I wasn't. I was far away with a volatile man who believed his death was coming, too.

"I'll call you when we get back, Dad. I'm sorry."

. . .

We settled in at a campsite on Hunting Island, South Carolina, where we had the beach to ourselves. For a couple of days we took long walks along the shore where we shared stories of our grandparents and our childhood. One day, we were treated to the wonder of seeing loggerhead turtle babies hatch, and on tiny flippers scurry into the sea. In pictures we took of each other, our smiles are bright.

Then, like thunderhead clouds gathering moisture, the darkness returned. One night he accused me of cramming too much into the shallow cupboards that lined the upper interior of the camper.

"You're so stupid!" he said, throwing things in fistfuls out the door onto the dusty ground. His harsh words pelted me again and again, as I shut down, cowered, and remained silent, waiting for the storm to pass. When it did, he overly indulged me with kisses and caresses, like a reward for taking his abuse. Accepting his care as a sign of remorse, I prayed for sunny skies.

Like a frog in hot water, I had become numb to his cruelty, detaching it from him and assigning it to his cancer, as if without it he would be nothing but kind. Whatever ground I had gained before we met in learning who I was without a man was lost as I grew further from myself than I had ever been.

. . .

"I'm having a blast, Mom," Zac said at the start of the second week. Cell phone service was spotty on the island, yet I spoke with him every day, sometimes twice. "And I'm going to see Daddy!"

Mimi called at the end of the first week to say she had convinced Jimmy to spend time with his son. Even though it cut his visit with Karen short, it was good for him to see his father.

"That's great, sweetie. I miss you so much, but I'll see you soon. Have fun and I'll call tomorrow."

"Okay. Love you, Mom.

"Love you more."

A few days before we were to head back to Tennessee, Mimi called. "Jimmy says he needs y'all to come get Zac early. He can't keep him for the weekend." Her tone was snippy.

"I'll be there on Monday night, like we planned. Tell Jimmy he needs to figure it out or I'll just have Karen come pick him up. I've taken care of him practically 24/7 since the day he was born, Mimi. If Jim doesn't like it, he can call me." The current tension between me and Liam fueled my outrage.

"Jimmy doesn't want to speak with you. I'll call you back." She hung up without saying goodbye.

As careful as I was to shield him from it, Liam was unnerved by this conversation.

"It's his kid, too! We're not going to cut our trip short for that asshole."

Worry of upsetting him swelled in my chest. "Karen would love to have him for the weekend. I'll take care of it."

A few hours later, my phone rang again.

"Lisa, I don't want you to worry, everything is going to be okay." *Uh oh.* "But you need to know that Jimmy is not going to give Zac back to you right now." Fear gripped me tight when I heard the tone in Mimi's voice become even sharper than before.

What? The sky and the sea and the ground all started swirling together in a blur.

"What are you talking about?" I said, trying to be calm. "You just said he couldn't keep him for three days. I don't understand."

"Well, he's worried that you'll take his boy up to Canada and he'll never see him again. And frankly, how do y'all even think you could have a life together with this child?" My knees buckled. "My God, all you did was talk about this man when you were here. Your son should come first."

Shock and horror blinded me. *She betrayed me again.* I felt sick with the stupidity of trusting her after she the way had checked up on me when Jim and I were divorcing. Of course, she couldn't be trusted. What a fool I was to think otherwise.

"I'm coming to get Zac right now." *I don't give a shit if Liam gets mad.* "I'll be there by tomorrow morning. Tell Jimmy to have—"

"You can't do that. Jimmy's not gonna give him to you, Lisa. He has rights under the law." *You bitch, my son belongs with me!* Panic seized me. *She has the power. Be cool. Be cool. Be cool.* The mantra roared through my head while I tried to get a breath.

"I will get on a plane and be there in a few hours." Feeling like I might throw up, my mind raced with the logistics. *What is the closest airport to here?*

"No. I'm sorry. You need to just calm down. Call your family and talk to them. They will explain it all to you."

"What?" *What did they have to do with this?* "My family?"

"They care about that boy, and you best talk to them about the deal Jimmy made with 'em when you wouldn't come get your son." She hung up.

Through gulping sobs, I dialed my mother. Liam stood by watching, furious.

"Ma, what the hell is going on? Mimi called and said Jimmy has Zac." I couldn't breathe.

"Jimmy called me very upset this morning. He said you wouldn't come and get Zac, so he doesn't want to give him back to you! Why wouldn't you go get your son?"

"Ma! I was getting him on Monday. Why didn't you call me? Jimmy can't do that!" Instantly on the defensive, they all acted as if I was abandoning my child. "First Jimmy wouldn't even see him, now he wants to keep him? He's crazy, Ma!" This was about Jimmy punishing me for sticking to my guns.

"Jim has decided that he will only give him back to your sister, and she is flying down there to get him tomorrow." There was a long pause. When she spoke again, her tone was more incriminating. "What were you thinking not going to get him when they told you to? Now Jim wants custody. He will only send Zac back by giving temporary custody to me."

"WHAT?! Custody? You're all going along with him behind my back?" *The man who has had practically nothing to do with his son wants custody?* Panic rose like bile in my throat. "It's inconvenient that I couldn't pick up Zac *early*, and he could have gone to Karen's where he was going to *begin* with, but instead Jimmy wants to fucking *keep* him? He refused to even take him for his visitation when I asked him to!" Rage and fear swallowed all the oxygen inside me. *Is this all my fault?* "I'm going to get Zac now. He's MY son! How could you all make these plans without talking to me?" My stomach retched. "Why the hell didn't you call me sooner, Ma?"

"Because I was afraid you would react like this."

Nineteen

My sister and I sit at my mother's table while Deena doles out five of Dad's watches with the efficiency of an auctioneer. "These are the ones you picked," she says, marking them off the list of dozens in his inventory. I was fourth in line to choose. "You get one of his rings, too." She opens a small box containing several pieces of jewelry. My father's familiar pinkie ring isn't in the box.

It's uncomfortable sitting with Deena, each of us on alert for the other's ire. I slide a gold ring with a rectangular diamond from a tiny Tiffany bag. "I'll take this one," I say, noticing there is a tiny chip in one corner of the diamond. "I don't remember him wearing it, though."

"Me neither. But that's fine." She starts packing up her things. Her stony silence hurts me.

"I know you have a lot of responsibility, Deen. I'm happy to help." It is still excruciating not to share the loss of my dad with my only sibling.

"Thanks, I know." She keeps her eyes averted. "I really appreciate that you're taking care of renting the apartment." A crack of light shoots through the wall she has erected between us, a fortress that isn't meant to hurt me, just protect herself from me and my big feelings. *I hate this, Deena. We're sisters. Our dad died! We should be crying together or something.* I don't say the words out loud. Instead, I tell her about the letter.

"There's a letter on Dad's computer called Lisa I found while looking for the lease. I'd like you to print it before you get rid of his computer."

She glances over for a second, furrows her brow. "Why would you want to keep that?" It's obvious she's read it, which surprises me. "Don't you think if he had wanted you to read it, he would have sent it to you?"

"I want it because he wrote it to me." Dust motes dance above the basket of artificial fruit in the middle of the table. I look right at my sister. "Do you know how hard all this is for me, Deena?" It's hard for her, too, I know. Maybe harder.

"I'm sure it is," she says without looking up. Her grief radiates off her like steam, mingling with something like impatience.

I stand up and give her a hug. "Thanks for that, Deen."

The entire 550-mile drive to Nashville, I thought I might throw up. Liam took a hard stance against everyone, especially me.

"It's your fault for letting your family be so involved in your life. Why would you even tell that bitch Mimi anything about us? You're an idiot." He went on and on that it was my fault for not having control over everyone and everything. I didn't fight back. I didn't say a word. *Please let me find my son. Please,* I silently begged. All the way to Tennessee.

When we arrived in the morning, we went straight to the police station near Mimi's. I didn't know where else to go since Jimmy didn't have an address. The police were understanding and called her house to see what was going on. She came down to the station, and from separate rooms we told our sides of the story.

"Your son's father has visitation rights so we can't just take him away," the officer said when he returned from fifteen long minutes in a room with Mimi.

"Please tell me where my son is right now, and I'll go get him. Please." That they didn't know exactly where my son was made me sicker. *Why couldn't Jimmy have spent his two weeks visitation with Zac, like I asked in the beginning? Now I look like a delinquent mother.* The thought that I had caused all this—that I was the bad parent— seemed unfair, considering how much of my life was devoted to my child.

"Apparently, he is at a motel, ma'am." *A motel?* I pictured my sweet son in a seedy Motel 6, confused and scared. The horror of it all made me dizzy.

"He's got him holed up in a motel? That's because he and his wife live in a camper!" *Like lowlifes.* "What motel? Please, I've got to find my son!"

"There are no laws forcing him to disclose where he is, ma'am. There was a restraining order filed against you at the courthouse. I suggest you go talk to them."

Guilt rose up in my throat. *Restraining order? How could I let this happen? What did I do that was so wrong?* All I wanted was a vacation with my boyfriend.

My hands shook as I stood in the courthouse holding the papers containing lie upon lie. According to Jimmy, I was a drug-addicted, negligent, reckless slut who was wanted for a DUI. None of it was true. Without legitimate cause, he concocted incriminating lies.

"These are all lies, Your Honor! I have never performed a field sobriety test. Never! And certainly not while driving with Zac." The words blurred before me. "I did not traverse the United States for six weeks with an unidentified male companion, and I do not do drugs. Please believe me. I take good care of my son without any help from his father!" My pleas to the judge bordered on hysteria. Stating that all these allegations were untrue didn't satisfy her.

"Your ex-husband has stated he will relinquish your son to your mother, and that your sister is allowed to transport him back to Illinois. I suggest when you get home you get yourself a lawyer."

The knowledge that my son would soon be on a plane with my sister without my knowledge or consent twisted inside me like barbed wire. As grateful as I was that Zac was headed home, I was seething at the betrayal of my family going behind my back. All I wanted was to wrap my arms around my son and take him home myself.

Liam's punishment added to my agony. He went on and on about how much control they had over me until he abruptly pulled to the side of the road. We were on our way to Karen's to pick up some of Zac's things on our way out of town.

"Get out!" he yelled, "Call Karen and let her deal with this bullshit. I'll drop your stuff in Chicago." Shocked, I sat on a park bench and dialed her number, sobbing into the phone to please come get me. Moments later he came back to retrieve me. I hesitated before getting back in the camper.

"I just can't take this, Lisa! I'm sick. This is not good for my health to have all this drama, and it's your fault. But I will take you back to Chicago."

Quietly crying in the passenger seat, I struggled to understand how my life had unraveled so completely. When we arrived at Karen's, I went in to get Zac's things while Liam stayed in the camper. When she and I came out of the house, he was gone again, my duffel bag and purse sitting on her driveway.

"Oh, my God! How could he—" I burst into tears and sat down on the smoldering asphalt.

"Lis, it'll be okay. Let's just try to get you a flight home." I couldn't move. *I hate him. I hate them all.*

Before she could get me up off the driveway, Liam pulled back up. My instinct was to tell him to go straight to hell. All the apologies in the world couldn't make up for leaving me behind, twice. But I went with him, thinking it was the fastest way to get to my son. I went with him because it felt like the only choice I had right then. I went with him and silently prayed for the whole seven-hour drive that my boy would forgive me for what he went through.

"I'm fine, Mom. Daddy was afraid you want us to move to Canada, but I kept telling him you don't." We were putting clothes away in Zac's room after washing his suitcase full of dirty laundry.

"That's right. We're not moving anywhere. Anything else you want to tell me?" Of course they had grilled him, so I was cautious to keep the conversation simple. God knows what Jimmy said about staying quiet.

He shrugged his narrow shoulders. "They kept asking me, 'Don't you remember the time you got pulled over by the police while your mom was driving?' I told them I don't remember that ever happening."

"That's because it never did, sweetie." I seethed with fury at Jimmy for planting seeds against me in my child's head, yet I didn't let Zac see it.

"I knew it didn't happen. They asked a bunch of other stuff, but I can't remember." His sweet face smiled up at me, melting my heart. *Thank God you're home.* "Then DeeDee came to get me so I didn't have to ride in the hot camper." He seemed okay, happily changing the subject to his upcoming birthday party, but I suspected some of his innocence had been left behind at his father's in Tennessee.

Pictures from that party show us all smiling and sun-kissed, but threaded underneath was a dark ribbon of resentment at Liam and my family, at everyone except my sweet birthday boy. Focusing all my attention on him was all I could do.

Even though I knew I had to let Liam go, abandoning someone with cancer still felt impossible. His pleas and apologies once we got home supported my belief that it was his illness that spewed ugly words from his mouth, not him. Overcome by an obligation to see him through it, I caved.

"Baby, I just felt sick, and I couldn't take listening to you beg them anymore. You know I wouldn't have left you. I love you." His teary eyes sucked me in, challenging me to think of how I would feel facing his illness alone. His beautiful words of love acted as a counterweight to the ugliness. *To have met you is the luckiest thing that has happened in my whole life,* he said in a note left behind when he went home. *To die now is not going to be as hard after knowing you.* It was a sick and twisted dance I begged myself to stop. Breaking up with him felt cruel, but I vowed to take a step back, to focus on life with my son and starting a new job. No more trips to Canada for me.

• • •

"Petition to Change Custody" was boldly printed across the top of a document that arrived a week later. It contained the same lies about me and my character that Jimmy had made up to share with the judge. It didn't mention that Zachary's father went months without speaking to his son, and the thousands of dollars he was behind on child support.

Scouring the papers for proof that maybe I really was a horrible mother, I found no truth in his allegations, but the accusations alone made me feel sick with remorse. My poor judgment had landed me here, and I was being punished for a selfish desire to put my own happiness first, even for a couple of weeks. It carried a hefty cost.

"Jim's claims aren't true! He makes it sound like I'm a strung-out slut who put my child in danger. A DUI? Never. It's lies," I cried on the phone to the lawyer I hired in Tennessee, a compassionate woman who did her best to calm me down. "I've taken good care of my son every day of his life, while his father has gone years without seeing him! How can he do this?"

"I'm sorry, but unfortunately the judge took him at his word. He will have to prove you had a DUI, which he can't. And he must pay the outstanding child support to proceed, so that should help with the legal fees. I can't imagine the judge will give him custody." She was kind and patient, and most importantly, she believed me. "We have a good case."

I typed up pages and pages of my response to the petition, telling my side of the story as honestly as I could, pleading for my son to stay with me. Dad wrote a check for the lawyer's retainer, an unexpected act of solidarity I sorely needed and appreciated greatly.

. . .

My personal growth books became my respite. Poring over them late at night became my ritual, as I grew ever more grateful for their lessons. Every single choice I had made led me to my current situation, and I reflected on how putting my own needs first, even for a time, had been calamitous. *How much are we supposed to give away to other people before we start losing ourselves?* It was comforting to know I had control of my next choice, and the one after that. I vowed to stay mindful of every choice I made.

When the authors I loved came to town, I went to their lectures at libraries and bookstores. I attended events with lesser-known local authors, including a couple of life coaches who had written a book about boundaries.

"As children, our parents keep secrets from us in order to protect us, sometimes telling white lies," the blonde woman said, her sturdy frame perched on a stool next to her husband's. He nodded, smiled, and continued, talking about the confusion that is created between how we feel about an experience and what we're told to feel. Like when you skin your knee and Mom says, "Oh, it's fine." Maybe it didn't feel so fine to you, but it's Mom so you believe her.

"A struggle begins between being vulnerable and letting others tell us how we should feel. This can lead to not trusting our own feelings, causing us to look to others for validation and approval."

It was as if a light bulb went off, illuminating how little I trusted my own feelings. With men, with Dad, with my mother. I fidgeted in my chair, glancing around as if others could see it.

"Often, while you're looking for other people to validate and approve of you, they are looking to you for the same validation and approval. This is a vicious cycle."

His words sounded like gospel truth as he offered the only solution: self-validation. He said that only by taking a hard, honest look at who you are and how you have processed what's happened to you can you begin to develop the self-esteem that leads to good boundaries.

All the tumblers in my mind clicked into place, unlocking the reality that my boundaries were miserable if I had any at all.

The coaches' words wouldn't let me go as my calls with Liam became less frequent. It had grown easier to be apart since I no longer yearned for a future. When we did talk, I was aware of being honest about my feelings instead of calibrating to his mood.

"My chiropractor hired me to do marketing, so I have something for now. It feels good to get back to work. But I'm not sure what I really want to do. I know it's not this."

"You can do anything, my love. I can't wait to see you." He wanted to visit for Christmas. Over the past several months his sweet demeanor had softened the sharp edges of the summer, so I agreed, knowing deep down it had to completely end between us.

The holiday itself was pleasant enough, with the usual suspects gathering at our house for Christmas Eve: Mom, Dad, my sister and Shannon, Zac, Liam, and me. Most of my attention was on preparations, and my son's excitement over opening presents. Mom and Deena were complicit in acting like things were fine, and Liam seemed to be on his best behavior.

"So, tell me about the early days in IT, Don. Lisa tells me you were a pioneer," he said, pulling up a chair in the corner of the living room where my father was sitting. Dad launched in, regaling him with his years at Honeywell in the sixties. Liam was a rapt audience.

"How about the computer world in Canada? Has that always been your interest? You have some pretty good remodeling skills looking at what you've done around here." Dad caught my eye and smiled. *He likes him.*

I smiled back, watching them sit side by side swapping stories, like bookends, their similarities so striking. *They're so alike.* Both wickedly smart computer programmers, they also loved home remodeling. Each had suffered a harsh diagnosis as a vibrant man in his prime, and it was clear their own well-being was of utmost importance to them. They both thrived on being the center of a conversation, yet their self-absorption could be excused because they were so interesting. Blessed with good looks that had opened more than a few doors for them, they each had a charming personality that loved to tease. Especially me.

Dad laughed heartily at something Liam said. Despite all the complications and drama this man brought to my life, it was clear my father enjoyed being with him. It was like looking into a mirror. *Like Narcissus.* The charm and abuse cycle of narcissism was a new concept I had begun reading about, yet I resisted labeling them emotionally abusive no matter how many of the tell-tale signs I could attribute to them both.

The way narcissists manipulate you by giving and withdrawing their love at will was what I knew most. Being ignored by these men made me feel so anxious because it was a cruel rejection meant to invalidate me. But on that Christmas morning, I didn't want to believe any of that. I just wanted to enjoy a moment of feeling loved by both of them.

With the custody case still ongoing, I was nervous to send Zac down to visit his father for a week after Christmas, but I didn't have a choice. The lawyer assured me Jimmy had to play by the rules, and Zac would be home before school resumed in January. While he was gone, Liam and I planned to work on a remodeling project to open up a wall in the upstairs hallway. It was a good distraction. At first, he was sweet and cooperative. *He's changed*, I thought, my guard down in the light of his kindness. But within a few days his rage returned like a bad dream.

"That won't work, you moron!" he shouted, pulling a plunger from my hand and throwing it against the wall. "You can be so fucking stupid. You're a fucking idiot." His words hit me like scalding water, but it was his face, contorted with disgust, that sent me over the edge.

"Fuck you!" I screamed at the top of my lungs. "I am not fucking stupid. You're a fucking asshole." My words shook me awake. It didn't matter that he had cancer. He had become the cancer, and it was killing me. "I'm done with this, with you. We're done."

Without another word he slammed his things into his bag and stormed out at two o'clock in the morning, driving off to Canada in the snow.

• • •

"I'm so sorry, baby," he said on the phone the next day when he got home. "I just reacted badly to you yelling at me. You've never done that before. I didn't like it." He sounded contrite, as he always did after his explosions.

"Yeah, well, I don't like how you treat me, Liam. Your outbursts are more than I can take. I thought it was the cancer talking, but it's you. It's you talking. This really is over. I gotta go." I stopped taking his calls.

He sent long, condemning emails about our summer trip, and how my family and Zac had ruined it. Just the thought of the entire debacle brought on nightmares that someone was trying to take Zac. Each time I tried to scream to Karen to grab him, nothing came out. When I woke up with a paralyzed jolt, it became clear the dreams were about how my voice had been silenced, and how that had compromised my son. I vowed not to let it happen again.

As a further reminder of that summer, the custody case ran in the background of the new year like a computer virus. For months I received emails from my lawyer, orders to Show Cause, and a huge stack of legal bills.

My books brought me solace. Fear of losing my son had awakened me to all the ways I had been unconscious about some of my decisions, and the ripple effect they'd created. *The drama of Liam fed the part of me that wanted to be in love like in a movie,* I wrote in my journal, admitting my impulsiveness in romance was selfish sometimes. But being selfish doesn't mean we can't still be responsible people, while caring for our own needs. *Like with Dad. He's selfish but he often means well. It surprises me how good we get along when I let it be all about him. He was thrilled to tell me all about his new profile on Match.com the other day.*

I read *The Four Agreements* and found comfort in learning my best today may not be my best tomorrow; striving for our best is the point. I learned that taking things personally and making assumptions was exactly what I did with my family, and as a result I was often defensive. Most of all, to be impeccable with my word meant I would keep telling the truth.

. . .

"Mom, I'm going to play soccer at Miguel's, okay? Oh, my God! What's all this mess?" Zac's voice broke my reverie, and I looked up to see his silhouette filling the doorway, golden sunlight pouring through the space around him.

"I'm cleaning my office. Did you clean your room?" He stared at me blankly, silent. This meant no. "I want it clean by the end of the weekend. Please be back by dinner and be careful." He dashed off as I added quietly, "Have fun."

I sound like my mother, I thought, as I sifted through old files and drawers of assorted office paraphernalia, filling a garbage bag with what I could let go of. *Mothers.*

It seemed like yesterday when my son took his first unsteady steps toward me, his chubby legs carrying him precariously, arms outstretched, reaching for Mommy. He was certain I would catch him if he fell. In a flash, it seemed, he was sprinting away from me in grocery stores and parking lots, then walking off to school and out into the world, eventually running full tilt away from me at every turn.

Be careful, my mother said to me each time I walked out the door. Like her, I've prayed for my child's health and safety, especially as he was on the brink of becoming a teenager. Once upon a time, a soothing lullaby came out of my mouth, now it was a shrill demand to clean his room, do his homework, pick up his mess. *Be careful,* I thought, *don't run him off too far.*

I dug through my mess to uncover an empty journal and opened it to a blank page. *I'm so hard on my mom sometimes. She treats me like a rebellious teenager. Well, maybe I am. With her, anyway.*

Ending my relationship with Liam had garnered me favor with my mother. Choosing to put the past behind us, the wound from my family's lack of faith in me slowly began to scar over, leaving a jagged reminder that I had fucked up by letting fear of my emotionally unstable boyfriend dictate my actions. My anger at them was partly at myself for letting Liam's illness nudge itself to the front of the line of my concerns that summer. While I always knew that my mother and sister just wanted to get Zac home to Illinois, it was their distrust that wounded me so deeply, creating a rage that blinded me to my own culpability. Of course, going back early to get my son was the right thing to do given the unpredictability of his father's family. I never dreamed demanding Jimmy step up to a few more days of parenting would backfire so spectacularly, yet I could have bet that Mimi was capable of betraying me again. When it came to my own family, the choices I made led to my every move being filtered through a lens of irresponsible parenting. It didn't matter if it was fair or not.

Taking responsibility for my choices didn't mean Mom and Deena would understand the betrayal I felt for their action behind my back. They didn't see how their lack of trust created a loop in my head that made me constantly defensive: Did they take over because I was a bad mom, or did I feel like a bad mom because they took over?

"The case has been dismissed," my attorney said when the court ruled in my favor weeks later. "They didn't have a case. Zachary will remain with you."

My knees buckled with relief. "Where he belongs. Thank you so much, Leann. I am so grateful." Tears of relief and gratitude filled my eyes as I dialed my father, to thank him.

"We won the case, Dad! I couldn't have done it without your help. Thank you." It was clear to me that his financial help with the legal bills had been an act of love to his entire family.

"It was worth it, honey. Zachary belongs with you. And your mother would be so upset if he had to go to Tennessee. I felt fairly certain the judge wouldn't give him to Jim."

"Me, too. But it sure feels good to be sure."

"It sure does. That vacation with Liam cost more than you bargained for, didn't it? Especially since it didn't work out between you two."

"Yeah, it did. Things worked out how they were supposed to." The weight of my relief felt exhausting, so I thanked him again and promised to talk again soon.

When we hung up, I thought about the cost of things, not just financially, but emotionally and mentally, and the family currency I had squandered because I took risks they wouldn't take. Rather, that Mom and Deena wouldn't take. Dad, I realized, took plenty of risks for love. It slowly dawned on me that when it came to romance, Dad and I were more alike than I cared to admit. As a single parent, he sought freedom and passion, sometimes putting his children's needs behind those desires. When I cried on the phone, distraught over him missing a Sunday visit, him being a parent carried more weight to me than him being single. It never occurred to me that he was a young man living true to himself for the first time, savoring the liberty of coming out, of sharing his life openly with a man. He took his responsibility for having children seriously when it came to providing for us, but once divorced he embraced his life separate from us. My harbored resentments over those past hurts ran deep, but I began to see the irony in that as my desire to be a woman first sometimes, and not just a mom, was often tied to passion.

Late at night, I slid under my down comforter and filled page after blank page, diving deeper into how I wanted to live my life authentically, to do work I was proud of, how I wanted my son to feel the kind of love that breeds confidence in himself, and how I wanted to attract the right man at the right time to love me. Then I snuggled further into the covers and caressed my silky skin, exploring the brilliance of my own sexual response so that when I shared my body with a man again, I would not be literally giving myself away.

Twenty

Free booze in first class is good and bad. After reaching a cruising altitude of 37,000 feet I am well into my second glass of wine. Lucky for me, Dad's miles have landed me a seat in first class on the way home. As we float over the puffy clouds below, it seems like we are barely moving, gliding through heaven.

Reaching into my purse, I pull out the small blue Tiffany bag and fish out Dad's ring. It slides easily onto my index finger. I thought it would make me feel closer to him, but it is uncomfortable, and unfamiliar. I take it off and put it back in my bag.

Leaning back, I let the past several days play in my mind like a film. Sitting at Mom's with Deena, finding the letter from Dad. Fighting with Mom over my feelings. Spending time with my son, such a man now. The highlight of my visit.

It's not fair to blame my sister for how she handled the power Dad gave her along with his antiques. What's upsetting is the way she shut me out over my open grief for what felt like so much more love offered to her. So much more trust. It may take years to sort out with each other the reactions neither of us could help at the time. Since I feel like I'm gliding through heaven, I send out a prayer we can do that before we have to say goodbye to Mom.

My eyes close tight against the thought of losing my mother, unable to imagine it. Tears hang there, waiting. The flight attendant pours more wine. Like truth serum, it helps me see more clearly my part in the strife of these past few months, how pouring my pain over everyone made a hard situation harder. We each hurt one another in our own way, mostly out of disappointment or fear or our belief that we are right. How differently we all see the world.

My mother's tear-filled eyes as I said goodbye this morning broke my heart. I know my departure brought up her feelings of loss, inviting grief back into the house. She was so happy to see me, to have her sensitive daughter there to hug her, spend time with her, but my presence was hard on her, too. My big emotions and truth-telling shook her up with each word I uttered about Dad, Deena, Zac, the will, all of it. The way it always does. They love me, I know they do; I'm just hard for them to be around.

Closing my eyes, I feel my deep love for them reverberate through me, like the hum of the plane as it takes me home.

"Time to get up, sweetie," I said from the hall on a snowy January morning. "C'mon, Zac, please."

"Five more minutes, Mom," he muttered, disappearing into a sea of blankets, one large foot dangling over the edge of the bed. "Good dream." *How did he get so big?* I wondered, then went down to make coffee before calling him again.

Each day I grew more aware of the ways I had sabotaged my own best good by believing that a man in our lives would make us a more complete family. As I became more honest with myself about how much space had been taken up by the love of a man, or the ache of not receiving it, my heart opened more fully to each moment I spent with Zac. As we grew closer, I felt his love deeper than ever before. It filled me up. I knew that in addition to the responsibility for his well-being, safety, and stability, I would provide the guidance he needed going into adolescence. He was in middle school now, and I cherished this time when he looked to me for every answer, holding me at the center of his orbit, because I knew it was fleeting.

The assured, cool guy he would be as an adult was already visible in his swagger; he was someone success would follow like the Pied Piper. He was popular in a way I had always wanted to be, with a parade of friends coming over to hang out in our basement while he held court. He took most things in stride, especially when he had my love and attention all to himself.

That night we made dinner and watched his favorite show, *Degrassi*, the edgy Canadian teen drama which launched many conversations about situations he would encounter, like drugs, bullying, gossip, and of course, sex.

"I will never get a girl pregnant in high school, Mom," he said, lying on the couch with his back to me when Manny tells Craig she's pregnant. "I promise. It's so stupid not to just get condoms."

"Well, that's good news, and you're right. Remember that sex isn't just for fun, though. It's a lot more special when it means something. Girls, especially, can get hurt when they think sex will lead to love. Like we talked about before, there are big consequences when it comes to sex, but it's a natural part of life so don't be afraid to talk about it." *Don't say too much. He hates when you preach.*

"Oh, I know." He nodded. "I'll be a good guy, Mom. Don't worry."

I worried plenty. I wanted to believe he knew this in his soul, that he really wanted to be a good guy, and wasn't just telling me what I wanted to hear. "So, Marco is gay, huh?" I said, venturing into another character's lane, wondering if it brought up any questions about DeeDee and Grandfather.

"Yeah, no big deal, except he got beat up that one time. That really sucked. And people called him a fag and stuff. But he's fine now. I think he still likes Dylan."

"You know those words aren't nice, right? Fag and homo. They're insults to gay people."

"Yeah, I know." He got up and went into the kitchen for a snack, my signal he was done with the Q & A. We watched the rest of the episode in silence.

Will & Grace and *Queer Eye for the Straight Guy* ran in the background of my son's childhood, like subliminal messages of acclimation and acceptance, though I had not told him his grandfather and aunt were gay. Dad not having a partner made the information unimportant to a kid, and I knew my mother was still uncomfortable with anyone knowing about Dad. My sister wasn't fully out to the whole family, so it wasn't my information to share, though I wasn't willing to lie about it. She and Shannon had always been discreet, and I knew Zac would ask questions if he was curious.

When my great-aunt Claire died, Dad attended her funeral with the new man he met on Match, introducing him as his partner to members of the extended family. Zac only overheard that Benny was moving in with him. Later, while pushing our cart through the aisles of Big Lots, he turned to me and said, "Hey, Mom, I heard Grandfather say his friend Benny is moving in. He's only got a two-bedroom house. Is he giving up his office to have a roommate? That's just weird."

Here we go, I thought.

"Do you really want to know?" I replied, watching his twelve-year-old sensibilities put the pieces together until he saw the big picture.

"Eww," he said, with mock horror, then smiled, "Actually, it makes so much sense. I can totally see it."

We continued our conversation in the car, and I answered his questions about when I found out about Dad and what that was like for me.

"It was a lot harder back then because no one I knew had a dad like mine, and I had to keep it a secret from DeeDee for a long time."

It seemed okay that he should learn about his family through his curiosity, the way I did. Especially since my family wasn't offering him this information about themselves and no one was lying to him.

About an hour after we got home, Zac came into my home office and sat in the chair across from my desk. "So, Mom, this thing with Grandfather, it's cool, I mean, I'm glad I know, and it's no big deal. But I do have just one question."

"What's that, honey?" He looked so grown up, his strong features taking over his little boy face.

"What about DeeDee and Auntie Shan?" His grin told me he knew the answer, and it was all okay. What had been an ugly secret in my story was not a crisis in his life. It was liberating to have it out in the open to the person who mattered most to me. Whatever shame I felt growing up would never be his to bear. The world had been changing as I raised him, inching toward openness and inclusion. Unlike me, he would know better, and would not be judgmental of the people he loves.

. . .

"You know that essay I wrote at the library about losing my job?" I said to Mom while we sat at the bar in her kitchen over coffee, our favorite ritual. "Well, it won me some free life coaching sessions. You know, like the women on that show *Starting Over*." She loved the reality show about women living in a house together while working with coaches on their problems.

"Oh, good! Can it help you find a real job?" Her anxiety had been mounting about my next career move since the job at my chiropractor's office barely paid the bills.

"Yes! I've had a couple sessions and I decided I want *her* job. I want to go back to school to become a life coach."

She looked confused. "And who is going to hire you to do that?"

"I'll find clients. It seems like every time I turn around, I meet more coaches. It's an exciting new field and I'd be helping people. I can keep working for Dr. Smith while I go to school. Imagine, me back in school!" My enthusiasm bubbled over as I explained how I would attend classes on the phone, not have to leave Zac, and would work with clients that way, too. "It will be good for me to be around when he comes home from school. Especially when he's in high school." For a moment, I remembered my own tumultuous teen years, and cringed that my son would be a teenager on his next birthday.

"But you need insurance! And what if you can't get clients? People are going to pay you to talk to them on the phone?" Her skepticism was understandable, yet it was tempered by a true appreciation for my excitement. In her usual way, Mom wanted me to be happy, but I would be going about it in a way she couldn't understand because of risks she would never take.

"I'll figure it out. We'll be covered, I promise." I kissed her cheek. "I'm gonna go call Dad."

"Well, honey, that's wonderful," my father gushed when I shared my plan with him. "You certainly have the personality for it. How much is this school?"

"It's almost three grand. I put it on my credit card." I didn't want him to think I would ask for money after his help with some of the legal bills. "It's time I do something I'm excited about again, Dad. You've always said how important it is to like your work. There's always been a part of me that loves helping people with their problems, you know, like my girlfriends. I'm so much better at that than solving my own." We laughed at the truth of that. "And God knows I love to talk on the phone." We laughed again, and I felt his sincere pleasure in hearing my new path included furthering my education.

His health had begun faltering, the result of back surgeries that did not help him much. During his recent hospital stay I visited him, but once he was on his feet a cursory check-in was all I could muster. Deep down, my connection to him still held the charge of my younger, hurt self, carrying the fear of investing emotionally only to be let down by his indifference. Knowing he would not return the intensity of my love made me hold it in a locked box from which I doled out portions, like tokens at an arcade. His support, sharing my excitement about school, granted him a nice payout.

· · ·

I wrung out every ounce of coaching school I could, drenching my soul with a new empowerment, one that had me believing in myself in ways that felt akin to my work in entertainment, only this time I was in the driver's seat. The only shotgun I rode was with my clients, navigating for them.

"You used all the pillars of coaching in those ten minutes, Lisa. Great job!" my instructor said. Nearly halfway through my program, not only was I mastering tools like perspective and powerful listening—it was intuitive. After acing my written and oral exams, I took on clients as an apprentice.

"So, what do I do?" my newest client lamented, "He won't commit, and I've given so much of myself to him. I became dependent on his support when my dad died, then I lost my job. It's so much. Even my mom told me I'm too obsessed with him."

Residual anxiety over yearning for a commitment of my own ran up the back of my neck, my own mother's disapproval of my romantic choices echoing in my head. As I started working with clients, I was a magnet to women who were struggling to maintain their identity in relationships. My empathy ran deep.

"It sounds like maybe you are obsessed with him, and your relationship is driving your life. What if that's true?" I paused, feeling her misery. "I know how desperate that feels." *Do I ever.*

"It probably is true. I am obsessed." The weight of her sigh came through the phone, a heavy revelation.

"Turning our power over to someone else is not healthy. That's why it feels so bad. The question is: Do you want to turn some of that attention on your own life? What if you could find things that make you happy outside of this guy?"

"That makes so much sense. I just wish there was something I could do to change this situation with him." She sounded both hopeful and deflated, wishing for a simple answer I couldn't give her.

"The hard part is that there is no answer but to take responsibility for your own happiness, Rita. We don't grow without discomfort. Make a list of things that bring you joy that have nothing to do with him." How much easier it was to impart that wisdom to someone else than to live it.

"I will. I promise to send it before our next call. Thank you." Each session carried the reward of knowing that energy had shifted, that wheels may have turned, that beliefs could be nudged and challenged. Including my own.

My weekly classes that year had been like attending a year-long personal growth workshop, each one insisting I look at my own shit. Realizations piled up about my external search for love, my need for a man's validation, my deep insecurity about my talent. Despite my strengths, pursuing men had made me weak with longing and distraction. I doubled down on my desire to change that, calling it out when I heard a client doing the same thing.

Melanie Beattie's *Codependent No More* was an elixir, soothing my need to try to force outcomes, urging me to let go of expectations of others. The traits of narcissism were present in Dad, but also in most of the men I fell in love with. I learned my codependency was what had brought me so much grief, and I could have control over it if set boundaries. The more I learned, the more I applied this new knowledge to my own life when setting limits with Zac or talking with my mom. I joined the Chicago Coach Alliance to surround myself with like-minded people, and I joined Toastmasters to hone my public speaking skills. Without the distraction of a man, my star was on the rise.

"What do you think of this?" I asked Karen over the phone, "You (Don't) Complete Me: Dispelling the Jerry McGuire Myth." I was test driving an article I was writing for a women's newspaper. "I have a whole workshop planned and everything."

"I love it. Read me the beginning."

"Okay, here goes. 'How many of us felt the tension as Jerry McGuire and Dorothy Boyd, fresh from Jerry's meltdown and Dorothy's impulsive support, stood in that elevator while the couple beside them shared those romantic words in sign language, "You complete me"? Dorothy's panic over what she had just done was momentarily usurped by the intimacy of that gesture and you could feel her longing for that in her own life. Fast forward to the end of the movie when Jerry rushes in to declare those very same words to her. Didn't we all want someone to feel that way about us? I know I did.

'I spent years of my life looking for someone to complete me, and to complete him, so I would feel whole. On the way I attracted "halves" like me who didn't have a complete sense of who they were— and that "half" needed considerable fixing. I signed up for the job and failed miserably. For a divorced mom dating is tricky enough. I have plenty to do raising a man; I don't need to fix one, too!' What do you think?"

She laughed, a trace of her southern roots ringing through. "And I was with you every step of the way! Read more."

"No shit. Okay. 'We are all whole on our own. The irony is that in seeking externally for that wholeness we are denying the very parts of us that will make us feel complete. Our unique talents and gifts get buried beneath others' expectations of who we should be.'"

"I love it. You finally get it, bestie. I'm proud of you." Her praise pierced my heart, flooding it with gratitude.

"Well, on paper I do. Gotta go. Love you, girl."

My *You (Don't) Complete Me* workshop attracted twenty-five women armed with their stories of complicated love and heartbreak. After that, in a brazen display of self-confidence, I invested in contributing a chapter to an anthology about purpose and passion. It paid off with radio interviews and speaking engagements that led to new clients. I applied to a coaching slot with eWomenNetwork and was accepted.

Mark resurfaced. He sent emails and the occasional letter. Our conversations became good coaching practice, given his unhappiness in so much of his life. We shared thoughtful exchanges, written late in the quiet night while our families slept. The ritual of sitting in the low light of my desk lamp with a cup of tea, primed to answer his woes, gave me a comfortable place to test drive my skills of perspective and reframing a situation. His support of my success was tinged with envy; he wished for meaningful work in his own life. We had arrived at a seeming reversal from our very beginning when he was the star.

From way down here the sight of you and your great life going higher and higher means that eventually I need to get back to my own rising star project, he wrote after I sent him a draft of my book chapter. *Problem is, when I open my workroom to build my own flying machine, the sight of all those parts strewn around, and the well-worn instruction manual missing a page, makes me feel a little stupid, a little tired.*

His words broke my heart as he shared how unhappy he was in his marriage. *It's a waste of a life to live this way. And what? Divorce? And give up half of everything, including my daughter? Forget it. That's a hell worse than this one.*

The final year of my marriage to Jimmy came rushing in. *I've learned to embrace the dark times, the painful stuff*, I wrote back, surprised that this man who I thought could manifest anything would find himself so miserable. *Those times when we are grounded with technical difficulty is when we can revise our flight plans. Just keep going back to the workroom.*

• • •

That summer, I took Zac to California to see Mary and her family. We were excited for our boys to finally meet each other. During our visit, I suggested to Mark we all get together, and invited him and his wife and daughter to join us for dinner. He declined, saying it wasn't a good time. Then, on our last night in town, I got an email saying he was unexpectedly free, that the girls went to a horse show for the weekend.

I have plans for dinner with Mary, I wrote back, *but you can meet us at Bruno's around 8 p.m. for a drink, if you want.* I was grateful to have Zac to get back to that night. I wouldn't be able to go too far off the rails and continue what we had started in that hot tub nearly five years earlier. His family being out of town was dangerous, and it was in everyone's best interest if we didn't share more than a drink.

I'll be there, he said.

When he walked in, the setting sun lit his silver hair like a halo. By the time he sat down I was enchanted all over again.

"Hi, ladies," he said, smiling at Mary and reaching for my hand to pull me off the bar stool into a hug. "Hey, Lis. You look great." Mary looked at him, then me, as he pulled up a stool to join us. He motioned for a server to come over. "Let me get us a drink."

Mary held her hand over her near-empty glass. "I'm good. In fact, I'd love to get home to Jeff and the boys. Would you mind dropping her off, Mark?" A knowing smile flashed between all three of us.

"Are you sure? I didn't mean to bust up your evening, ladies."

"No, no. We've spent days together. You guys have a nice night. I'll see you at the house later, Lis. Have fun." She gave me a swift hug, whispering, "Be careful, it's Friday the 13th."

Once she left, I felt a little self-conscious with the unexpected time alone together, my attraction to him surfacing. Like the last time, once we had a glass of wine the conversation was flowing easily.

"How about a walk?" After he paid the check, we ventured into the neighborhood. As the light in the sky disappeared, we strolled through the residential streets while a crescent moon hung softly from the clouds.

"We had such grand illusions about love twenty years ago, didn't we?" he said.

The youthful fantasies of future bliss that we had conjured up over wine chats in our twenties bubbled to the surface. We talked about how they didn't match the reality of our grown-up choices. Especially the romantic ones. Under the dark sky we confessed the deeper truths of where we were in our lives, sharing our disappointment over not being where we thought we would be after passing our fortieth birthdays.

"When I was young, I thought I'd be settled in my forties," I said, walking close beside him, the warm night thick around us. "Married, a nice house, a good job I loved. Maybe with a family. Yet here I am embarking on a new path alone, starting a business, raising a man without one around." He curled his arm around my shoulders. "I thought I would be in love," I said softly.

"Me, too," he said, drawing me closer.

When he dropped me off, we made out in his truck like the idealistic young people we reminisced about, then he hugged me tightly and whispered, "You feel like home to me." After he drove away, I sat on the porch in the moonlight, savoring the evening, not ready to let it go.

"Well, the minute he walked in, and you looked at each other, all the air sucked out of the room," Mary said the next morning over coffee on her patio. "Whew, it was really something."

"Yeah, we have quite a connection," I said, remembering the smile that bloomed across his face when he saw me.

"It made me want to get home to Jeff and snuggle on the couch. Seriously, I was happy to give you guys some time to hang out without me as a third wheel. The boys were having fun when I got home; I made popcorn and we all watched a movie."

She swooned as I recounted the evening, of our confessions of longing on a hot summer night. "Honest to God, Mary, it felt like the most romantic thing in the world."

Just then Mark called to tell me about a dream he'd had just before he woke up that we were together in a villa in Italy.

"It felt so real," he said. "Incredibly real."

I imagined us bathed in the ochre light of Tuscany, surrendering to love. It was risky to entertain the fantasy, the internal movie featuring us as star-crossed lovers.

After I returned home, Mark popped in and out of view like the special guest on a favorite TV show. It was easy to keep him simmering on the back burner of my attention, given the distance and his marital status. Mostly, we shared newsy letters over email comparing philosophies and desires, stopping short of making pledges about the future. We tiptoed around our erotic thoughts of each other like land mines, weaving the fantasy about being in Italy together into a short story we wrote back and forth for days.

Just like his dream it felt incredibly real.

. . .

"What about sex? Having any?" The practitioner asked while

doing some energy work on me for severe low back pain. Lying face down on her table, I was calmed by the scent of lavender from the candle burning on the windowsill. Her touch was soothing.

"It's been a long time, about a year," I told her. "Not that I wouldn't rather be having some." She pressed on my sacrum, and I nearly jumped off the table. She released her fingers and gently moved them up my spine.

"And your father? Is he living? How's your relationship?"

I was startled by her question. "Yes." Tears sprang to my eyes. "We've had a complicated relationship but we're pretty good at the moment, I guess." I swatted away my dad's voice talking about his new pain management doctor in a recent phone call. Most all our conversations lately were about his pain, and I had decided to accept how much easier it was to relate to each other when it was all about him.

She pressed the tender spot again, her finger stabbing like a hot poker into my tailbone. "Sometimes when someone has what they call 'daddy issues' it implies that a person was hurt by their father, and in some cases, they carry that wound in their second chakra, using sexuality to soothe the pain left behind."

All my striving to be loved by being sexual with men who were unworthy or unavailable came rushing in, then poured out of me with the sorrow I felt over giving so much of myself away. I sobbed into the tissue paper draped over the head of the table.

"It seems clear this pain could be connected to your father. Is there anything you need to forgive him for?"

After her treatment I was couchbound, nearly unable to move until I wrote the letter she had suggested might ease my pain.

Dear Dad,

My lifelong fear of abandonment was born the year you and Mom separated, I guess. That fear felt fresh and raw now, my ten-year-old self quietly crying in the background as I shared the truth with the first perpetrator to scar her fragile heart.

Waiting for your call on Sundays felt like torture. When you guys got back together, and we moved to Oak Park, I was so happy to have you back. It was shocking when you guys got divorced and Terry took our place in your life. I was devastated that you would leave Mom for a young man. It was so hard to lose you that way and no one would talk with me about it. Which meant it must be bad. As I got older, seeking the attention of men replaced chasing after yours. Men who dismissed me easily. The way you did, sometimes.

Admitting that my struggle with love had to do with our relationship felt dangerous, and freeing. I knew better than to blame him.

I know you did the best you knew how, and admit I wasn't always the easiest daughter. Finding out you where gay was confusing and painful; I was young with no understanding of a life different than the one I grew up in with you and Mom. I had to keep it a secret, so I thought you were doing something wrong. But it's just who you are. In the end, our issues really had nothing to do with that. I just wanted your attention. For you to be there for me and to love me.

I forgive you for not always being there when I wanted you to be, Dad, and I appreciate everything you've done for me. Thank you for being the best father you knew how to be. I love you.

Like every other birthday card I'd bought for him, I found a generic one, then stuffed my letter inside and mailed it, relieved to put down the heavy anger I had carried for far too long. What used to send a wave of shame through me made me smile. Time had softened us. My father wasn't a man on the prowl in the Castro hitting the bathhouses anymore, willing to share his conquests with me over Sunday brunch, and I was no longer that twenty-something disapproving daughter who wished for a worthy role model for a husband. He was just my dad. A good man, unashamed of his life.

My resentments and disappointments got tied up in a bundle of forgiveness and were sent packing.

As I vowed to let go of the hurt my back pain subsided.

. . .

Dad never responded to my letter. A couple of years later I mentioned it to my mother.

"He was furious about it," she said. "He had no idea what you were talking about. He thought he was a good father, and you had no need to forgive him for anything."

My inclination was to write an outraged letter to him then, this time to call him out again for not coming over the bridge to the ICU or acknowledging his grandson's birth. Yet, the desire to issue indictments against him was tempered by the fact that he had remained silent. When he received my letter of forgiveness, he had not sent a nasty reply arguing with me, seeing my feelings as unfair or unfounded accusations. He just bitched about the letter to my mother and let it go.

Instead of making me angry, I let my forgiveness settle deeper into my bones. I realized that the release of my ancient fury at my father, the clemency I granted him for all I had held so tightly, wasn't really for him.

It was for me.

Twenty-One

Dad thought he would live to be eighty-eight. A gypsy fortune teller read his palm and told him that in his forties. He believed her so fervently it became insurance against his carelessness with his health. His death is fifteen years shy of her prediction, so I keep telling myself that's why he never changed his will once we became closer.

A copy of his nasty letter did not get saved. My sister thought since he didn't send it to me, it wasn't mine to keep. Probably just as well. It feels better to choose to remember the good stuff: his assurance that I would be successful even if I quit high school; that if I loved coaching enough, I should pursue it; that if I wasn't happy in a relationship, I could leave it. Beside every time I judged him for not being there for me, I can point to a time when he backed me up.

His death has tempered the edges of our past, a sharp object I have learned to handle gingerly. Time has given me the gift of accepting this man who hurt me again and again, and my mother for being complicit in her devotion to him. I've stopped resenting them for loving each other more than I thought they loved me. And for not seeing me because my choices didn't look like theirs, and even when they did. The truth is, Dad saw me in the moments of pride that he loved to associate with his daughters, when our successes were a fine reflection of him. And by extension, he offered his kindest generosity to my son.

By becoming a parent who wants to live her life as an individual, I have learned to see my parents as individuals, with desires and disappointments that have nothing to do with me. I see them now as people with strengths and flaws that define their worlds apart from their children—just as I would like to be seen by my son.

Empathy for my father, who showed little empathy for me or anyone, came as I watched him succumb to an addiction to pain killers he denied because they were doctor-prescribed. The meds made him frail and obsessed with his pain, weakening his system. Pity replaced my resentment once I understood his narcissistic personality, and that my dad's self-involvement, his inability to take criticism, and need to be right were symptoms of a syndrome. This allowed my acceptance of him to fill some of the holes in my heart, like Japanese kintsugi, the art of creating precious scars from mended pieces. With forgiveness, the need for his approval diminished; I could finally talk to him without having to prove anything to either of us. Surprisingly, even the email I stumbled upon, his slap from the grave, can be forgiven. Because the truth is, we can only be damaged by those we love if what they say is more powerful than what we believe is true.

"Hey, Dad," I said when my turn came to say a private goodbye to my father on the day he died. I crept into his room timidly, as if death were a living thing squatting in the corner. I took my dad's hand. "I don't know what to say. Can you imagine that? Me." I felt shy, wanting to say the right thing in case he could hear me, feeling like I could get this wrong. "I love you, Dad. And I know you love me, too." I wanted so badly for him to reply. My father always had the last word.

"I have so much to thank you for. And some things to forgive you for, which I have already, I really have. I sent you that letter a long time ago, remember? You never replied, but it helped me to write it to you." I took a breath, rubbing my fingers gently over the thin skin of his hand. It felt like tissue paper.

"Thank you for taking such good care of my mother all her life. She could always count on you. Always. Even though I was sometimes jealous." Sobs rose in my chest. "I know I was, but I didn't need to be. You were good to me, too. You were. Even though you could really disappoint me." I wiped my eyes, struggling to find the right words. "There are things I'll wish I said to you, but I can't think of them now. This is the first time I get to talk to you without hearing your opinion and I don't know what to say." This made me laugh, settling my tears. "I'll miss you," I whispered, realizing I really would. "Just know how much I love you, Daddy."

After everyone spent their time with him, the doctor removed all the tubes. In a moment of surprise, Dad opened his eyes. I jumped to his side, as did his partner Benny, and for a second or two we wrestled for his attention. "Dad! Dad," I pleaded, as Benny leaned into him from the other side. His eyes darted around for a second then closed again.

The last time I saw Dad had been a month before. I remembered a mischievous glance between him and Benny, an inside joke they must have shared. *A couple of old queens,* I'd thought, affectionately. They were rooted in the comfortable ease of longtime love. I was so happy my dad had found that.

I backed away, leaving Benny to the intimate moment with his partner that he deserved. I sat beside Deena and my mom, noticing that Zac had disappeared, probably to the family lounge to get a break from the sadness in his grandfather's room. It was the third time my family sat together waiting for God to take someone we loved. The last time had been Gram, thirteen years to the day before we were all gathered to say goodbye to Dad.

"You're not dying on my mother's anniversary, Don," Mom had

said softly, hours before, in the lovingly bossy tone she used with my father. It was around 3:00 a.m. now, and I watched her grief come on like a fever, more acute as the minutes ticked by. She was losing the love of her life, too, though it was Benny who sat right beside him, whispering in his lover's ear as his breathing grew more labored. My sister sat quietly, saying next to nothing, staying close to Mom.

"I'll go get us some coffee," I said, "And see if I can find Zac." I squeezed my mother's shoulder.

"That's a good idea. Thanks, Lis." She looked like she had aged a decade, painfully aware of all the loved ones she had lost. This one might hurt the most.

Zac was sitting alone in the dimly lit lounge when I walked in. I poured myself some coffee. "How're you doing, sweetie?" He didn't shrug me off when I draped my arm around his broad shoulders.

"I'm okay. Just really can't believe it. I mean, Grandfather will be gone just like that." I pulled him into a hug as he broke down. *My sweet boy.* As I held him, I thought about that visit we'd had with Dad, the last time I saw my father alert and talking, the joy I felt that day with my father and my son. *It was only a month ago.*

"It'll be all right. He'll be out of pain, in a better place. I believe that anyway. We'll miss him, but he's still a part of us." My son nodded and wiped his eyes.

"I just posted this." He handed me his phone, open to his Facebook page. He had simply posted the Lord's Prayer on his wall. Raising him with a relaxed faith—not much church but plenty of God—it touched me deeply that he had reached out for comfort in his own way, as I had been doing all day.

"That's beautiful, Zac. Prayers are good right now. Grandma will like that a lot." He nodded. "We'd better get back in there." I poured a cup of coffee for my mother, and we slowly walked back to Dad's room to join the others until his last breath.

• • •

Walking into the lobby of the funeral home I couldn't help but think of the wakes of grandparents, aunts, and uncles I had come to pay my respects to over the years. Knowing the family owners my whole life, I had been to Saxx Funeral Home many times, including the Halloween party I attended in the basement when I was nine years old. None of that prepared me for the jolt of seeing one of my parent's names on the wall outside a viewing room. *Dad always liked to be on a marquee,* I thought as I walked in, carrying the poster board of pictures I had assembled. I placed it on an easel next to the podium at the front of the room as an 8x10 photo of my dad looked on. The photo—a professional shot from his executive days— stood beside a pale blue box, presumably containing his ashes. *Oh, Dad. You were so handsome.* I ran my fingers over the wood frame and was suddenly grateful he had chosen cremation, sparing us an embalmed, heavily made-up version of him. It brought tears to my eyes, remembering my father young and healthy. Once everyone was seated, I joined Zac and Benny on a couch in the front. Deena and Mom shared the other one.

"Thank you, everyone," Stephen, the funeral director, said as the murmur in the room hushed. "Thank you for coming today to celebrate Don's life, the contributions he made to his family, and to the world." He said a few more words, then introduced me. "Don's daughter, Lisa, would like to share a few words with us."

I took a deep breath as I got up and stepped to the podium, cleared my throat, and began.

"Generous. Organized. Controlling. Responsible. Irritating. Really, really smart. And picky, picky, picky... These are just a few of the words we would associate with my dad. He was a man of many strong opinions and he delivered them with the kind of authority that would make you want to do your homework before challenging him. And boy, did we do our homework! Right, Deen?" I glanced over at my sister, then looked away quickly so I wouldn't cry.

"My father's generosity came with the understanding that we better have researched whatever it was we wanted. As irritating as that could be, it was an incredible gift he taught us: Be educated on the quality and value of the things we choose, and to know what we are getting when we choose them." *I wish I had done that with men*, I thought. *We both had some doozy boyfriends, didn't we, Dad?* "His tenacity in being thorough drove us crazy, but because of it none of us will ever get screwed over on a used car." A chuckle bounced around the room.

"His marriage to my mom, Peg, brought me and my sister Deena into the world, and though their marriage wasn't meant to last forever, their love and friendship surely were. I learned what true best friends looked like from my mom and dad." I fought tears while looking over at Mom.

"Yet my father still believed in romance. He gave me a copy of the book *Bridges of Madison County* twenty years ago and inscribed: *From one incurable romantic to another. Love, Daddy.*" I took a slow breath. *Don't lose it. He's somewhere watching this. Make him proud.* "And he kept that hope alive until his partner Benny came into his life nearly a decade ago. The devotion they shared carried Dad through to the very end." I looked over at my father's shell-shocked widower. He nodded, barely.

"His only grandchild, Zachary, was a source of pride to my dad, and he recently told Zac how important it was to love what you do for a living." That day a month earlier felt so long ago now, but I could still feel the joy of it as I caught my son's eye. He smiled, though I could tell he was trying not to lose it.

"Professionally, my father was a hardworking man who loved what he did. He was a pioneer in the computer industry back when a computer filled an entire room, never dreaming we would all eventually carry one in our pockets. Self-taught, he ran a computer division at twenty-four years old while supporting his young family and delivered pizzas at night. He later became a community college professor though he had never attended college himself, and when we all thought the world would turn upside down at the millennium, he was in charge of Y2K security for an international bank. The clock struck midnight without a hitch or a hiccup."

Like the many times I had given inspirational talks, I felt myself get carried into the stream of words, fluid and true, coming from a place beyond me. Or maybe it was the Xanax from Benny kicking in.

"Over the years, my dad had many passions. He could rewire a house, build a deck, wallpaper a room, and upholster a chair. He could MacGyver almost anything, a holdover from his days as an Eagle Scout. He was a member of Mensa, until he got bored with it. He loved to dance, and he and Mom once did an award-winning rumba. During his musical theater period, he played lead characters in *A Christmas Carol* and *Anything Goes*. While living in Oak Park and San Francisco he could be found singing Broadway show tunes at the piano bars."

I flashed on him at the Galleon in the Castro, perched on a stool in front of a Steinway, nursing a beer while singing *You're the Top*. I already missed him. How much fun he could be when he was in his element, being himself. I paused and took a deep breath.

"Later in life my father's fascination with clocks and watches, most of which he found on eBay and fixed himself, created something of a time museum in his small house.

"He liked to think he could cook—and he made a mean pork roast—though in later years he was pickier than ever. He didn't eat much unless it was a filet at Tom's, Peg's rigatoni, Fannie May chocolates, or Jewel English muffins...until they changed the recipe.

"He drank an ocean of coffee in his lifetime and smoked thousands of cigarettes. He lived life on his terms, calling the shots where he could. I know he is in a better place now and feeling no pain. That, indeed, is the blessing of today as we celebrate his life and remember the knowledge, love, and beautiful memories he leaves with all of us. We'll miss you, Dad."

I gathered my notes, stepped away from the lectern, and burst into tears.

After the memorial, Stephen gave Benny the rose containing Dad's ashes. He had split the rest into temporary containers for me and Deena to take home with us.

"I'll take his brains and heart," I whispered.

Epilogue

A full blue moon is set to rise at 7:15 p.m. It is my father's seventy-fourth birthday, the day I will scatter his ashes in the lagoon behind my home. *Dad would just love the theatrics of this*, I think as I begin my day preparing for the memorial at sunset.

As I gather all the materials I want to include, the home movies of my childhood play in the background, 8mm film my dad had transferred to DVD as a Christmas gift to all of us years ago. What is most stunning about the footage is how normal it all is—moving images of a wholesome mid-century American childhood, complete with blow-up swimming pools, family holidays in my aunt's basement, a Holy Communion, and a little sister who my dad filmed with me walking up and down our driveway in matching red velvet coats at Christmas, and yellow ones at Easter.

In the footage before they were married there are subtle clues to the future: Dad's meticulous positioning of the candles on my mother's nineteenth birthday cake, and a slightly seductive shot of him looking at his friend Daniel at the lake while stretched out on a towel. Mostly, I can see the friendship between my parents and the love they had for each other.

Watching the movies, I see myself on my third birthday on my daddy's lap, his attention all mine. Deena is an infant and much less interesting to him. My days as the only apple of his eye were numbered and I didn't even know it. We look joyful as he bounces me on his lap, my eyes shiny with glee.

Another frame a few months later shows a family of smiling faces in our elegantly decorated living room, and it dawns on me that my dad really did give us a wonderful life. Regardless of what he wanted secretly in his heart, or what he did on Monday nights, my dad was a devoted husband and father when we were children, providing for us and protecting us. Loving us.

My heart swells as I turn my attention back to the ritual, feeling peaceful about sending Dad off into the next world. *No tears today. Just beautiful memories. Today he will rest in peace.*

The purple silk shawl I pull from my closet to create an altar on the dock gets put in a basket with a collection of photos from my father's life. Added are his baby shoe, the blue globe paperweight, and the red chipped heart. When I get down there, it all gets arranged on a tile tray with the blue box, a few candles and the inkwell that will contain some ashes to keep. A photo frame Dad had created of him and his brother, and their parents, stands beside a photo of the four of us—Mom, Dad, Deena, and me—as a young family. A bottle of tequila sits on the worn plank of the dock ready to toast the ancestors, one of which my father has now become.

Mark arrives as the sun sinks low in the sky. We've spent a lot of time together since I returned to California a few years ago. We're both free now to say *yes* to the love story the Universe has had in store for us all along. He softly plays a ceremonial rhythm on his djembe drum while I pick flowers. Once I place them on my make-shift altar and light the candles, I'm ready.

"We honor you, Dad, on this day of your birth. Not just any day but on the full blue moon." The sound of my father's voice singing "Blue Moon" plays in my mind as I scatter herbs—rosemary, lavender, rose, and sage—to mingle with the light sparkling on the water, sending fragrant wisdom, remembrance, and love into the golden glow of the lagoon.

I pull the plastic bag from the blue box I have so carefully decorated and open one end. A flutter of excitement fills my chest as I feel the weight of my father's brilliant brain and generous heart in my hands. A few pinches of each go into the inkwell. Joy and grace, not sadness, fill me up, as my father's spirit smiles down on my ritual.

"I release you back to the Earth with love and honor, Dad." A silent moment passes, then another, as the sun slips past the horizon and disappears. I tilt the bag and watch his remains flutter in the breeze and fall to the water. *You're free of the body that caused you such pain*, I think, as my father's ashes dissolve and disappear.

Mark's rhythmic drumming softly punctuates the cool air for a bit longer, while the round, fat moon rises higher in the eastern sky. Enveloped by dusk, I pour an inch of tequila into each of the crystal glasses I've brought down with me, then we raise them in a toast to the man who gave me life. "Here's to you, Donald Haute. Go in peace." The clink of our glasses rings through the darkening evening, then I savor the warm burn of the liquor as Mark resumes his drumming.

I'm free, too, Dad, it occurs to me while I sit quietly listening to the heartbeat of the drum as it echoes across the still water, *to love you like we both always wanted.*

Gratitudes

While the process of sitting and writing a book is solitary, I have many people to thank for helping me get my story onto the page and into the world.

Thank you to my memoir teachers: Wendy Dale, your guidance as I wrote my first draft was exceptional. Brooke Warner and Linda Joy Myers, you offer so much information and encouragement to memoir writers. I truly learned so much from you both.

To my editors: Laura Munson and Chelsey Clammer, I appreciate your thoughtful suggestions which undoubtedly made this book better. Magdalena Bartkowska, I offer you my deepest appreciation for your tough love and dear friendship. You truly have an eagle eye—and a huge heart.

Thank you to my publicist, Lexi Rose, for showing up like a fairy godmother ready to work her magic. To my designer, John Edgar Harris, thank you for your creativity and a willingness to collaborate with mine. Your generous patience and good humor got me over the finish line.

Jordan Budd, you and COLAGE offer such incredible community to families like mine, each with a different story. Your support of this book is deeply appreciated.

To all the readers who read this book in its many iterations: I couldn't be more grateful for your time and feedback. Special thanks to Libra, Nancy S., Darcy, Gay, Carolyn, Abigail, Nancy A., Melissa, Julie, Mary, Debi, Barry, Laurie, Kathy, Pamelah, Christina, Susan,

Brian, Marise, Eleanor, and Selimah. Extra love to my 93-year-old black sheep role model, Auntie, who was an early reader and a great cheerleader.

My undying love and gratitude go to my creative midwives, Kim Waters, Alexia LaFortune, Janet Petrine, Kathy Knowles, and Amy Ferris. You all helped me birth this labor of love with joy and grace. I could not have reached the end without you.

To my bestie, Karen Krattinger, who has read every page a dozen times: I love you, girl.

My sweetheart, Mark Mathias, has been quietly in the background all along, just like in the story, with his abiding love, beautiful meals, and true belief in me. Ti amo, baby.

Writing memoir often means risking family relationships to tell your truth. While the early stages of this process carried some tension, ultimately it has fostered great healing. Much love and gratitude go to my mom for her understanding support, and to my sister for becoming a champion of this story. You have no idea how much it means to have you guys on my side.

Zac, you are a central character in this story and in my life. Being your mother is vital to who I have become. My pride in who you have become is endless. Love you more.

And Dad... your voice in my ear carried me through the journey of writing our story. You may not have agreed with all of it, but I know you would be so proud that I wrote it. The inkwell on my desk is a reminder that the love between us is indelible.

About the Author

Lisa Lucca's work has been published in several publications and anthologies, most recently in *Crone Rising*. She is the co-author of the epistolary memoir, *You Are Loved*, with her partner, Mark Mathias, a love story she will continue telling in her next book.

She shares a home with Mark in the high desert of southern New Mexico where she continues her work as a life coach, and hosts a weekly public radio show, *Live True*, bringing insightful and engaging interviews to her listeners. The show streams globally at lccommunityradio.org where the shows are available in the archives. Visit her website at lisalucca.com.

Made in the USA
Middletown, DE
07 November 2021